The Folk Who Live In The West

Tales from the West Coast

Kathleen MacPhee

Published by New Generation Publishing in 2020

ISBN
        Paperback   978-1-78955-846-3
        Hardback   978-1-80031-974-5

www.newgeneration-publishing.com

New Generation Publishing

Recent titles by this author:

<u>Scottish History</u>

Somerled, Hammer of the Norse
Call Yourself a Scot?
Dalriada, Heartland of Scotland

<u>Education</u>

Maths and English Basics Manual
Parents' Guide to the Basics Manual

<u>Other</u>

Recipes and Tales from a Highland Smokehouse

To all of us --- the cousins!

Ronald   Sheila
(Alas, we have now lost them)

Thig crìoch air an t-saoghail
Ach mairidh gaol is ceòl

Anne	Kenneth
Barbara	Gill
Celia	Marjorie
Evelyn	Kathleen

Translations of the Gaelic quotations are on the back page.

Acknowledgments

I am indebted to the following for their kindness and generosity in allowing me to refer to them or their families in the Tales:

Mr Niall MacNeill of Campbeltown and Glasgow
Mr David Barbour of Aucharua Farm, Southend, Kintyre, Argyll
Mrs Maria Gibbons (Miss Maria Grumoli) of Southend and Campbeltown

Some people, places and events have been transposed in time and place.
Some names have been changed and some are purely fictional.

I have made every effort to contact all the actual persons named in this book. In some instances I was unable to obtain permission to quote them as I could no longer trace their whereabouts. In the event that any reader can help me to trace these people, I would be extremely grateful if information could be passed on to me via the publisher.

Special thanks to Ms Laura Currie of Oban for bringing so many scenes to humorous life with her wonderful drawings.

Grateful thanks to Runrig for kind permission to quote from their lovely song, *Cearcall a'Chuain*.

Also, my grateful thanks to Mr Andrew Hutchinson of Sandbank, Argyll, for his endless patience and considerable computer skills during the production of this book.

Very many thanks, also to Webster's of Oban for skilful photographic assistance and for bringing so many old slides back to life again.

i

Table of Contents

Preface

I started to write the tales about events in Kintyre, but found that I was often straying into the entire west coast area, and from there, inevitably, into Norwegian territory --- so I just let it all happen!

After all, it's all the west coast, and I didn't want to be accused of being parochial.

This book is a celebration of people and places from the era of Myth and Legend right up to the present day, and is written as thirty stand-alone tales which may explain the repetition of certain anecdotes.

It remembers, not just the times of happiness and hope, but also the true story of the dark times which affect all people at some time in their lives --- unless they are very fortunate indeed --- and which can't be just swept away into oblivion at will.

But I hope that the humorous tales will lift the spirits enough to make a break from unhappy thoughts and, hopefully, bring a smile where before there was none.

Tha sinn uile air cuan
Stiùireadh cuairt troimh ar beatha
A' seòladh geòla dhorch
Air chall an grèim na mara
Tha a'ghaoth air ar cùl
Tha a' gheòl' a'cumail roimhpe
'S cha dèan uair no an cuan
Toinisg dhuinn no rian

Ach tha mi'n dùil, tha mi'n dùil
Nuair a bhios a'ghrian dol fodha
Chì iad mi a'stiùireadh 'n iar
Null a dh'Uibhist air a'chearcall
Cearcall a' chuain
Gu bràth bidh i a'tionndadh
Leam gu machair geal an iar
Far an do thòisich an là

Runrig :- *Cearcall a' Chuain*

Tale no. 1: "Sheena" and the Orca

Southend was green and blossoming in the warm June sunshine, and the sea was the same blue as the sky, and so still that the Mull of Kintyre was reflected perfectly in the unusually calm waters of the North Channel.

John and I had "looked the nets", dealt with the many and varied tasks associated with salmon fishing, and now were inclined to bask indulgently in the sunshine of our own approval.

We decided to give ourselves a little holiday from hard work, and take the *Sheena* for a short cruise down the coast towards the looming headland of the Mull, an inhospitable place at the best of times, but always dramatic in its rocky splendour, and looking enticingly harmless on this blissful day.

We put aboard some fishing lines baited with rubber sand-eels which we knew would invariably attract the attention of the lythe and saithe which frequented these waters.

Ancient Myth and Legend declare that seven tides meet at the Mull this, no doubt, being the only way the ancient peoples could explain the frequent, sinister, deep surges of ebb and flow around this headland, when it has been known for a sailing boat to remain in one spot, not answering her helm, no matter how much the wind was filling her sails, or under bare poles with her engine struggling against the powerful ocean currents, until the tides changed and released her from the grip of the ocean.

Sheena was very sound, having had her engine recently overhauled and her entire hull thoroughly checked. We felt satisfied that we were setting out on a sensible expedition.

In those days communications were pretty casual for us in the commercial salmon industry and we tended not to bother telling the Coastguards what we were about, as we were in and out around the coastline all day long. We were pretty sure, anyway, that they had tabs on us, as usual, as they watched us, from their cliff-top eyrie, sail out of the Conaglen River and turn to starboard around the impressive bulk of Dunaverty Rock and the ruins of its ancient castle.

Before we left the mouth of the river there was a shout from behind us and, looking back, we could see two of the Coastguards' young boys racing down to the water's edge, waving their arms frantically. Inevitably, as sailors' sons, they were very interested in everything to do with the boats. We liked to take Neil and Calum aboard with us as they were such good-natured, likeable youngsters, and very well-behaved (which we couldn't say about some of the holiday-makers' children!). When in the boat they did exactly as they were told without argument or question, having been well warned by their Coastguard fathers about always obeying the captain. In any case they both hero-worshipped John and would do anything that he asked.

John waved the boys over to "the back of the Rock", the spacious, rough, grass-covered mound behind the half-ruined old fisherman's stone cottage which we used as a store, and always referred to as "the hut".

"We'll pick you up off the Horse Rock," shouted John, and a couple of minutes later he drew the *Sheena* carefully in towards "the back of the Rock" where an outcrop of petrified volcanic debris, surprisingly flat on top, projected out into the sea. This was the Horse Rock where horses, long ago, had had to walk along precarious planking from the decks of ships on to the dry land at Dunaverty, and vice versa. No doubt many a one fell in during this dangerous manoeuvre.

"We're going down the Mull a bit. Do you want to come?" shouted John.

Did they want to come!

Nobody even mentioned the possibility of maternal disapproval -- - it was like that in those days. Of course their mothers wouldn't object! In any case weren't they the Coastguards' kids and experts in all matters naval?

Local children enjoyed the priceless privilege of absolute freedom to roam about the countryside and the coast at will, as long as they turned up at home in time for the family evening meal.

Our agile young adventurers leaped fearlessly off the Horse Rock and collapsed, giggling, on to *Sheena*'s deck.

"Oh, thanks, Mr Cameron" they said, picking themselves up and going obediently to sit forward of the engine casing where John directed them.

We were now passing the mouth of the Roaring Cave, a deep hollow in the rock where there was always an eerie, booming noise of the sea echoing off the walls of the cave, no matter whether the sea conditions outside were calm or rough.

As soon as we drew near the mouth of the cave the air erupted with the sudden, violent clapping of many wings and the shrieking of hundreds of pigeons as they catapulted off their roosts on the cave ledges and rocketed out past us, in a thunderous black cloud, like the clap of doom. Everyone ducked, but fortunately no-one was hit by a feathery missile.

The boys looked impressed. There would be plenty to tell their envious pals the next day at school and no doubt things would be slightly exaggerated in the telling.

Sheena continued at a sedate pace over the now deeply covered Bow Reef --- no dangers lurking there today --- and around the base of the great Rock of Dunaverty from which, alas, many unfortunates had been thrown, or had fallen, to their deaths during ancient troubles.

Dunaverty's beautiful, golden sandy bay now spread out before us, and we watched happy holiday-makers relaxing, playing, picnicking, swimming and basking in the unaccustomed summer warmth, Neil and Calum looking faintly smug because they were out in the big motor-boat, and none of these other folks had that privilege and pleasure. Only special people got out in the boat with John.

"Right, boys, we'll put out the lines now and see if you can catch a fish for your tea," said John. The grins of delight on the two young faces said it all. You had to be one of the "in" crowd to be invited out fishing with John, and this was their first trip. What excitement! No doubt the boys would have preferred to eat their fish and chips out of the Campbeltown chip shop, but they knew they would get lots of brownie points from their mothers for bringing home a fresh local catch caught by themselves, and the next day, in Southend School, their fishermen's tales would be recounted with a certain amount of drama, thus greatly increasing their status among the other kids.

What more could you ask?

We knew the folk in the district who liked fresh lythe, or pollock, to give them their other name, and I was usually given the task of delivering parcels of newspaper-wrapped fish to certain village houses and local farms on our return to the Conaglen River.

I used to flit about the place in the dark of the night dropping the soggy parcels on doorsteps and window-sills, like a fishy Robin Hood. Some parcels, alas, were discovered first by the local cats, and the intended recipients found only the bones of the intended gifts scattered about their farmyards in the morning.

We gave all our saithe, or coal-fish, to Archie, John's brother, for use as bait in his lobster creels, as no-one really liked the texture of their soft, white flesh.

Sheena's engine was slowed right down, the boys threw their lines into the sea on either side of the boat, and we trawled slowly along hoping for our first bite. It came unexpectedly quickly, on Neil's line. He was caught unawares and pulled halfway over the gunwale with what was obviously a good, big fish on the end of his line.

"Hang on tight," shouted John, who gave me the tiller and moved forward at the speed of light to grab the young fisherman round the waist in order to stop him being pulled out of the boat by his lively catch. It would look really bad to lose a passenger overboard while out on a dead calm sea!

"Keep a hold of him and we'll bring him in slowly," instructed John, wishing to let Neil bring in the fish himself. The lad had his pride, and this was his very first fish after all. And what a fish! Lythe are extremely strong, lively creatures and fight quite ferociously against any attempt to pull them out of their natural environment. Calum dropped his line in his excitement and rushed over to watch the battle at close quarters.

"Don't let him go, Neil," he yelled.

Neil was doubled up over the gunwale, hanging on to the threshing, twisting line for dear life and hadn't a single breath to spare. Gradually, with John instructing his every move, he managed to get the fish over to the boat's side, but couldn't pull it inboard.

"It's too big for me," he almost sobbed, but John got a hand on the line where Neil couldn't see, and between the two of them the big, golden-streaked fish was lifted, still violently struggling, over the gunwale and into the boat. Neil collapsed, completely breathless, but grinning from ear to ear, on to the bottom boards beside his magnificent trophy, while the enthusiastic Calum danced a jig of delight around the fish box containing the now motionless fish.

"What a beauty --- wasn't that just great--- wait till your dad sees this --- fancy you catching this big one on your very first trip---

they'll never believe this at school, you know--- what a shame we didn't bring a camera---" etc, etc.

"Wait you," said John, and produced the spring scale from under a thwart. "Let's get him on this and we'll see what size he is."

John held up the scale while Calum eagerly helped Neil lift up the heavy and incredibly slippery fish to hang by its gills on the blunt hook.

"Look at that! He's a thirteen-pounder," shrieked the ecstatic Neil. "No wonder I couldn't pull him in! Now, all we need is another one for Calum," he added generously, happily ignoring his now liberally fish-scaled jersey.

We trawled for quite some time as the boat crossed Dunaverty Bay and, fortunately, Calum did manage to get a reasonably sized lythe, but nothing as grand as Neil's leviathan. Several more were added to the count in the now well-filled fish-box, which was protected from the sun's rays by a canvas cover, then the lines were pulled in and carefully coiled and stowed as *Sheena* left the sheltered waters of the bay. Flasks of tea, thick sandwiches filled with beef and tomato, and generous slices of deliciously moist fruit cake--- courtesy of Mrs Cameron, John's wife--- were produced from somewhere, and we sat, happily munching as we sailed along, looking at the glorious scenery of Southend, in a state of perfect contentment.

John pointed out the various features of interest ashore.

Neil and Calum sat up in the bows, gazing with rapt attention as we passed the once elegant, but now sad, abandoned shell of Keil Hotel, originally a lovely five-storey, white-painted Art Deco building built by Captain James Taylor just before the Second World War. Before the hotel was even finished it was immediately requisitioned by the Royal Navy in 1939 as a hospital for wounded servicemen. It was, of course, returned to the Taylor family after the war in 1947, but in a sad state, and requiring a lot of expensive attention. It had also played its part in the war effort, not just as a hospital, but as a navigational aid to ships and aircraft as its white shape on the cliffs at High Keil provided a welcoming beacon when the lighthouses were forced to switch off their lights in order to hide from the enemy.

Once returned to its former white-painted perfection it was managed with skill and flair by the Captain's daughters, Sybil (now Mrs Kelly) and Mary, and became the venue of choice for many

Kintyre social events, as well as a favourite holiday retreat for hundreds of holiday-makers over the decades.

I told the boys of High Teas that were to die for, with daily home-baked soda scones made with Mary's secret ingredient--- buttermilk straight from the farm (I watched her bake them on the top of the huge Aga cooker), wonderful fluffy sponges (described by my father as "Dunlopillo sponges"), lobster salads, straight from Archie's creels and enhanced with melt-in-the mouth home-made mayonnaise, jugged hare and other delicacies, all eaten at tables laid with pristine white linen cloths, sparkling cutlery and elegant china, all carefully spaced out along the long picture-windows of the dining-room. There was the added bonus of incomparable views of the entire Dunaverty Bay, Machribeg, Brunerican and Conaglen River coastlands.

I recounted happy memories too, of winters at Keil, when the hotel was closed over the winter months and limited social events took place in the cosy confines of the spacious dining-room. Sybil was a wardrobe mistress, and Mary an actor, with the local amateur drama group, Dunaverty Players, directed by the well-known Southend author, Angus MacVicar, of Ach-na-mara.

I got to know that dining-room carpet extremely well, having spent many a happy evening kneeling on it, enjoying myself thoroughly, scissors and pins in hand, with swathes of cloth spread out flat over the large expanse of floor as Sybil directed my efforts at costume design and construction without the aid of the usual bought paper patterns. We drew our own, on squared paper, having first measured the actors fore and aft, and copied the necessary designs from library books! What luxury to have such space to work in.

During the day the energetic and talented Taylor family set about cleaning, painting, decorating and generally renovating the hotel ready for re-opening in the springtime. It remained in business for many years until, alas, all good things inevitably came to an end when Sybil, her husband Charlie, and Mary retired to enjoy well-deserved retirement in the district, at Macharioch House and Keil Point respectively.

Situated below the hotel were Keil Farm and the burned out ruins of the former Keil School.

"What happened there, and why is it called Keil?" asked Calum.

"Well," said John, "Long ago this place was called Kilcolmkill, which means the cell or preaching place of Saint Columba, and it was a holy place right up to the 16th century. Over the generations the name was shortened to Keil, and much later a beautiful mansion was built, which became the place where the school was originally established, on 29th November 1915, as Kintyre Technical College, by Sir William MacKinnon, 1st baronet of Loup and Balinakill.

Keil School ruins, Southend

He had the idea that a school should be built to provide a decent education to deserving Highland lads, and would be open to boys, from the age of twelve, who had passed their Qualifying Examination from the primary schools."

Calum and Neil looked puzzled.

"They don't have that exam any more," explained John, "but in my day we all had to sit it before going on to secondary school--- Campbeltown Grammar in my case. Around 200 day and boarding pupils were to be enrolled from the counties of Argyll, Inverness, Bute, Arran, Western Isles and the rest of the Highlands. Their education would be free, paid for by bursaries from their local councils, and they would stay at the school for three years while they followed a course in mainly engineering and agriculture--- very suitable for farmers' sons and country boys at that time, and much sought after."

"How did they know which boys to take?" asked Neil.

John smiled. "The pupils were found, a bit like junior footballers today, by talent scouts who went out on bursary tours, and by recommendations from local ministers and such like important folk in each parish.

You two might have really liked the school, learning how to grow crops, fruit and vegetables, and look after farm animals, though you might not have liked having to do all the household chores, apart from cooking, around the big house. And, of course, you didn't see your family and relations for weeks on end. Even at only ten miles' distance Campbeltown was declared to be too far away for parents to come visiting. At the end of the three years you had to pass exams, written and oral, before you got your certificate and they let you go!

But it was a great school, and many a Kintyre boy was glad of the chance of such a good education.

Sadly, the building caught fire on the night of 7th December 1924, and burned out. The pupils escaped just with the clothes they stood up in, and maybe a few small possessions, and that was the end of the school in Southend. The insurance money wasn't enough to rebuild it as it had been, so it was moved up to Dunbartonshire, to Helenslee, the house once owned by Denny of Dumbarton, the famous shipbuilders."

"That's quite sad," said Calum, "and what about the big house I can see among the ruins?"

"Oh, said John," that's the present Keil Farmhouse--- what's left of the original Keil House. In 1926 the whole of Keil, including the ruins of the school, were sold to a farmer called James Barbour, of Gartfern in Stirlingshire and his descendants are still farming right here to this day."

By this time *Sheena* was passing the impressive cliffs of Keil with their several caves, the Great Cave, the Piper's Cave and the Hermit's Retreat.

"Did folk really live in these caves?" asked Neil, open-mouthed. "They must have been frozen half the time."

"Yes, think of the awful draughts, and maybe bad folk were able just to walk in if they wanted to," said the scandalised Calum.

"Well, people have left evidence of living here away back as long ago as Neolithic times--- that is, prehistoric times," said John.

"Maybe the dinosaurs got them," uttered the irrepressible Calum.

"Don't be so daft, there weren't any dinosaurs left by then, but there must have been murderers and thieves and highwaymen all going about then," shivered Neil.

John leaned forward and, with a serious face, said, "The only person you hear about from long, long ago was the Piper of Keil, who was walking past the caves with his dog one dark night, on his way home from Carskiey to Southend, when he was grabbed by Something and dragged into a cave along with his trusty dog."

Caves of Keil

John went on in a low voice, "He disappeared for a long, long time, and was eventually found, wandering and mad, in a field near Inveraray, the dog still with him, "but," whispered John,"do you know what?"

"What? What?" shouted the boys, shivering with terrified delight.

John bent down and whispered again, "There was not a hair left on the poor dog--- not a single one! And if you pass the Piper's Cave on a black winter's night you might just be able to hear the faint sound of the pipes and the barking of the poor dog over the soughing of the wild wind through the terrifying darkness---".

The boys were suitably impressed, but weren't unduly scared on this bright, warm afternoon when it seemed that nothing frightening could possibly ever happen in Southend.

Obviously the next tale was about the ancient chapel dedicated to Saint Columba, and its holy well, along with what are described as Saint Columba's Footprints. These are just beside the caves, and visited by lots of tourists.

St. Columba's Footprints

John explained that the footprints weren't really those of the saint, but that one had been carved in 1856 by Daniel McIlreavie, a local mason, along with the date 564, which he wrongly thought was the date of Columba's landing in Kintyre. The other was very old --- dating from when Kintyre was still part of the Scots kingdom of Dalriata, later Dalriada, during the Dark Ages, and modern Argyll hadn't yet happened. It was where a chief or king stood with his foot on the footprint, at the time of his inauguration, and took an oath to protect and care for his people in return for their allegiance to him.

"Oh, yes," said Neil loftily," I know all about Saint Columba. "My dad says that soon there will be a big open-air meeting on the hill over there beside the Footprints."

"I know," added Calum importantly, "It's called the Saint Columba Conventicle, and it's always held in June, and the old minister, Mr MacVicar, will speak in Gaelic, because the new minister can't speak it."

Tale no. 15: Explosions, Cauldrons and Other Delights

I couldn't sleep. It was June and the sun hardly had time to set before it began to rise again, so the room was more or less continuously bathed in a diffuse, soft glow all night long.

But it wasn't just the sun that was keeping me awake --- my mind was going like a train as I unwillingly contemplated all the things I had to do before the end of the school term in a couple of week's time. I tossed and turned as I worried about my forthcoming piano accompaniment of the school choir at the ceilidh arranged for that very evening. They were to sing a medley of Gaelic songs among which was a set of Puirt-a-Beul, or songs for dancers to dance to.

I felt I hadn't really got the speed of the first Strathspey right, and it kept rattling through my mind while I tried, unsuccessfully, to make myself go back to sleep.

Eventually it became clear that I wouldn't, and couldn't, get back to sleep.

"I might as well get up and practise," I told my unwilling self, and struggled in a bleary haze through to the piano in the sitting-room. Fortunately there was no-one else in the house at the time, so I could practise without disturbing anyone.

The piano sat in the large bay window which overlooked the garden which, in turn, overlooked the open countryside. By this time it was almost four o'clock and the room was bathed in the rays of a glorious sunrise, giving me plenty of natural daylight to see by.

The neighbouring farms were still deep in blissful silence before the noisy clatter of morning milking would begin. Everywhere seemed completely deserted. I felt quite secure in the privacy of the sitting-room. There was nothing to distract me from a good, stimulating practice of the Puirt, especially the Strathspey.

I started up, and became quite engrossed in the music as I gained confidence and got faster and louder in my efforts.

"This is much more like the thing. This is how it'll be tonight at the ceilidh," I told myself, and swept on through the entire programme in happy anticipation of the evening's performance.

It was while I was proceeding at speed through a lively reel that I became aware, in the corner of my eye, of movement on the front lawn, and looked away from the piano to see, with utter astonishment, a little man dancing what looked like the Highland Fling, in the middle of my mother's rose garden.

He was keeping excellent time to the music, and dancing light-footed like a leprechaun. He saw me gazing, open-mouthed, at him and waved cheerily in the midst of his dance. I was forcibly reminded of the Hollywood film, Brigadoon!

Abruptly, I stopped playing, and the leprechaun stopped dancing. I gazed at him, thunderstruck, not knowing exactly what to do next.

He smiled at me, bowed solemnly from the waist, waved again, and vanished out of the garden before I could utter a word. I never saw him again.

Was he real, or was he a delusion of my over anxious mind?

I went around all morning completely bemused by my mysterious visitor, and told the staff of the school about the incident. They all laughed loudly, and told me I must have been making an awful lot of noise for someone in the garden to have heard me, but I had the feeling they were humouring this poor soul who was obviously in need of a good rest during the forthcoming holidays.

Happily, the ceilidh that evening was a resounding success.

Life goes on, and I had, the next day, to make the journey northwards to Lochgilphead High School where I would be attending an Outdoor Education Summer Course for Teachers as soon as the summer holidays began. We did extra educational courses in our own time, and mostly, at our own expense, in these days.

I was the liaison for teachers who wished to take part in the course, and had to discuss many details before the arrival of the participants.

The road, which wound through north Kintyre was, in those days, full of bends, broken down edges, bad cambers and narrow stretches. Many construction firms had taken on the considerable task of rebuilding the road and had gone bankrupt in the attempt. The latest firm had been working on it for several weeks and was still in business, so we were full of optimism that the new highway would soon be successfully finished.

I drove carefully through the various road-up hazards and now reached the area where trees crowded thickly on to the verges on both sides of the road.

Suddenly a man appeared through the forest and waved energetically in my direction. I looked around to see if he was waving at anyone else, saw no one, and waved cheerily back.

At that moment the entire roadway in front of me blew up and I was caught in a cascade of falling masonry, branches and mud. It thumped and clattered down on the roof and bonnet of the car, which was completely enveloped in the debris. For some illogical reason I thought I should not stop in case anything else exploded, and drove hesitantly on, peering through the curtain of mud on the windscreen, which the wipers quickly turned into a thick, black tide. No amount of water from the windscreen washers would remove this mess. I crawled on, agonisingly slowly, towards the head of West Loch Tarbert.

At last the welcome sight of the West Loch Hotel, just south of Tarbert, hove into view and I slowly turned the car into its front drive and drew up thankfully at the front door.

People in the hotel dining-room stared out aghast at the sight of the car which looked as if it had been through a war zone, and mine host rushed out of the hotel, yanked open the driver's door and helped me out. By this time shock was beginning to take effect and I started to shake, especially when I saw the state of the car.

A kindly visitor brought me a cup of tea in the hotel lounge, but I was shaking so much I couldn't hold the cup steady, and it clattered against my teeth when I attempted to drink. I soon gave that up.

"What on earth has happened to you?" questioned mine host. "I think I'd better phone the police."

Of course, he should have done, but I was in such a state of confusion that I said I didn't want the police and would be alright once the car was cleaned up again. After some arguments he gave up on calling the police and instead got some of his underlings to go out front with him, with buckets of water and sponges, and examine the car for structural damage. Miraculously, there was no damage but some scratches to the paintwork and a bent windscreen wiper.

Now I knew why the man was waving to me so energetically from the forest. Why there were no barriers, lights or people to warn the motorist I have never found out, but I did recognise that the firm's almighty carelessness was inexcusable. There could have been a devastating accident on that road --- and there could easily have been yet another firm going bankrupt.

Looking back, I also don't know why I didn't take some legal action against them myself. I suppose it was because there was, as yet, no Health and Safety legislation, and people tended to be much more accepting about dangerous happenings in our part of the countryside. The American habit of suing had not yet arrived from across the Atlantic.

At any rate kind folk helped to clean the car and, after an hour or so of rest and recuperation, I ventured forth timidly to resume my journey to Lochgilphead, much later than planned.

Once there everyone commiserated with me over my bad fright on the road, but soon we were all engrossed in plans for the forthcoming Outdoor Education Course. I was pleased about this as I didn't want to dwell on the incident.

Soon the day came when the summer course was due to begin, and we welcomed Primary, Secondary and specialist PE teachers into Lochgilphead High School where the course was centred. It had been decided that it would consist of practical applications of outdoor education theory in Loch Gair, Loch Sween and the Sound of Jura. In other words there was to be no mere armchair theorising and everyone would have to take physical part in the various activities over the ten days of the course.

I found myself fully involved in the sailing activities, mainly because I had my own Don Class, gunter-rigged sailing boat, *Catriona,* which doubled as the sixth boat in our salmon fishing fleet at Southend in Kintyre. I knew a lot about sailing (and fishing!) and was none too pleased to be told that I would just be part of a crew, with Sam, one of the PE teachers, in charge.

I knew for a fact that he himself didn't own a boat and I had a feeling that his knowledge of sailing was mainly theoretical but, for the sake of peace and harmony, decided to go along with the master plan.

Off we drove the next morning to the village of Achnamara beside beautiful Loch Sween. The weather was ideal for sailing and the four of us in the boat were looking forward to a brisk sail down the long sea loch. There were two novice women sailors, Sam and myself, and we set out with himself at the helm, instructing everyone in the theories of sails, sheets, halyards and the various sailing manoeuvres. The novices were pleased to get the instruction and carried out all tasks with concentration and alertness. I let it be known that I had been sailing boats since I was nine, but Sam kept issuing instructions to me as if I knew nothing at all.

We tacked back and forth across Loch Sween until about noon when we beached the boat and had a picnic lunch on the shore while basking in the hot, breezy sunshine. Sam was in his element with two admiring women hanging on his every word, but I was fed up listening to him.

After an hour's break we climbed back into the dinghy and this time Sam magnanimously allowed me to take the helm. Although hot onshore, there was a brisk wind blowing out on the water, and we sailed down the loch on a broad reach, the fastest point of sailing, at an exhilarating speed.

The two ladies were thoroughly enjoying themselves, but the bold Sam was beginning to look a bit green about the gills in the slightly choppy sea. Nevertheless he continued to issue patronising instructions to me every two minutes while sitting boldly, in a rather precarious position, on the boat's gunwale, rather than sensibly inside the hull.

I suggested to him gently that he might like to change his position and sit safely right inside the boat, but he passed off my suggestion nonchalantly, and said he would be fine where he was.

I mentally shrugged, and decided it was time to go about and put the boat on to the other tack, as we were getting rather close to the shore.

"Ready about. Lee O!" I sang out to my crew, and swiftly turned the dinghy up through the wind on to the next tack --- a perfectly correct procedure.

The next minute there was a yell, and Sam, who had been sitting with his hands grasping the edge of the gunwale, did a complete backwards somersault and disappeared into the sea with a loud splash.

At first I wasn't sure whether he had done it on purpose for a laugh, but when I saw the dark head emerging, spluttering from the waves and the arms waving wildly, I knew that he had learned the hard way how not to behave in a fast dinghy. As the skipper he should have known better, especially when there were novices in the boat. I knew I had to get him out of the water as soon as possible for, although it was July, the loch itself was very cold, being an inlet of the Atlantic.

I brought the dinghy round towards him, then pointed its bow up into the wind with sails flapping, in order to spill air and stop it sailing. Our awestruck novices were given wholly unexpected instructions on what to do when there is a man overboard.

Our combined efforts brought Sam in over the stern and he lay, puffing like mad, until he got his breath back. Then, shamefacedly, up he got and, finally recognising that I knew what I was doing, meekly let me take the boat back to her mooring at Achnamara without uttering another word.

"Thank goodness you knew what to do," said one of my female crew. "What would we have done if you hadn't been here, and we had been left alone in the boat?"

I desisted from the temptation to tell her exactly what would have happened, and set about getting Sam, who was now shivering in his saturated clothing, ashore and up to the camp where the rest of the group was waiting. He absolutely insisted on staying with us and resisted all suggestions to go back to the school for dry clothes.

That would obviously be just too much loss of face.

A great deal of good-natured ribbing went on but eventually we all sat about on the grass enjoying the warm, breezy sunshine and assumed that Sam, having been given a thick, fluffy towel, somebody's car rug and a hot mug of tea, would dry off nicely in a short time.

About fifteen minutes later one of the men who was sitting near him, called to me,

"He's not answering when I speak to him. In fact he won't even look at me."

There was anxiety in his voice, and we all went over to Sam. I didn't like the look of him. He had stopped shivering, which was a bad sign, and sat with his forehead resting on his upraised knees.

"Sam, can you hear me?" I asked anxiously. No response. "Sam, speak to me," I urged. Absolutely no reponse.

It was evident that he had gone into a state of hypothermia, and could be in danger if we didn't do something about it, and quickly.

"The hospital is just down the road at Lochgilphead," I said. "We'll need to get him over there right away."

There were no mobile phones at that time, so the men got him up and half carried him to the nearest car, hoping to get him to medical help as soon as possible. Off they went and I was left with the rest of the group, who had now gone very quiet.

I thought to myself that no amount of lectures from the organisers on the dangers of hypothermia would have been half as effective as actually seeing it in front of their very eyes, but what a grim way to learn that particular lesson!

That evening we all trooped over to the hospital where a much recovered Sam was sitting up in bed, surrounded by flowers, fruit and concerned lady teachers. He was thoroughly enjoying all the attention, but later admitted to me privately, that showing off in a boat is not a good idea, and he apologised for causing such a commotion, and for not accepting that I had had a great deal more experience than he in the actual handling of sailing boats.

I was immediately promoted to the rank of instructor. About time too, I thought.

Unfortunately I became known as the Holy Terror, who ditched anyone who did not obey orders fast enough!

We were due to do a long sail and take the big day-boat, which was anchored in Loch Gair, right down the coast of Kintyre to Southend. Obviously I was delighted at the thought of showing my home waters to the group, none of whom had ever been in south Argyll before, and happily pointed out all the landmarks of interest on the way.

We had a glorious day for our sail and that evening anchored in Dunaverty Bay where everyone went ashore in my boat, *Catriona,* which had been pressed into service as a tender, some to be fed and watered at the Argyll Arms in the village, before going back on board the day-boat for the night --- at least, the men did.

As the accommodation was cramped and limited I took the ladies home to the house with me. My wonderful mother didn't bat an eyelid when a band of strange young women turned up on her doorstep, looking for a bed for the night. The only thing was that there wasn't enough food in the house to satisfy our, by now, ravenous appetites, so back to the shore we went, fishing gear was fetched from "the hut" --- the old fisherman's cottage on the shore, now our net store. *Catriona* was relaunched, and the girls got their first lesson in trawling for lythe. With typical beginner's luck they all managed to catch at least one fish each and squealed with delight as they brought their haul into the boat. Of course, they didn't, or said they didn't, know how to gut the fish, so I had the task of cleaning all the lythe in the river when we went back inshore.

"That's the first fish I have ever caught," announced a delighted Sally to my mother back in the kitchen.

"Well, you can now tell everyone that you caught your own supper", said my smiling mother.

Out came the frying pan and in went the fish. Soon we were sitting round the big kitchen table, with delicious fresh fillets of lythe --- also known as pollock --- large cups of tea and thick slices of bread and butter.

"I bet this is much better than what the men got for their tea in the hotel," sighed Janet contentedly through a mouthful of food. "Talk about fish fresh from the sea! You couldn't get fresher than this. No wonder it tastes so great."

Soon afterwards a very tired group wandered upstairs and into beds all over the house. For once there was no lively conversation, just a few sleepy murmurings, then silence descended. I think they all fell asleep as soon as their heads touched the pillows.

The next morning Ronald took pity on us having to carry our heavy rucksacks all the way down to the shore, and arrived on a tractor at the back door.

"Shove all that stuff on to the trailer, he announced. "I'll take it down to Machribeg beach for you and it's only a step over to the jetty from there," and off he went, allowing my visitors to enjoy an unencumbered stroll down to Dunaverty to join up with the rest of the crew of the day-boat that morning.

When we got aboard the skipper called us all together for a "conference". This was rather a misnomer as he had already decided what we were going to do but, as he proposed quite an adventure, nobody raised any complaints about not being properly consulted.

"The weather forecast is good for the Inner Hebrides," he said, "so I suggest that, instead of just retracing our steps back up the east coast to Lochgilphead, we sail round the Mull of Kintyre and up the west coast, through the Sound of Jura to Loch Crinan, then ---" and he stopped for major effect --- "if the calm weather holds and the tides are right, we'll sail through the Corrievreckan."

"Garry," I spoke in hushed tones, "Do you think that is wise, with this inexperienced crew?"

"Don't worry," he reassured me," I won't take even the slightest risk with the boat's safety, and it'll be such a thrill for the crew to go through the Whirlpool. They will be able to dine out on the story for years afterwards!"

"Well, okay then, but no risks, mind!" I said.

"Absolutely no risks," he reassured me.

The reason for this discussion was our potentially dangerous west coast, exposed as it was to the open Atlantic. In particular, the mention of the Corrievreckan gave me a sudden cold thrill of apprehension. These were not waters for the inexperienced sailor, and required local knowledge and sailing expertise even from the "old salts".

Sally asked me why I was looking so serious.

"Well," I said, "going round the Mull of Kintyre is, in itself, to be taken seriously. This is a notorious ships' graveyard. Okay in the present weather but always to be treated with great respect. Once round the Mull we are then sailing in the open Atlantic. That too, is fine in calm seas but it's when we get up the coast past the island of Islay and enter the Sound of Jura that things can start to get a bit rough."

"What do you mean, rough?" asked Sally, rather apprehensively.

"Loch Crinan is fine --- a good anchorage, but it's when we sail back out into the north end of the Sound and into the narrow channel between the islands of Jura and Scarba that we enter the notorious Gulf of Corrievreckan."

"Why is it notorious?" asked another member of the crew who had overheard our conversation and anxiously joined in.

"It's all to do with the Whirlpool," I explained. The two girls looked appalled. "The tidal race formed in the straits, or narrow channel, between the north of Jura and the south end of Scarba, causes a very intense flood tide which can reach speeds of up to 8.5 knots, or around 10 miles per hour. This collides below water with a deep hole and a high, basalt rock pinnacle and produces tremendous standing waves, up to 30 feet, or about 9 metres, high, and also the infamous Corrievreckan Whirlpool."

Sally had turned quite pale. "Is that dangerous? Can you sail through it?"

"Yes, you can sail through it, at certain stages of the tide, when it is quite safe even for a sailing boat," I explained." It is the third biggest whirlpool in the world. Its name, in Gaelic, is *Coire Bhreacain* , meaning speckled pot or cauldron, probably from the white-topped waves breaking and foaming over the top of the disturbance. And like a boiling pot it makes a loud noise, only in this case the roar of the Whirlpool can be heard from sixteen to twenty miles away!"

"Help," muttered Sally, almost inaudibly. "If I'd known I was going to have to sail through a whirlpool I wouldn't have come on this course."

"Don't worry," I added. "Garry is an accomplished sailor. He won't take us into any danger."

Sally looked almost disbelieving, but smiled bravely and went off to coil down a loose rope.

We sailed in placid blue seas right round the Mull of Kintyre, up the glorious west coast and entered Loch Crinan, as planned. After a delicious evening meal at the Crinan Hotel we all wandered off for a stroll around Crinan Basin which is at the outer end of the famous Crinan Canal. All kinds of small vessels use the canal as a shortcut from the waters of Loch Fyne to the outward end at the Sound of Jura and points west. Lots of yachts and other interesting boats lay moored or anchored here.

The *"Vital Spark"* in Crinan Canal

"Look, here's Neil Munro's *Vital Spark*, "shouted Garry, and we all trooped over to look fondly at the sadly rusting hull of the gabbart, or "puffer", which featured so prominently in Neil's wonderful series of tales about the mythical little steam lighter skippered by Para Handy around the west coast of Scotland. This was, of course, not the original *Vital Spark,* but one of many which were used in the various film versions of the tales. We looked at the forlorn little ship languishing, forgotten, amid the wonderful scenery which she had undoubtedly sailed through many times, during her life as a working "puffer" on the west coast.

Another excited yell from Garry brought me running to his side. He was standing beside an unexceptional, even faded-looking yacht tied on to a bollard at the head of the basin.

"Look at this," he almost squawked, pointing to her starboard bow.

I looked. There, in faded black letters was the name of the yacht --- *Seewolf.*

I didn't need any explanations from him as I knew exactly who she had belonged to. The rumours had gone around the boating fraternity for years, and there she was, in front of my very eyes --- the disappeared, former personal property of Field-Marshal Erwin Rommel --- "liberated" from a north African port by a British officer after the battle of el Alamein, brought to Britain and now lying in sad neglect in Crinan Basin.

The crew came running to see this prime example of wartime memorabilia, and were noticeably silent after their first exclamations of surprise. We almost felt the presence of the famous German general, and I reflected on the fickleness of the power-mad dictator who had accepted devoted, even if misplaced, service from this man, then destroyed him in a fit of vitreolic madness.

The next day brought more calm, settled weather and the decision was made to sail out into the Sound of Jura and turn westwards through the eight mile long gulf of Corrievreckan. It was slack tide as we sailed out of Loch Crinan, past Ardnoe Point and the entrance to Loch Craignish with its scatter of little islands and skerries and passed, on the port side, Barnhill, the house on Jura belonging to George Orwell of *Nineteen Eighty-Four* fame.

I hadn't liked to mention to the crew, in the passing, that Craignish Point was the spot where the world-famous *Comet,* the world's first passenger paddleship, was wrecked due to the powerful currents around the area of the Whirlpool.

To everyone's surprise Garry, our skipper, then shinned up to the top of the mast and surveyed the waters ahead of us. We were now entering the infamous Corrievreckan.

The subdued, but eagle-eyed, crew looked anxiously at the sea around the boat. There was really nothing to see except for a few small eddies and ruffles on the otherwise smooth surface of the ocean. Garry remained vigilant at the head of the mast and we proceeded safely through the infamous strait. Soon the small island of Colonsay appeared to the west and the long peninsula of the Ross of Mull to the north. We were through.

"A bit of a damp squib," breathed Sally in relief as Garry slid quietly down the mast to the deck.

and became mildly infected themselves, at least Teddy did. It became a case of "If you can't beat 'em, join 'em" --- in any case "Health and Safety" hadn't yet been invented.

On one occasion, after the long, wearisome trail down through Lowland Scotland we arrived at our designated hotel in Castle Douglas, clambered out of the bus laden with luggage, props and bits of scenery and trudged into the hotel. After a welcome dinner we had a rehearsal of our play, with Angus getting uptight as we inevitably forgot our words and moves. How many times did we say, "It'll be alright on the night," which just made him more irritated than ever.

However we were eventually released and went off to relax in our usual way. This shouldn't have, but always did result in an impromptu ceilidh till the early hours, much to the justified annoyance of the other hotel guests. Angus then chased us off to bed uttering dark predictions about our not being fit to take part in the festival the next evening.

The young farmers, however, were happily off the leash, had no cows to milk the next morning, and were determined not to waste a precious moment of their freedom. As a result the bar did a roaring trade until the wee small hours, and all the usual songs were sung (over and over and over again!) Ceilidhing continued in small groups in various bedrooms until exhaustion finally set in and a blessed silence settled over the hotel.

The next morning I heard guffaws of laughter coming from the direction of the top corridor, and, going up to see what was going on, discovered a group of our young farmers holding their sides as a rather bedraggled Teddy appeared, hopping about helplessly all over the corridor. On awakening in his slightly befuddled state he had somehow managed to get both his legs into the one trouser leg. Naturally he had tried to extricate himself from this undignified condition, without success, set off out of his room in order to obtain assistance, and to avoid the scolding of his wife but, after staggering around for some time, completely lost his balance, crashed into a large plaster statue of some unclothed Greek deity, causing it to rock alarmingly, and finally fell to the floor where he was eventually confronted by an irate Olive.

"Edward Herbert!" she commanded, "Get back to the room immediately and dress yourself properly!"

Teddy knew things were serious when Olive gave him his full and proper name instead of the usual "Teddy". Obediently, he gathered himself up somehow and staggered off in a zig-zag course back to their room, still hampered by the offending trouser leg, not to mention the unseemly mirth of unsympathetic onlookers. Even Angus was heard hooting away in the background.

All day long poor Teddy had to endure the ribald comments of players and crew, and the next morning was confronted by a large notice attached, by who else, but Alf of course, to the front of the unclothed Greek statue, bearing the words of Andy Stewart's jokey song --- Donald, where's yer troosers?

That was another hotel we wouldn't be allowed back to!

Several of us in the cast used to become extremely nervous before and during these competitions at semi-final level, which caused us to experience a temporary cessation of reality.

Florrie Niven, our wardrobe mistress, was requested by Angus to take a walk-on part in a scene, as a member of a crowd at a garden fete, as at the last minute he felt we were a bit short in number.

"All you have to do, Florrie, is take off your glasses so the stage lights don't make them flash, then wander around the stalls at the fete, admiring the merchandise. After a minute or two go up to one stall and pretend to bargain with the seller for an item on the table and then come off stage. There's nothing to it, and you don't have to say a word. It's dead easy."

Florrie, who had never appeared on stage before, never mind in a national competition, went into a complete flap, but tremblingly did as she was told. She duly arrived at the table and started to make bargaining actions with the stall-holder.

Watching from the wings, we wondered why the stall-holder firstly looked shocked and then appeared to be stifling some strong emotion, before a flushed Florrie hurriedly left the stage and joined us in the wings.

"What is it, Florrie?" asked Angus anxiously. She said nothing, but merely held out her hand. Nestling in her palm were, not her glasses, but her dentures!

In her all-encompassing stage fright she knew she had to take something off, but couldn't remember what, so, in a panic she had removed her teeth thus giving the unsuspecting stall-holder the full toothless gums treatment. No wonder that scene was later described by the adjudicator as "slightly unreal"

I, too, played my part in the confusion stakes during that same competition when, in another play, and dressed to kill in full medieval gown with the obligatory long, flared, pointed sleeves I accidentally flicked a sleeve point full into the eye of the young hero, rendering him temporarily blinded and stumbling about the stage with tears pouring from the affected eye.

We didn't get into the finals that year!

But several years later, in 1967, after many mishaps along the way, Dunaverty Players did reach the Scottish Finals and covered themselves with glory.

In spite of his irrepressible sense of fun, Alf was a serious businessman when it came to his shop, post office and cafe, as well as all matters to do with Dunaverty Players. He took it upon himself to do something about the parlous state of the floor in the hall.

This had so many exposed knots in the wooden planking that people constantly tripped over them, especially during the village "hops". One night Alf announced to the assembled drama group that he had bought a floor from some newly closed theatre, and that it would be installed in the village hall very soon. This absorbed him so constantly that Maria, his daughter, when asked where her father was, would usually say, "He's up at the hall, playing with his new toy."

When all was duly installed and settled in we moved the drama rehearsals up to the hall, which had a proper stage and much more room, but, in spite of that I missed the comforting cosiness of the cafe.

I always felt that winning the awards was not really what we were about, wonderful though that undoubtedly was, but more important were the memorable nights down at the village hall, when we all got together during the winter months, despite distance, bad weather and the unreliable cars of these days, and thoroughly enjoyed the company, the craic, and the antics on stage, even if Angus did rule us with a rod of iron.

"This is a democratic club," he boomed "but I am in control!"

As he was the published author of many plays as well as detective and children's novels, we believed him and tended to do what we were told, though, truth to tell, we did christen him The Grim Reaper --- behind his back, of course.

Angus, however, continued to find it very difficult to control our mischievous business manager, Alf.

During the club's early days Port Ellen Dramatic Club, on the nearby Hebridean island of Islay, issued an invitation to Dunaverty to come over and join them in a little drama festival simply for the enjoyment of the local island folk. Logistics were a considerable problem, involving bus, then ship, followed by bus again or, alternatively, bus, aeroplane and bus. The latter course was deemed more straightforward and less time consuming so the club set off, having chartered a BEA flight for the outrageous sum of £100. They were to fly from Machrihanish to Machrie in Islay, where a fleet of buses and lorries would collect the visitors and convey them to Port Ellen. At some point during the rather bumpy flight nervous passengers were cheered by the appearance of a notice, in what looked suspiciously like Alf's handwriting declaring, as on any Campbeltown bus: PASSENGERS ENTERING OR LEAVING THIS VEHICLE WHILST IN MOTION DO SO AT THEIR OWN RISK.

Apparently the pilot was so pleased with the relaxing effect of this humorous notice on his nervous passengers that he insisted on the notice being left exactly where it was for long afterwards.

A wonderful time was had on Islay --- naturally!

Like most producers Angus always had a struggle to get us all together in the hall and start the rehearsals on time. As many of the cast were dairy farmers, with an evening milking to attend to, this was not always possible.

One evening we awaited the arrival of three members of the cast, John, Maggie and Janet from Aucharua farm, and Angus was beginning to frown a bit.

"Where's Aucharua?" he demanded.

After half an hour of waiting we heard a car being driven up to the hall door.

"At last!" growled Angus, and in came the Aucharuas, not apologetic in the slightest for their late arrival. Maggie came in first, grinning from ear to ear.

"Sorry we're late," she said," but we had a bit of trouble with the bull."

Then John himself arrived and, in the self-deprecating way of the local farmers, told us what had happened.

After the milking he had gone to usher the cows, accompanied as always by the bull, out of the dairy and back to their field, and the animals, as they had done hundreds of times, walked sedately

towards the entrance to the farmyard. The door which led to the cheese-loft in the farmhouse had been left open, as it had been on many occasions, and the cows wandered past unconcerned. But, for no discernible reason, the bull, for the first time in his life, took a right turn into the open doorway and started up the stairs to the cheese-loft, unfortunately getting himself jammed in the turn of the stairs on the way. He could go neither up nor down, and started up an ear-splitting bawling, which brought all the farm folk out at a run. John, approaching with care from the rear, decided that he would have to get a ladder, climb up through the loft window and try to push the clearly distressed bull backwards down the stairs. All the farm folk had by now taken refuge in the farmhouse and were peering fearfully out of the windows.

This, apparently, had been a sight to behold, with John trying to shove the thoroughly upset, extremely heavy bull backwards and the animal, frightened by all the commotion, seriously resisting his efforts. Eventually gravity took over and the bull half fell, half scrambled down the stairs. John, having lost his balance, followed precipitately, and there was a tangle of man and beast in the farmyard until order was resumed and the bull, his dignity restored, rushed away still bellowing, to the calm and safety of his harem in the field. Miraculously John was unhurt but needed a complete change of clothes before his sisters would allow him into the car for the journey down to the hall.

John's straight-faced, matter-of-fact telling of the story had us all in fits of laughter, and the Aucharuas were instantly forgiven for being late!

I used to sit quietly in the semi-darkness of rehearsals, looking up at the players on stage, and the others waiting off stage, and thinking how much I cared for these folk and how privileged I was to be living and working among them.

The place itself was always a source of delight to me, and even nature put on a show for me one night as I left the hall after rehearsal. It was pitch black, as there were no street lights in Southend at that time, and it was a freezingly cold night in November. I caught my breath as I left the lighted hall and turned to walk up the dark road home, for the sky was alight with the brilliance of the Aurora Borealis, pulsing and blazing over the hills of Kintyre with endless waves of flickering, glowing colours. I was spellbound with the display, and wandered off up the road, nearly

walking off the edge several times, so entranced was I with this magical scene. When at last I arrived at the manse entrance I was loath to go inside, but at the same time, anxious to tell my family what I had seen and hope they had experienced it too.

I remember thinking, at the time, "Always hold this in your mind, for the memories of this place and these people will be precious to you for ever."

I had seen the Aurora only once before, at Dunoon, again on a freezing cold November night when I had sat up late correcting the first-term history papers of my third-year pupils. It was about two in the morning when at last I finished and, getting up stiffly, stretched up to pull back the curtains for the morning. I got a shock at the waves of light pulsing over the hills of Cowal, and at first had the horrible thought that there must have been a nuclear explosion somewhere near, for this was the era of the Cold War when nuclear annihilation was not in the realms of the impossible.

When it dawned on me that I was experiencing a wonderful, natural phenomenon that most people never get the chance to see I stood for a long time enjoying it all, but eventually had to drag myself away from the window and get some sleep before facing my pupils later in the morning.

On both counts it was unusual to see the Aurora as far south as Argyll, but the western sky was clear of the light pollution that many places suffer from nowadays, and still is.

"The drama", as everyone called it, was not the only social outlet in south Kintyre, and I happily found myself in three choirs, all at the same time. Kintyre had a well-deserved reputation for choral singing --- as well as a great deal of informal ceilidh singing --- as did the districts of Oban and Connel, and so I sang in Southend Church Choir, originally directed by Florrie Niven, in Campbeltown Gaelic Choir under the direction of Charles Bonnar (Chick) and in Kintyre Singers, established and directed by the blind music teacher and organist, James MacTaggart, a Coll man who had tragically lost his sight as a young child on the island while watching a stone mason at work.

This provided a wonderfully varied musical experience before the unexpected arrival of the Beatles' songwriter and singer, Paul MacCartney in our midst. As is the usual case in Kintyre no-one made much of a fuss of Paul and his then girlfriend, Jane Asher

except, of course, the Grammar School girls who ran screaming after him whenever he appeared in the town.

Once he was forced to take refuge in MacIlchere's grocer shop in Main Street where a shrieking crowd of girls had ambushed him. Paul had to retreat to the back shop where Mr Joe MacIlchere kindly hid him until the arrival of Mrs Kate Black, the farmer's wife from Tangy Farm, a next-door neighbour of Paul's, fortunately shopping in Campbeltown that morning. She smuggled Paul out of the back door into her car and hastily drove him out of reach of the screaming mob.

Paul and Jane, however, were treated with quiet hospitality by adults in Kintyre society and soon received an invitation from Campbeltown's Gentlemen's Club to a dance in the club premises. Ladies had to receive an invitation before entering the hallowed portals --- rather like a golf club --- and I had received an invitation myself, so duly turned up, only mildly interested in being in the company of a pop-star, as we called Paul, and really more impressed by the cream of Campbeltown society. Paul and Jane behaved with becoming modesty and decorum, even when I, unfortunately, banged Paul on the head with my elbow, during a spirited version of the Eightsome Reel. We had no idea at that time just how stratospheric the Beatles, and Paul in particular, would become in later years. In fact, I cringe when I remember how I rather loftily told my school pupils that the group were only a flash-in-pan and would never last. How wrong can you get?

I also can't forget Paul's kindness to my boss's three young sons, while on a visit to Tangy Farm, when he had the patience, and took the time, to teach them the basics of guitar playing. They, of course, were mightily impressed and kept on telling everyone who would listen that Mr McCartney had said this, and Mr McCartney had said that, until their jealous young school friends could stand no more of this boasting and took radical measures to shut them up.

It was like that in Kintyre. Although it certainly had its landed gentry it was a pretty well classless society, where you were valued for what you did and not for who you were, socially.

The bad old days of master and servant, when farm workers were paid a pittance for a lifetime of slavery to the land, were well and truly over, and now they had living wages, employee's rights, their own cars and county council houses, with government pensions

when their working days were over --- and, most importantly, the respect of their employers.

The Rev. Angus MacVicar, our drama producer's father, used to tell of the days of Queen Victoria, when Southend had a social hierarchy, from the humblest of farm workers, to the top of the aristocracy.

Living in its midst Ina, Dowager Duchess of Argyll, on the death of her husband, the 8th Duke, built herself a dower house at Macharioch on the south-east coast of the peninsula, and lived there almost as a recluse, until her death.

Macharioch House and farm, together with the gardener's lodge and two farm workers' cottages formed a small community of between 35 and 40 people, all involved in maintaining the Duchess in her chosen lifestyle. As well as her elegant mansion, she erected on the shore a magnificent memorial to her late husband, and provided two beautiful stained glass windows in St Blaan's Church (now known as Southend Parish Church).

Le'arside road down to Macharioch

The Duchess was driven about the place in a big, maroon, open car chauffeured by Broadfoot, her butler. The children stood aside respectfully when the car passed them on the road, while the boys

saluted and the girls curtsied, but she never acknowledged their presence by nod or smile.

On the sudden death of one of her farm tenants and the subsequent removal from Macharioch of his young family with no apparent means of support, the Duchess gave to the new widow a small pot plant, not by her own hand, but that of her butler.

Noblesse oblige!

Tale no. 4: All Things Bright and Beautiful

The widespread nature of Southend parish, and its distance from Campbeltown meant that, in order to have any kind of meaningful contact with the rest of the community you had to have a car, and be able to drive it on all kinds of unusual terrain.

As we didn't even live in the village, but two miles in the countryside to the north of it, the day inevitably came when I was obliged to learn to drive my father's pale blue Ford Consul, as he was heavily engaged in his parish duties and had neither time nor inclination to drive us around whenever we requested a lift.

Driving was no trouble to my brother Ronald, who had been driving tractors on various farms since childhood, and transferred this skill to cars with absolutely no difficulty whatsoever, but wasn't always around to act as chauffeur.

But, with one mind, we banned my mother from taking driving lessons as we reckoned her speed and distance judgment were hopeless, and she would be a menace to the rest of the community if allowed behind the wheel of a car, especially the Consul which had only three forward gears and a very large turning circle. The mysteries of double de-clutching were, we felt, completely beyond her. So she declared that as we were all so unkind I would have to learn to drive and chauffeur her around wherever she wished to go.

I made the mistake of asking my father to teach me to drive as it was a bit of a bind to have to be taken the eight miles from the house into Campbeltown for a professional lesson when, as I mistakenly thought, I could pick it up just as well here at home in Southend. That was a major error on my part and nearly caused a rift in the family.

The inevitable happened --- Dad and I argued constantly about my driving and he seemed to me to be insufferably bossy:

"Why couldn't I avoid crashing the gears? Why couldn't I treat the clutch more carefully? Why didn't I see that it could burn out? Why was I driving so fast for a learner --- a full forty miles an hour!"? etc, etc.

I put his fussiness down to the fact that he had been taught to drive by an ex-RAF pilot, Squadron Leader John Galbraith --- one of his congregation.

One day we were driving back from Campbeltown with me at the wheel, arguing continuously as usual about my driving. In the middle of the open countryside I decided I could stand all this unjustified criticism for not a moment longer. I jerked the car to a standstill at the verge, threw open the door dramatically and stepped out on to the empty road, bristling with anger.

"That'll teach him," I thought, furiously. Then, of course, I looked around me. I was slap in the middle of nowhere, and wondering where on earth I was going to go next and how I was going to get back to Southend. Reluctantly, and with complete loss of face, I climbed back into the car, crashed into first gear as always, and we resumed our journey in an atmosphere of strained silence.

Fortunately I did, in fact, pass my driving test in Campbeltown some weeks later but had to admit that, in the interests of family harmony, you should never have a family member teach you to drive.

Nowadays the test that I sat would be regarded as a complete dawdle as the town had no traffic lights and very little road traffic compared with a big city. The down side was that many indifferent drivers passed their test first time round, and were subsequently let loose on the unsuspecting public.

One of my teacher colleagues, physically shaking so much with nerves during the test that the loose change in her pocket rattled continuously, was told to draw the car up at the kerb. She did so, and waited in trepidation for the next instruction.

"Now, Madam, would you please empty the loose change out of your pockets," instructed the tester. "All that rattling is driving me mad."

The poor girl hurried to appease him, but still didn't manage to stop shaking --- in silence this time. Fortunately she passed her test and didn't have to go through that ordeal again.

Dad, of course, could be extremely courteous where lady drivers were concerned.

One afternoon he had been driving down the east coastal road from Campbeltown to Southend, known as the Le'arside, a narrow, twisting single-track road with steep gradients, when he came across an apparently abandoned Riley blocking a notorious bend, its back wheels embedded in the muddy bank. With some foreboding he stopped the Consul and got out to look, as he thought, for potential casualties. Some yards on he came across two middle-aged ladies in floods of tears, and asked what he could do to help.

"Oh, please, could you drive our car round that dreadful bend," sobbed one. "It's stalled and we are afraid it's going to run backwards into that peat-bog."

So Dad had first to reverse the Consul safely back out of the way into a far distant lay-by then, with engine screaming in high revs he got the Riley's wheels off the bank. The tyres finally gripped the road and it lurched clumsily out of the mud but alas, immediately dived, nose first, into the opposite bank. How Dad wished his ex-RAF pilot was around to take over. The situation was saved when, blessedly, the tractor from Glenahervie appeared and the farmer, quietly and efficiently, hitched a rope on to the Riley and towed it safely on to the middle of the road. It seems he was used to finding stranded cars on that bend.

The roads were really quite hazardous throughout the entire peninsula of Kintyre and the cars, too, were not up to modern standards.

The Consul was awful to learn on, what with double de-clutching and trying to perform the impossible task of doing a three-point turn on our narrow country roads, when the car wanted to do, at the very least, a five-point turn. In addition, driving round some of our tighter corners was a positive nightmare,

I remember trying to take the car up the narrow path from Keil to High Keil, with its sharp bend in the middle. It couldn't manage it, and I had to reverse downhill in order to get the wheels round far enough to take the bend. Reversing downhill is a dangerous manoeuvre.

A similar situation happened to my father on a notoriously bad bend on the Carradale road. We were all in the car when it stalled while trying to climb the inside turn of an infamously steep brae, and all of us passengers had to get out and start pushing the unwilling vehicle up and around the badly engineered corner. My unhappy father struggled to double de-clutch the engine into first gear, while the car, held and no more on its handbrake, indicated that it would really prefer to run backwards down the hill. Dad decided to let it do just that so that he could get a good run at the brae. We scattered out of the way and kept a wary lookout for anything approaching from the rear. Eventually, with the engine roaring, he got the car to struggle up the steep corner in first gear. It was impossible to swing wide there in case you found yourself nose to nose with any vehicle coming downhill. As he didn't want the car to stall again he continued his laboured ascent of the brae for quite some time, while

we all plodded resentfully up after him until the road was level enough for him to risk stopping for us.

"And this is your idea of a nice run to Carradale?" said my mother in acid tones as she fell into the back seat and concentrated hard on getting her breath back.

But the most dangerous place of all for driving a car was at the Mull of Kintyre lighthouse. This, first lit in 1788, was one of the two lighthouses in Southend district, (the other being on the island of Sanda) and my father obviously had to visit them both as well as any other dwelling in the parish. It was many miles from Southend. Most people mistakenly think that the village is at the Mull, but the actual headland is about seven miles from the Drumavoulin turn-off, which itself is a couple of miles from the village.

Angus MacVicar kindly offered to take us to the lighthouse in his big Morris car and he manoeuvred it along the twisting, single-track road, with the skill born of long practice, to a wide open space at the top of the Mull of Kintyre.

"Normally we would stop here at The Gap," said Angus, as we gazed in awe down the narrow, twisting slope with its hairpin bends, which led to the lighthouse. But all that stood between us and utter disaster were the good brakes of Angus's car, and his undoubted skill at coping with the sharp bends.

"What happens if we meet something coming up the way?" I quavered.

"Oh, it's okay," replied our hero, "I'll just reverse uphill to the nearest lay-by and let him through. That's what we always do, you know. You can't expect anyone to reverse downhill on this road. It's too dangerous."

We arrived at the lighthouse, pale and shaken, with a completely unfazed Angus blithely leading the way in.

Then, of course, there was the return journey. This was just as bad, if not worse, as the big car seemed to be standing on its hind legs while we crawled laboriously back up to The Gap. I later had nightmares about being in a car which was being reversed down the lighthouse road, only for the driver to lose control and fail to take the first bend, with subsequent horrific results!

Nowadays it is forbidden to take a car down past The Gap, but people just got on with things then, and driving down to the lighthouse was all in the day's work for most folk.

I did it myself several times over the years with frequently terrified passengers, when I remembered the advice of an outspoken female friend who remarked, "If you want to know what a man is really like, take him out sailing in a rough sea and just see how he behaves."

This basic idea is equally useful when quelling the pretensions of any loud and boastful person, whether male or female. As going sailing is not always feasible I thought of a useful alternative --- drive the source of annoyance down to the lighthouse from The Gap, preferably when there is a car coming up the way, so that you have to reverse uphill round a bend or two to the nearest lay-by and again, just see how the boaster behaves.

I actually did this on occasion --- it had much the same effect as rough sailing. The annoying person was always paralysed with fright into respectful silence, and annoyed me no more!

The trouble was, of course, that I often found myself in the passenger seat, when the situation was reversed. There were some truly dreadful drivers in Kintyre, mainly those who had never sat a driving test in their lives. Youngsters learning to drive were usually taken out to the airport --- known locally as "the drome" (the aerodrome), where they learned to handle their vehicles efficiently on the spacious, empty runways before venturing on to the public roads. This was, of course, before the airport became part of NATO. But the older generation who learned to drive before the Second World War, hadn't been required to sit a driving test, and drove everywhere quite legally, but with little, or no, instruction.

Elderly farmers, often with failing eyesight, could be observed weaving all over the road as they drove along, interestedly inspecting the crops and animals in the fields on the way, and even falling into a doze if they were tired or had been up very early in the morning.

I vividly remember a hair-raising drive to Muasdale on the west coast of Kintyre, with just such a driver at the wheel. I was a passenger in the back seat on the shore side of the car, which was full of ministers going to an evening service in the parish church on the hill. The driver was full of chat and paying scant attention to the twisting, winding road which bordered the beach. Every time we came to yet another bad corner I looked down in horror, as the offside wheels ran along the grassy verge, not the road, and was a nervous wreck by the time we arrived at Muasdale Church. I couldn't concentrate on a single word of the service, so worried was I about the return journey, which would be in the dark. Never were

heartfelt prayers for a safe return uttered more sincerely than mine that evening, and I hoped that the presence of so many of the clergy would guarantee divine intervention and a journey without disaster on the way home. Mercifully, it did.

As soon as we young folk passed our driving tests we quickly got used to driving long distances at all hours of the day and the night, in all kinds of weather conditions, in pursuit of our very enjoyable social activities.

Once my mother complained that she hadn't seen me for three weeks on the trot, as I had been a-roving from Southend to Campbeltown, to Tangy, to Peninver, to Carradale, to Ifferdale or to Machrihanish on every single evening.

On one particularly busy night I attended three different venues, rushing from the one to the other in quick succession. I started out driving twelve miles from Southend down to Davaar, south of Campbeltown, to collect friends for a squash competition. This was to be held at RAF Machrihanish --- "the drome" --- eight miles from Davaar, courtesy of the service personnel who generously allowed twelve civilians to use the squash courts at night. This involved driving up to the guardhouse, signing in and being warned not to get out of the car before reaching the courts as the Alsatian guard dogs were on the loose, then making a quick dash from the car into the safety of the courts. All this was an adventure in itself, before we even took on the very athletic RAF squash team. As usual we were beaten hollow by the experts, but enjoyed the company.

Afterwards I hustled my friends back into the car, signed out at the guardhouse, drove them the eight miles back to Davaar, where I left them, turned the car and hastily drove the two miles back into Campbeltown. I arrived late and somewhat dishevelled at Gaelic Choir practice in the Grammar School, apologising profusely to Charles Bonnar, our conductor, and my colleagues in the alto section. I had felt obliged to make the effort to get to rehearsal as the National Mòd was looming on the horizon and I needed all the singing practice I could get.

No sooner was choir practice over than I rushed away again as Angus had declared an extra necessary drama practice at Southend later that evening. So it was back the ten miles to the village hall, and more profuse apologies, to our producer this time, for my very late arrival.

Who said that life in the country was dull?

My father was totally reliant on his car for visiting all corners of his parish, which began at Killellan bridge and ended at the Mull of Kintyre, north to south, and stretched right across the entire peninsula, east to west, which made for some hazardous journeys, especially on the single-track roads.

His predecessor, the Rev. Angus MacVicar, our drama producer's father, had only his bicycle and his own two feet, with occasional pony and trap journeys, and, later still, lifts in someone's motor car --- still a rarity in his day.

A minister of the parish, many years after my father retired, regularly visited his congregation on horseback. Jimmy was a retired Forestry Commission Clydesdale horse and became a popular feature of the minister's visits, though Angus complained that Jimmy's "big feet" made an awful mess of his front lawn.

The minister obviously didn't mind in the slightest what Jimmy's hoofs did to the manse lawn, for the horse was often seen to be grazing there while waiting for his master to go out again on a visit. It all looked like a scene straight out of Jane Austen.

The Georgian Manse of St Blaan had its full complement of stone outbuildings, built round a square yard, with stabling for three horses, a large barn, a coach-house, a spacious byre with hayloft, a walled midden and two smaller outbuildings used as a washing-house and coal cellar.

Manse of St. Blaan

The small, original ancient manse, christened by the MacVicar children, Peter's Barn, stood between the later Georgian building and the road, and still had its roof and roof beams though no windows or doors. This was the home of a beautiful barn owl and one of next door's farm tractors.

House and farmyard were a true example of a Georgian country manse and were the most attractive of the type that I have ever seen.

Around this were two acres of walled garden with a large vegetable plot and fruit bushes, a screen of mature horse-chestnut trees, a small plantation of larch trees, and a line of beautiful lime trees stretching along the roadside wall. The extensive and sheltered back garden contained the church hall, and parking for this was always in the manse yard.

The lovely grassy area in front of the house was graced by a magnificent copper-beech tree where the MacVicar children played on their swing. We inherited that same swing, and enjoyed it as they had done. Also in the front garden were the one hundred and fifty rose bushes belonging to my mother, which in no way took up the whole lawn. These had originated in a Northern Ireland nursery because the weather conditions over there were more like ours than any other area of Scotland. How they flourished --- fed regularly with bone meal, and blood from the Campbeltown butcher's, and watered by the plentiful Kintyre rain!

Across the road and down a slope was the manse glebe for grazing the minister's horse and possibly, cows and sheep, with the waters of the River Conaglen running through it. The incumbent minister had the salmon rights in this stretch of the river, but we never saw any salmon. In any case we got ours from the sea fishery.

Long ago this was the usual country arrangement for the independent maintenance of the minister and his family, in the days when stipends were almost non-existent and most people had to live mainly off the land. The Manse was also used as an unofficial hotel for any visiting officials to this remote parish.

I have never loved any house as much as I loved the Manse of St Blaan. It had a happy aura about it, due in some part, I am sure, to the MacVicar family who lived in it for over forty years, and I was shocked, on revisiting, after my father's retirement, to find that radical changes had been visited on the old place, in the form of demolition of all the outbuildings except, strangely enough, the stable.

My mother's roses had been ploughed into the ground and the copper-beech tree had been cut down as had been the lovely lime trees. The former walled garden is now a barren car park for the church hall. Pheasants no longer strut through its long grass, nor do the hares play and spar with one another in the springtime and the wild snowdrops, daffodils, bluebells and primroses no longer bloom in among the larch trees.

The house is still the parish manse but, tragically, has lost a great deal of its original character. A listing order was belatedly placed on it, but that came too late to save the outbuildings from destruction.

I found it absolutely heartbreaking.

The garden was always associated in my mind with the local animals and birds, domestic and wild.

We had a semi-wild little Manx cat, called, unimaginatively, Cat, who arrived one day in the back garden when I was hanging out some clothes. She was a beautiful, brindled, grey and white colour with white paws, longish hair almost like a Persian, the ear tufts one associates with the Scottish Wild Cat, and the traditional Manx stump of a tail. I had never seen her before, and thought she must have come off the hill or from one of the farms.

I looked at her appealing little face upturned towards me and reached down to stroke her. She immediately sank her very sharp claws into my hand and spat ferociously. I jumped back in dismay, licking my bleeding hand, and threatening to banish her for ever from the garden. This was, I thought, a part-bred Wild Cat, and therefore untameable. But she kept coming back and I soon fell under her spell --- just one melting look from these golden eyes and one soft little miaow, and I was lost. She became an integral part of our family, but we could never take any liberties with her, and never touched her back or she would turn into a snarling tigress. We thought someone must have hurt her back at some time in her youth.

Ronald and "Cat"

Typically of her Manx breed she had only seven kittens during her lifetime, four of which were Manx and three were tailed cats. She was, however, a rotten mouser. I came into the kitchen one day to find Madam Cat, paws folded neatly under her, reclining lazily on my father's chair while idly watching a mouse running to and fro right in front of her nose. She made not a move to catch it, and looked like a spectator at Wimbledon.

I loved her to bits, but always hankered after a dog. This, however was deemed inadvisable as the fields around the house were frequently full of sheep or cattle, and we recognised that it would be catastrophic if a dog of ours started to chase these animals.

In the spirit of, "If you can't beat them, join them", my mother managed to get the farmer from Keil to lend her a beautiful brown and white calf, who was promptly christened, Belinda. She was kept in a fenced-off section of the spacious front lawn and fed and watered faithfully by my mother. It was believed that Belinda would help to keep the grass down in her domain, and provide much needed manure for the roses. She stayed with us until the inevitable sad day when the farmer arrived to take a well-grown Belinda back to rejoin the herd

She was not our only bovine visitor.

Early one morning I heard a commotion in the back garden, and struggled out of bed to see what on earth was going on outside.

There I beheld my mother tentatively attempting to shoo a number of fully grown cows out of the vegetable patch while banging a pot lid with her wooden spoon and shouting, "Go away!" at the top of her voice. Naturally they took fright at this strange apparition and scattered all over the garden. Ronald then took over and calmly, as a good agricultural student should, got the cattle into some semblance of order, and herded them out of the garden, and safely down the road to the farm.

Ronald, agricultural student

Apart from pheasants and occasionally, grouse, which wandered in and out of the garden at will, we were not so pleased to have visits from a corncrake, for the noise it made, especially around dawn, was unbelievable. The bird is well named, for its harsh, repetitive call

"Just the prayer at the end," put in Neil in a flash, determined to score one over his friend.

Fortunately at that moment there was a happy diversion, just before the rivalry got too heated.

"Look at the cliff face, boys," I interrupted.

Just above the cave entrances the cliff was scarred with ledges each just big enough to hold a family of fulmar petrels.

The cliff was full of nests, with a constant movement to and fro of birds in that distinctive flight of theirs. We watched as the little dove-like bodies glided on rigid wings across the cliff face, using the updraughts from the soft, warm breeze to keep themselves aloft, then breaking into rapid, flapping flight again when necessary.

John was very fond of these little seabirds, and always called out to them when passing," Aye there --- yes, I see you." And then he would laugh at himself, probably a little embarrassed at showing his sentimental side.

Moving along to the westward *Sheena* had now passed Keil Point with its little sandy coves, and was about to cross Carskiey Bay, yet another of the lovely golden beaches of which Kintyre has a profusion, but this one rarely has a crowd on its sandy shore for, unfortunately, the beach drops away quickly as you enter the water. This could be dangerous for children and non-swimmers, most of whom prefer the shallower bay at Dunaverty where everyone can splash about in safety.

By this time the great bulk of the Mull of Kintyre was right in front of us --- no more sandy beaches on this rocky headland. On the right we passed Port na Cuisle, a tiny inlet just below Garvalt. Its name is Gaelic, meaning *a narrow passage of the sea through which the tide runs swiftly*, then along the cliffs to Port Meadhon, Gaelic for *middle port*, another inlet where fishermen of old could gain shelter and land their catch.

Most of the place names hereabout betray their ancient Gaelic origin, such as Carskiey itself, Garvalt, Feorlan, Glenmanuilt, and so on but we were heading for Borgadale, or Borgadel, which is a pure Norse name meaning *fort dale* --- really just a steep cleft in the coastline, with its ruined dun and enclosure, of course --- reminding us that the Norwegian Vikings first swept down on these unsuspecting western coasts in the year 794AD. Over succeeding years many of them arrived and settled around the British and Irish coastlands. They were to remain for the next almost 700 years.

Indeed, some are still here today, and are now "more Scots then the Scots". The names give them away, such as MacLeod, MacAulay, Morrison, MacAskill, MacAuliffe, MacCorquodale, Cotter, MacIver, MacKitrick, etcetera. (The Mac prefix, being the Gaelic for *son*, showed that they had assimilated some of the language features of the Scots in whose lands they had settled.)

Neil was surprised and really quite gratified to discover that his surname of Morrison showed an exciting Viking ancestry, and was not inclined to apologise for all the looting and pillaging carried out by his long-ago ancestors.

"Maybe you'll grow up to be as good a seaman as your ancestors--- anyway, your dad's a sailor," I said. "Seamanship will probably be in your blood."

Calum was slightly put out at not having the undoubted cachet of such romantic forebears. He was a MacMillan, and definitely within the Celtic, rather than the Viking, orbit.

Sheena was now approaching Borgadalemore Point and the boys' attention was riveted by the huge, strange object lying in the water just ahead.

"What on earth is that?" demanded Neil, his newly found Viking bravery being seriously put to the test.

"Wait till we get closer and then maybe you'll guess," replied the ever calm John. Both lads were now right up in the bows, peering forward rather apprehensively towards the shapeless, dark mass lying so close in to the cliff.

As we drew nearer it could be seen that the mass was, in fact, a large ship's engine block. It looked as if it had been melted in some gigantic oven, for the dreadfully twisted and contorted metal had been melted in what had obviously been the ferocious heat of a catastrophic fire.

"Wow, what kind of a fire did that?" asked Calum. "It looks like a block of chocolate left out in the sun."

"It is all that remains of a cargo vessel which was lost during the Second World War," said John. "She crashed on to the rocks of the Mull where she burned out, and her cargo came ashore along the Southend coastline. Folks hereabouts were able to get cloth and oranges, and even bicycles, and all sorts of other things that came in on the tide."

John looked at me and winked. "They said that everyone in the district had lots of marmalade and lots of new curtains that year --- very welcome in wartime!"

Over the years the engine block had become covered by seaweed and other marine growth, and now constituted a man-made reef which all kinds of sea creatures frequented, from the smallest crustaceans to the fish-hunting seals we were so used to at Southend.

We cruised gently around the wreck, allowing the boys to have a good close look at such an amazing phenomenon --- even their dads were bound to be impressed by this --- then John turned the boat in towards the large cleft in the cliff face which was, in fact, the entrance to Borgadale. He brought her carefully in towards an apparently impenetrable jumble of rocks, one of which turned out to be flatter than the rest. I picked up the mooring line, climbed up on to the gunwale, and jumped ashore where I tied the line around a conveniently spiky rock.

The boys followed me ashore while John threw out an anchor over the boat's stern to keep her steady at right angles to the coastline, then he came ashore last. We clambered up the steep, rocky slopes, disturbing nesting seabirds and sheep on the way, until we had gained enough height to see across the bleak headland of the Mull itself.

It wasn't long before Calum spotted the first of the brown and white feral goats that range freely over the Mull, while Neil, not to be outdone, was sure that he could see a pair of Golden Eagles wheeling high above us. We certainly heard the mewing sounds made by eagle chicks in the nest, coming from the direction of a nearby cliff face, but John said that we should not disturb them, so we went off in the opposite direction.

It was an unforgettable afternoon, but all good things come to an end, and eventually we had to make our way back down to the boat, as the tide was on the make and *Sheena* might be starting to jib at her mooring. The boys were rather reluctant to leave, but, "All good seamen have to put the boat first before their own enjoyment," explained John to the young adventurers, who soon cheered up at the prospect of a nice, long sail back to the Conaglen.

Soon we were back aboard, John watchful as usual at the tiller and the boys lying half asleep in the sunshine on the forward thwarts. I sat dozing on the floor of the well behind the engine casing as we started on our return journey back along the steep-to coastline with the feet of the cliffs lost in the deep water of the Mull.

After about ten minutes John tapped my arm with his foot, and, before I could utter a word, placed a warning finger over his lips while shaking his head. I gathered he was telling me not to call out, and got slowly to my feet. I wandered casually over to him and pretended to be admiring the passing scene.

John said nothing but nodded out towards the open channel. I followed his gaze and saw, in the distance, the black, almost vertical dorsal fin of a large sea creature apparently keeping pace with us along the coast.

"It's a basking shark," I thought, then remembered that the fins of these sea giants were triangular, and so large that they resembled a sail. I was not unduly worried as they are not dangerous in themselves but are apt to charge at anything that touches them, like a boat, or a fishing net --- or the *Sheena*!

"It's got to be a dolphin, or a porpoise," I whispered to John, wondering why he was keeping his voice down.

"No, no, can't you see the colour of its body? I'd know that black and white shape anywhere, but definitely not around these waters," he went on. "It's an orca, a Killer Whale --- which some folk call a Black Fish --- and a real big fellow, about 30 feet long, I think --- longer than this boat! Don't say anything yet to the boys. I don't want to alarm them in case they think it might attack us. There has been so much adverse publicity about orcas --- there are recorded incidents where whales have been kept captive in these American sealife parks, and have gone on to attack and even kill their so-called handlers right in front of the spectators. Didn't you ever hear about that?"

I did remember hearing reports of around seventy attacks over the years by captive orcas, on their human "handlers", including at least three fatalities. These highly intelligent ocean-going animals had been driven mad by such cruel and unnatural captivity in the restricted areas of the pools in which they were confined, whereas in the wild they can travel up to a hundred miles daily in the open ocean.

It is the orca equivalent of going "stir-crazy".

Notably, however, there has never been a single reported incident of Killer Whales attacking humans in the open sea, but I could see John's point of view about not alarming the boys unnecessarily.

"John, why do you think this one is on its own and not swimming with its pod – they usually hunt in groups of up to 40, don't they?"

"Aye, but in the wild the male orcas sometimes leave the pod for a while to go off hunting on their own --- I think this must be one of them. I don't want to take any risks when I have the boys in the boat, so let's get a move on and get out of this deep water," he muttered.

Sheena's engine was gunned and she came back along that shoreline faster than she had ever gone before. All the while the orca, probably just curious --- but we couldn't know that for sure --- kept station with us at a distance of about 50 feet.

The increased engine noise and vibration caused by the faster speed inevitably woke the boys up. Naturally they wanted to know what was going on, and soon saw for themselves our enormous companion.

"Gosh, Mr Cameron, what's that? It's about the size of a bus!" they squeaked, probably thinking it was just another delight laid on by John, their friend and hero, who could always be trusted to produce all kinds of thrills, imaginable and unimaginable.

John and I played it down as much as possible, hoping desperately that we were not destined to become yet another orca incident!

"It's just a very nosy whale," said John in a fake calm voice, while I tried to look unconcerned, as if keeping company with a potentially ferocious sea creature was all part of the day's work in the salmon fishing world.

Eventually, and thankfully, we reached the shallower waters of Dunaverty Bay and never did they look so inviting. We shot inshore at Dunaverty jetty instead of going for the deeper route around the Rock and into our usual anchorage in the Conaglen River.

To our immense relief the orca moved off at last on a ploy of its own.

Archie, John's brother, was standing there, watching, as we tied up and hastily got the boys safely out of the boat and on to the blessed dry land of the bay.

As was to be expected they thanked us excitedly for a "really smashing trip", obviously thinking that all the thrills had been specially arranged just for their delectation, and, with the parcels of lythe firmly tucked under their arms, rushed off up the beach to the Coastguard houses in Southend village to regale their parents and friends with the gabbled tale of their adventures.

"Did I see what I think I've just seen?" said Archie, looking serious.

"You surely have, and I'll never take anyone, especially a child, down the Mull again, as long as I live," replied poor John, mopping his brow with his neckerchief. "I've only seen the like of that in these waters on one occasion, years ago."

"That's all very well," said Archie, "but I've got to go down the Mull myself with the *Ace* and a party of golfers next week. They're going across to Red Bay in Antrim for a charity match. I hope that big fellow has pushed off by then. The sight of that in the water would be enough to really put them off their game!

Tale no. 2: Boats and Benedictine

I sat huddled in oilskins in the lee of the bank below Archie's house of Dunaverty, watching apprehensively as the swollen flood waters of the Conaglen River tried their utmost to carry the *Sheena* out of the river mouth and away out to sea. Her white wooden hull was pulling hard against the restraining ropes which were just holding her and no more, against the outgoing flood. The boat was trussed up like a parcel, being festooned with ropes, two on either side of the bow, two amidships and two at her stern, all of them attached firmly to both banks of the river. If she broke away from these lines we could do nothing to save her as she sat completely out of our reach in the centre of the heightened waters. Floods from landward meeting an exceptionally high tide from seaward had caught her in between and put her in danger. I vividly imagined the nightmare of having to inform the Coastguard station that John's white motorboat was adrift in the stormy Sound of Sanda, out of control and causing a hazard to shipping or, horror of horrors, smashed against the rocks by violent seas!

I also checked John's little, nondescript clinker-built boat which was the maid of all work around the shore. It was commonly known as "the punt", though it had been christened with the most unlikely name of *Silvery Dawn*. During the annual spring painting of the boats it was this poor little Cinderella that was given a coat of any old paint that was lying around in the boat shed. The resulting effect was quite multi-coloured, so much so that it had now been re-christened *Herbacious Border* by an irreverent holiday-maker.

These dismal thoughts filled my mind as I sat there watching the boat and wishing John would come to relieve my acute anxiety. A boat is like a child and I had been baby-sitting this particular child since first light that September morning when I had wakened in the dark, unhappily aware of the howling of the wind outside the Manse of St Blaan and thinking of the vulnerability of our little fleet of six boats. Unable to sleep any longer, I had got up, dressed and, leaving a brief note for my mother on the kitchen table, had driven quickly down through the apparently deserted village of Southend to Dunaverty and the storm-tossed mouth of the Conaglen. No one else seemed to be around and I felt the desolation of the empty, sodden landscape without even a glimmer of sunlight in the sullen sky. Was I the only person left in the world, I wondered, in full self-pitying mode?

Conaglen River mouth in a storm

Of course, there were plenty of folk alive and well and busy milking their cows in the many dairy farms in the district, as well as Archie and John preparing for the day in their respective homes that morning. I just couldn't see them, and my imagination was running riot.

Now I arrived at the shore, checked the boats and impatiently awaited John's arrival. When I heard the welcome note of a car engine, and John appeared over the hill above the Conaglen I struggled stiffly to my feet and greeted him, gabbling on about how the *Sheena* was in such danger.

As usual he was reassurance itself.

"It's alright, don't worry. Why do you think I left her with so many lines on her last night? That's why we listen so carefully to the weather forecast, you know."

My fears lifted immediately at these calm words, but I felt, as an Irish friend of mine would say, "a right cod", at having given way to such panic.

John must have caught my mood for he smiled kindly at me and said, "Anyway, thanks for looking out for the boat this morning. But the tide's on the turn now. We'll soon get her safely back among us again and we can get all these ropes off her."

Archie had heard John's car and now appeared on the hill.

"What about your boats this morning, Archie?" I called. "That was some wind last night."

Kintyre folk are used to the violent winds of winter, the peninsula being open to Atlantic gales, and they know how to protect people and property with down-to-earth common sense, taking boats, caravans, cars and other moveables up from the open beaches and tying them down well away from the shoreline. The larger boats are taken into safe anchorages and secured with heavy ropes.

Occasionally, though, nature bares its teeth and shows us feeble humans just how powerful it can be.

One stormy morning my boss tried to walk out of the bus shelter in the village of Drumlemble, near Machrihanish, and climb on to the school bus. He was caught by a terrific gust and blown on to his knees. Having tried in vain to stand up again, he resorted to crawling on to the bus on hands and knees, much to the raucous mirth of the young passengers going in to Campbeltown Grammar School that morning --- a complete loss of the gravitas expected in a senior teacher!

In the meantime Archie had assured us that his boats were quite safe. Like John he had taken steps to ensure that they were out of harm's way.

In Dunaverty Bay, where his boats were moored, *Zena,* the brown varnished launch, had been floated on to the old bus chassis that Archie kept in the former Lifeboat house, and winched carefully up the shore into the safety of the building, from where she could easily be run down into the sea again when conditions improved.

White-painted *Ace* and grey *Rex* --- (not *Wrecks* as an incomer author unbelievably called her. As if any self-respecting fisherman would ever tempt fate by giving his boat such a name!) --- were esconced in the old Lifeboat shed perched precariously at the end of a long jetty which was no longer in the Lifeboat service. The boats were protected by tarpaulins from the attentions of the local starlings which roosted in the shed, and would be scraped and painted by us in the spring. Meantime the gallant *Zena* did sterling service as a lobster boat, and as a ferry taking supplies, post and lighthouse keepers across the two mile strait between Southend and the island of Sanda with its farm and lighthouse (though her lines were as fine as a river launch).

Assorted small craft also lay in the shed along with lots of miscellaneous gear, which "might come in handy some day". The place smelled of paint, varnish, tar, thinners, linseed oil, timber, tarpaulins, fish, the dust of ages and assorted seabirds --- delightful! And the noise was incredible, with the noisy chattering of starlings, the squawking of gulls and the whistling of even the lightest breeze through the myriad gaps in the timber walls and roof. Very draughty it was too when we stood there working on the boats for hours on end!

Meanwhile, in the teeth of the gale, all three of us struggled up the Conaglen shore to check on my boat *Catriona* where she lay, smothered in tarpaulins at the side of "the hut" --- the old fisherman's house. A tarpaulin was loose at one side and flapping enough to take off in the gale so we re-swaddled her, tying the knots in the restraining ropes more tightly. She was perfectly safe there for the time being, and would no doubt be restored to the river as soon as the tide and wind went down. She usually remained there over the back end of the year as did the *Sheena*. I didn't usually take her off the shore until the early spring when she would have her woodwork sanded down and varnished and any necessary repairs made to her beautiful fibreglass hull.

When *Catriona* had first arrived from the builders in Inverness she was delivered by accident to Southend Smiddy and decanted on to a straw bed in the stable until she could be collected. Katie at the Smiddy, the blacksmith's wife, phoned my father to let him know the boat had arrived and was in her stable. She was appalled, and let him know in no uncertain terms what she thought about the whole thing:

"It's a glass boat, meenister! You're never going to let her go out in a glass boat! Well, tell her she's to keep in to the edge."

To Katie all boats must be wooden, should rarely go to sea and should be kept as near to the shore as humanly possible. When I went over to the Smiddy with the trolley Katie was still muttering dire predictions and I thought at one point that she wouldn't let me take the boat away.

"It's alright Katie," I said, "The boat is made of strong, double-strength fibreglass --- not glass! I won't fall through it. It is formed in a one-piece moulding so it can have no leaks. And it's got a lovely drop keel which gives it weight and keeps it steady. It's a smashing boat."

I realised just after saying it that I shouldn't have used the word "smashing", as that started Katie all over again!

Catriona was a colourful addition to our six-boat fleet, and my pride and joy. She had spruce stringers and keelson, moulded in and hermetically sealed, resulting in a hull of tremendous strength, silver spruce oars and mahogany bottom-boards and thwarts. She was particularly useful for checking the salmon nets as we could lift sections of the net out of the sea and over her broad, flat stern in order to remove any salmon caught in the skirts of the net and even the bag of the net itself. The larger, heavier *Sheena* was needed when John had to lift the big stake nets each Saturday night, then set them again early on a Monday morning out in Brunerican Bay.

When not at work at the fishing *Catriona* reverted to her main purpose as a sailing boat. Her mast would be stepped amidships, side and forward stays attached and the spar holding the top of her mainsail hauled up to extend the mast in the unusual gunter rig. This meant, of course, that she couldn't sail as close to the wind as a Bermudan rig, but she certainly could plane spectacularly with the wind dead astern and the drop-keel raised judiciously.

One breezy morning my poor father was standing on the front steps of Angus MacVicar's house at the opposite end of Dunaverty Bay from the jetty when *Catriona* came whizzing round the Rock with sails goose-winging, and planed across the bay like an express train, her bow clear of the water. Angus later told me that my father turned pale as the boat kept disappearing completely in the trough of each heavy swell, but emerged unfailingly again on the crest of the next comber.

"I was sure you wouldn't be able to stop her before Ireland!" he exclaimed.

It seemed as if I were destined to frighten everyone with my beautiful blue boat.

Anyway, I loved her, but only one of the local farmers ever dared to venture out for a sail in her. The Southenders tended to be golfers rather than sailors and hardly any of them could swim. So much for having access to some of the most glorious beaches in Britain!

I recalled a plain-speaking female friend of mine declaring, "If you want to know what a man is really like, take him out sailing in a rough sea and just see how he behaves!"

As it happened the first man I took out in my boat was my father, who was not really an enthusiastic sailor. It was on a New Year's Day that we decided on a brisk sail in order to clear the mind and refresh the body after the excesses of the festive season. With the usual vagaries of winter weather in south Kintyre it was unusually mild with a light breeze --- perfect sailing weather --- but, to our annoyance, we were attacked by swarms of midges right out in the middle of Dunaverty Bay.

"You'd think we could get away from these pests out here on the water in mid-winter," grumbled my father. "Let's go inshore."

I thought that, in fact, he was feeling rather insecure out here in deep water, in a fourteen-foot boat which could heel over uncomfortably when under sail, so I brought *Catriona* up into the wind, allowing the boom to swing freely and letting the air spill from her sails in order to stop her sailing, and went forward to bring down the mainsail and jib.

We would row her in.

In the near silence that followed we heard the unlikely sound of heavy breathing in the sea in front of the boat. Alarmed, in case someone had fallen into the water unbeknown to us, we looked over the side, to be met with the bland stare of a big, male seal. As is often the case with seals he was very inquisitive and soon his harem gained enough confidence to cluster around him. They were quite enchanting and completely unafraid of us. Big round eyes in whiskery faces looked up at us, and they seemed to be wanting to make friends for they swam ever closer to the now motionless *Catriona,* the only sound being that unnerving heavy breathing. When hauled out on the rocks it's a different matter --- they can sound as if in distress, and I was once alarmed at Portnahaven on Islay when I heard what sounded like a dog howling in pain. In fact it was a group of amorous seals simply communicating with one another.

Folk tales of seals being enchanted by singing human voices are indeed just so many fairy stories, at least in my experience. At any rate whenever I tried to draw seals close to the boat by singing to them they all dived immediately and disappeared for good. Maybe it was just my singing!

Anyway, on that sullen September morning it suddenly dawned on me that it was Sunday. I was expected in church in order to take my unwilling turn playing the organ for morning service --- my father having arbitrarily volunteered my services in my absence --- and there I was, muffled in oilskins, wellingtons and sou'wester and still down at the shore. I had exactly half an hour to get myself home, changed and transformed into the respectable church organist the congregation would expect.

I rushed up the road to the house where my mother and father were anxiously awaiting my arrival. Thankfully they went off to church while urging me to get a move on. I quickly tore off the oilskins, donned a suitably modest garb for church and hastened off in their wake. I got there just in time, but slid unhappily behind the organ console out of breath and with a fast-beating pulse.

Mr MacKinlay was the visiting minister this morning --- a young, self-important man who had never preached in our church before and rather impatiently didn't listen to the beadle telling him that the pulpit door was rather stiff and needed a really good shove to open. He strode out confidently for the high pulpit and stepped with great dignity up the stairs in his longish cassock. He leaned forward to push the door open, couldn't move it, so stepped ever further forward and pushed again. Unfortunately, during this manoeuvre, he got both feet caught in the hem of his cassock, stood heavily upon it, and thus found himself trapped in an undignified bending position by his own garment, and unable to move. There was a hastily smothered ripple of laughter throughout the congregation.

After an ungainly hop, step and jump backwards he managed to free his feet and this time carefully hitched up the cassock out of harm's way. He finally made it into the pulpit where he sank into the big chair in an attempt to regain his composure.

By this time the choir, who had followed him in, can only be described as positively smirking, but fortunately the service then began.

All this had unsettled my precarious confidence and I hadn't really calmed down after my rapid dash up from the shore. I hated having to play the organ but had to take my turn among the four of us "volunteers", and tried, as usual, to hide behind the large floral decoration which usually festooned the top of the organ casing. The first hymn was announced and I nervously started out on the first verse but, in my excited state, soon lost track of which verse I was on.

"Where are we?" I hissed at the tenors who were nearest to me.

"Third verse," they hissed back, but unfortunately in my shaky state I managed to lose track again.

When I thought we had reached the end of the fifth verse I played the first two notes of the Amen then realised that the congregation were still on their feet with mouths open, already launching forth into a sixth verse. There was a lot of shuffling and looking around at one another as I cut them off in full flight, but they dutifully sang an unexpected and ragged Amen while subsiding uncertainly in uneven little groups on to their pews. The tenors obviously thought the whole thing hilarious, but I was dreadfully mortified.

Knowing I would be able to have a breather and calm my ruffled nerves during the sermon, I switched off all the power to the organ, glared at the tenors and sat back in relief, hoping, for once, that the minister would be inspired to give us a nice, long sermon so that I could recover before the end of the service.

This now proceeded as planned and eventually we arrived at the last hymn.

With infinite care I switched on the power on the console and placed my hands on the keys in what should have been the first chord. The organ did not make a sound. Puzzled, I hit the keys harder this time --- again, not a squeak. Mr MacKinlay was now peering down at me over the edge of the pulpit and announced the hymn again, in a firm, commanding voice.

"What on earth is the dratted thing doing?" I muttered, barely under my breath. Panic arose in my unhappy soul as I pressed and prodded every switch in the immediate vicinity, with absolutely no result whatsoever.

I imagined that the next thing would be me breaking out in a cackle of hysterical laughter, making a run for it up the aisle, out of the church and back up the road to hide myself in the house, closely pursued by a posse of furious Elders.

A cold sweat was breaking out on my feverish brow when I caught sight of my father frantically signalling to me to switch off everything and start again; firstly, and most importantly, switching on the power at the mains switch on the wall before the one on the console. It seemed an eternity before I accomplished all this, and everyone waited with bated breath as I feverishly rushed through the correct procedure for electronic organs.

It started!

I shed a huge sigh of relief and sallied forth on both manuals and foot pedals with the cautious confidence of one who knows that very soon the ordeal will be at an end. I determined not to cut the congregation short this time. We duly arrived at the end of the fourth verse, and I set out righteously on to verse number five --- only to realise, two seconds later, that there was no verse five!

"Merciful heaven," I prayed. "What did I do to deserve this?"

In my miserable state I just kept on playing the non-existent verse and the long-suffering congregation had to sing verse four all over again.

By this time it wasn't just the tenors who were choking with barely stifled mirth.

Eventually my ordeal was at an end. I managed to struggle through an attenuated final postlude then scuttled up the aisle making for the sanctuary of the vestry. Mr MacKinlay had already changed into coat and hat, obviously feeling as uncomfortable as I was, and fled out to his car and the reliable sobriety of Sunday in Campbeltown.

After the service the congregation usually stood about in little groups chatting on the gravelled area ouside the church door. I hung about furtively, peering out of the vestry window, and wishing they'd all stop blethering and allow me to escape back to the house and decent obscurity, but no, they were full of the recent unusual events in Southend Parish Church and were obviously re-living every detail with great relish and a lot of unholy glee.

Eventually I just had to leave the church as the beadle was agitating to get home for his dinner, and wanted to lock up.

I emerged, cringing, into the daylight, and the varied comments of my fellow Christians.

"Well," said Angus, clapping me on the shoulder, "You certainly know how to keep us on the hop. We'll never get the chance of a good snooze when you are behind the organ!"

I slunk off home for lunch and hoped-for sympathy from my dear family who were recounting each awful detail with howls of laughter.

"It's all your fault, Dad," I complained bitterly. "You volunteered me for this job against both my will and my better judgment, and it'll just get worse after the disaster of this morning. I hereby resign!"

Needless to say my resignation was not accepted, and I continued to be a volunteer organist by unanimous decision of minister and congregation alike. They apparently wanted to retain my unwilling services as they found it most entertaining, never knowing what I was going to do next.

St. Blaan's Church, Southend

That unhappy Sunday ended on a much lighter note when I fled to my reliable haven of Dunaverty after lunch. I wanted to check on the safety of *Sheena* and *Catriona* now that the wind had abated and the tide was well down in the Conaglen River. Of course, John and Archie had got there before me. All was well with the boats so we adjourned to "the hut" where John produced the usual bottle of Benedictine, an unrivalled solace for mariners landing, frozen with cold off the sea or, as he twinkled, for the shattered nerves of organists fleeing from church.

The fire of driftwood was lit in the little tiled fireplace, giving off glowing warmth and a faintly salty, tarry tang; the paraffin lamp cast a soft, mellow glow on the three of us sitting on bundled up, dried-out stake nets with small glasses of aromatic Benedictine in our hands. The damp nets which were still hanging up to dry over the rafters threw shadows on a scene that must have been repeated unnumbered times in this same small place over the decades. We huddled, warm and contented, as the last of the gale blew itself out in the autumnal gloaming, enjoying that priceless gift --- the companionship of old friends. No wonder I loved every sight and sound of this blessed place.

After the usual discussion of local events --- but tactful avoidance of my catastrophic performance in church --- I remembered that someone had asked me for the words of an old Kintyre song --- Flory Loynachan. It was a love song written in the part-Kintyre Gaelic, part Lowland Scots of generations ago and very few people still knew it. John had been known to sing it in select company now and again, so I asked him to give us a rendering there and then. After considerable persuasion on our part, and reluctant assent on his he began, in his pleasant tenor voice:

O, it buitie be an ogly thing
That mougres thus o'er me,
For I scrabed at myself thestreen
And could not bab an e'e.
My heart is all to muillins minsh'd,
Brye, smuirach, daps, and gum,
I'm a poor cruichach, spalyin' scrae
My horts have strok me dumb.

Dear Flory Loynachan, if thou
Through Sanna's soun' wert toss't
And rouchled like a shougie-shoo,
In a veshal with one mast,
Though the night were makin' for a roll,
Though raillaich were the sea,
Though scorlins warpled my thowl pins,
My shallop would reach thee.

Thou'rt not a hochlan scleurach, dear
As many trooshlach be;
Nor I a claty skybal, thus
To sclaffer after thee ---
Yet haing the meishachan, where first
I felt love's maiglan' smart,
And haing the boosach dyvour, too,
Who spoong'd from me thine heart.

O! rhane a Yolus Cronie --- quick ---
Across this rumpled brain!
Bring hickery-pickery --- bring wallink
Droshachs, to soothe my pain!
Fire, water --- fire a spoucher full ---
These frythan stouns to stay!
For like a sporrow's scaldachan
I'm gosping night and day!

Were I the laird of Achnaglach,
or Kilmanshenachan fair,
Crockstapplemore, Kilwheepnach,
Foechag, or Ballochgair;
Did I inherit Tuyinroech,
Drumgary or Ballochatnee,
Creishlach or Coeran --- daing the bit,
I'd fauchat them for thee!

O, the Clabbydhu, it loves the Trinch,
The Crouban, the quey-neb,
While the Anachan, and Brollochan,
They love the Mussle-ebb.
The Muirachbaan the Dorlin loves,
And the Gleshan, and Guildee,
They love to plauder through the loch
But, Flory, I love thee.

This old ballad was sung by Dougie MacAlreavie, of Corbat's Close, in Bolgam Street, Campbeltown, for the members of Kintyre Literary Association, as an illustration of the common conversational idiom of many years ago, and shows the linguistic influence of the "plantation" of Ayshire farmers to Kintyre in the 17th century, on the orders of the king. It was always popular, referring, as it did, to farms in the local area, though rarely sung at Southend ceilidhs simply because so few people actually knew the words.

These are the folk treasures which must never be allowed to get lost.

In "the hut" the fire had died right down so we finished our Benedictine, checked that all the nets were ready to be put out the next morning and went out, locking up behind us.

The kindness and consideration of friends meant that I was now relaxed and restored to equanimity after my stressful day. I pondered on the way home about how unbelievably fortunate I was to live in such a place and to count such folk as John and Archie Cameron among my friends.

Tale no. 3: Dunaverty Players at Large

Our anchorage in the Conaglen River was just south of the small building on the headland of Rudha MacShannuich (MacShannon's Point) from which the Coastguards kept their constant physical watch over shipping in the wide sea area of the North Channel, the north Irish Sea and the wide estuary of the Clyde, though they were in touch by radio with shipping and other Coastguard stations, northwards towards Oban and southwards to Portpatrick.

The men were all ex-navy in those days and we became very friendly with many of them. A particular favourite was the Yorkshireman, Teddy Wadsworth, who was, as we say nowadays, vertically challenged, but made up for his lack of inches by force of personality and a great sense of humour. Teddy could always tell a story against himself and did not stand on his dignity when away from official duty, but as Chief Coastguard in the district he was well aware of the importance of his position at all times.

I met him one July day on the way up Main Street from Campbeltown New Quay on his way back from an official visit to an Ayrshire Coastguard station. He had travelled on the turbine steamer, *Duchess of Hamilton* from Largs to Campbeltown, dressed, of course, in his dark Coastguard uniform. As it was July and the Glasgow Fair, the ship was packed full of holidaymakers milling about the decks in their hundreds. The ticket office was surrounded by impatient queues harassing the unfortunate pursers, the dining-room was completely full of people who could afford a substantial three-course lunch served by stewards in immaculate white jackets, and the cafeteria in the stern of the ship was jammed with hungry and thirsty passengers demanding teas, coffees, sandwiches, sausage rolls, sticky buns and other delights.

Teddy started out on the difficult journey from the crowded gangway to the companionway leading down to the forward passenger saloon, narrowly avoiding being overwhelmed on the stairs by a mob of people coming up the way.

At last he made it in one piece and, pushing open the door, thankfully entered this haven with one aim in mind --- that of finding a comfortable armchair, sinking in to it, and passing the journey in peace and quiet. As he stood in the doorway surveying the busy saloon a large lady, seated in a basket chair near the window, looked over at him and called out in a strident voice, "Hey you!"

Teddy gazed about him to see who she was talking to.

"Me, madam?" said the ever polite Teddy.

"Aye you. Wha did ye think ah wis talkin' tae?" she questioned aggressively. "Whit time does this boat get intae Brodick?"

Teddy cleared his throat and replied mildly, "I think about 2.20, madam." and turned to leave in search of a more peaceful haven.

"Ye think!" she shouted. "Dae ye no ken? Whit guid are ye in yer fancy uniform when ye cannae tell me the times o' the boats? An' ye can jist get me a cuppae tea while ye're at it, mister!"

This was too much even for a polite ex-Royal Navy officer. Bristling, Teddy drew himself up to his full diminutive stature, and uttered, "Madam, you are speaking to a senior officer of Her Majesty's Coastguard."

Unabashed, the lady declared, "Och, ah thocht ye were a waiter. Could ye no jist get me a cuppae tea while ye're aboot it?"

Teddy immediately removed himself from the saloon in silent disgust and went off to seek solace elsewhere.

On visiting my school at Tighnabruaich some years later Teddy arrived in a convoy of three large cars along with several underlings and a lot of life-saving apparatus. He and his henchmen had come on an official school visit in order to bring the vital life-saving work of the Coastguard to the notice of the general public and the school children in particular.

I noticed that when Teddy emerged with great dignity from the first car the underlings dutifully lined up behind him in order of seniority, then the passengers from the second and third cars. They marched into the school in that order, Teddy leading the way. On leaving at the end of the visit the situation was reversed exactly --- the lowliest rank left first, and got into the car, then next in rank, and so on, right up to the most senior person --- Teddy, who left the building last.

"Got to observe protocol on these occasions," he muttered as we said goodbye at the door.

This rather stuffy image disappeared when we met at Alf and Morag Grumoli's cafe and shop in Southend village. The cafe was closed during the winter and Dunaverty Players, our local dramatic club, met there usually twice a week, with local author, Angus MacVicar, as our original producer.

Dunaverty Players had originated in 1952 when the local WRI ladies had asked Angus to write and direct a play for them, which they then entered into the local Scottish Community Drama Association's Festival, as Southend WRI Dramatic Club. They were so successful that they continued for six years, until the menfolk agitated to get in on the act, literally, and the club had to be renamed Dunaverty Players.

Olive, Teddy's wife, was an enthusiatic member of the cast, and Teddy became a useful Assistant Stage Manager. We spent uncounted happy evenings in the cafe, courtesy of the irrepressible Alf and the long-suffering Morag. They were a wonderful host and hostess, always lit a big fire in the huge fireplace (which is still there), where we huddled in front of the comforting blaze when not out "on stage" in the middle of the cafe floor, and produced tea and biscuits whenever Angus allowed us a small break.

We took enthusiatic part every year in the national Scottish Community Drama Association Festival, or SCDA, for one-act plays, the first stage being held, in early spring, in the Victoria Hall, Campbeltown, where all major social events were held.

The competition among the clubs was fierce, but we had a high reputation and frequently won this first stage which meant we went on to the next level, usually held some distance away in the middle or south of Scotland.

Players, supporters, scenery and sets were loaded on to one of West Coast Motors' largest buses, invariably driven by Jock MacKay from Campbeltown, and off we would go, leaving the cafe in the dark at five in the morning when we had to travel as far afield as Castle Douglas or Kirkudbright. The only persons awake and alert at that ungodly hour were our numerous farmer members, some of whom had already done the morning milking before getting on to the bus. Special favourites were the Aucharua twins, Maggie and Janet Barbour, who were already in comical form and beaming at everyone. Angus, our Producer, would boom out, "I want to sit behind the twins", so that he could enjoy their humorous comments at close range. Naturally he got his way.

A stop was always made at Tarbert Hotel, Loch Fyne, for a substantial breakfast for those able to face a fry-up before dawn. By the time we reached Ardrishaig and decanted into the big hotel on the seafront most of us had wakened up and were chattering away like budgies.

The men usually disappeared in ones and twos at some point during this break, then emerged from the back premises of the hotel looking positively furtive, followed by mine host clutching a large bottle of some colourless liquid. It turned out that this was whisky in some early stage of its development --- nobody ever seemed to question its provenance, but the men were always very cheerful as we clambered back on to the bus, while the ladies were happy enough having sustained themselves with the hotel's finest coffee.

Lunch was usually taken at Tarbet, Loch Lomond, or Balloch at the foot of the loch. By this time Alf was really into his stride, and got up to all sorts of tricks. On one visit we emerged from the hotel after lunch to find Alf on the roof of the bus dancing a jig. Jock commanded him to to get down immediately, having a vision of Alf falling through the roof, and himself having to explain to his employers exactly what a passenger had been doing on top of the bus.

Alf on the bus roof

Jock and Maria help Alf down

But Alf reserved his best ploys for the crossing of the River Clyde as we travelled down through the Lowlands towards Glasgow. In those days there was no Erskine Bridge --- just a small vehicular ferry which chugged slowly across the river.

On one unforgettable occasion Jock duly drove the bus aboard and it was at this point that Alf, having got off the bus, appeared on the bridge of the ferry, to the speechless astonishment of the crew, dressed in khaki shorts and shirt, a pith helmet on his head and carrying a mock rifle. He then "took over" the bridge of the vessel from the astounded skipper, declaring to the disbelieving passengers that he was going to save their lives and shoot the crocodiles in the River Clyde. He then proceeded to aim the "rifle" and fire it at the monsters in the water. So paralysed with shock were the crew that they let him continue until we reached the Renfrewshire bank, no doubt afraid to challenge this dangerous lunatic in case he really got out of hand.

The following year Alf repeated this happy ploy, and was greeted by the ferry crew with a certain amount of wary resignation, "Here's that mad fella frae Campbeltown again!" they shouted to all and sundry.

But by this time they knew he was really quite harmless.

Our English contingent, Teddy and Olive, quickly became reconciled to Dunavery Players' growing reputation for eccentricity,

On another occasion Ronald stopped an incipient fight among two gangs of youths at a dance in Southend village hall, in a most unusual fashion, by wading straight in through the potential participants, right up to the main instigator who was posturing aggressively in the middle of his gang. Ronald grabbed him by the hand and, pumping the hand up and down vigorously said, genially, "Hello Lachie. How are you? I haven't seen you for I don't know how long."

The said Lachie was so taken aback that he forgot he was supposed to be starting a fight, and was totally deflected from his original purpose. The two started an animated conversation, and the proposed fight was cut off before its prime and melted away before it had even begun. The trouble-makers drifted sheepishly out of the hall without causing any trouble, peace having broken out and ruined their hoped-for melée.

Para Handy would have approved.

Even at the top echelons of society this propensity for eccentricity reared its head. One of the most respected members of Kintyre society was the Baroness Naomi Mitchison of Carradale, a charming lady who was completely unbothered by the petty dress rules upheld by polite society.

I met her coming down Sauchiehall Street in Glasgow one Saturday morning, right in front of that beautiful emporium, Daly's, where fashionable ladies bought expensive items of dress and many other exotic things.

There was the Baroness, sailing along purposefully past the main doorway of the store, inevitably mingling with the beautiful people coming and going about the shop, while apparently oblivious of the stares of shoppers and bystanders alike.

She was dressed in an ancient gabardine raincoat, belted in at the waist with a length of binder twine, and shod with a disreputable pair of wellingtons, all of which she had possibly worn earlier that morning in a field on her Carradale estate. Her face wore an expression of sweet amiability as we met and exchanged greetings. What a whimsical, lovely lady she was, as well as having a very sharp and clever mind. The worlds of literature, politics and social work benefitted immeasurably from her active involvement.

Another much loved soul, John Cormack, one of my father's brother ministers, was an incredible stickler for politeness and was known throughout the burgh for raising his hat and half bowing to everybody he met, parishioners and non-parishioners alike.

Maverick waltz

Mischievous Grammar School boys would greet him in the street, await the usual polite hat-raising, then run round the corner and meet him again whereupon the hat was raised for a second, or even a third time, as the poor soul couldn't see very well. It was even wickedly rumoured that he had been seen raising his hat to a Clydesdale horse, standing patiently at the kerbside.

I do know for a fact that my father observed this behaviour at first hand on the island of Gigha, which lies offshore from Kintyre, and to which the local Presbytery members had been summoned on business concerning a local church vacancy.

Dad was in the island's little hotel awaiting the arrival of the other ministers, including John. Looking out of an upstairs window he saw the island ferry come in and tie up. John came ashore alone and wandered up the deserted lane leading to the hotel, which was bounded on each side by fields of sheep and cattle grazing peacefully on the other sides of the fences.

Dad tapped on the window to let John know where he was and his colleague, true to form, gazed rapidly and short-sightedly around him, trying to find the source of the tapping, was unsuccessful so, no doubt hoping to cover all eventualities, smiled benignly all round and politely raised his hat to every grazing animal in sight.

Dad, choking with laughter, opened the window and shouted out, "I'm up here, John. Come into the hotel and the manageress will show you to the room."

"I couldn't believe he was actually raising his hat to all the animals," Dad told us later. "Poor John really does need a new pair of glasses."

But the same John was a man of acute intellect in matters which really interested him --- everything to do with religion and the Presbyterian Church --- and in another life would probably have been a first class lawyer.

Strangely enough our collective Kintyre eccentricity actually led to a change in education policy in later years.

It all began when Miss Julia Brown, designated Sole Teacher of one of the little country schools, and a fervent animal lover --- particularly of dogs --- considered that the pillars at the entrance to her school looked sadly lacking in something --- she wasn't sure just what. A visit to one of the larger primary schools in the nearby town showed her exactly what she felt was needed, so she sent for the Clerk of Works and explained,

"The entrance to the school lacks any kind of dignity or presence. It just looks like a farm. I feel that the pillars on either side should have granite, or some other kind of stone balls surmounted on each pillar. It would make the place look more like a proper education establishment, don't you think?"

The Clerk, who was secretly quite fond of Miss Brown and her two big Airedale dogs, didn't dismiss the idea out of hand, but promised to look into the matter and give it his earnest consideration, but was out of luck in the matter of the cost to the Authority.

"Out of the question," boomed the Director when it was put to him. "We haven't got money to throw around on trivialities like that!" and the Clerk retreated, temporarily at a loss.

He went around for several days, mulling over the problem, and at last came up with a brilliant solution after a visit to his house by the local plumber.

Miss Brown was thrilled to observe, the next Monday morning, that her pillars had been graced over the weekend by two dignified, painted stone balls which certainly enhanced the entrance to her school.

The Clerk was thereby greeted warmly by a smiling teacher and profusely thanked for his sterling efforts, thus gaining many brownie points with the lady. He was cheered by the pupils, patted the two dogs, and was invited to stay for school lunch --- a real compliment rarely bestowed on Education Department officials, one of whom visited the school the next day, spotted the new addition to the exterior décor, and inquired of the Clerk how he had managed to swing it with the Director for the cost of the stone balls.

"Oh, that's okay," said the Clerk. "I didn't need to ask the Director. The plumber just gave me a couple of second-hand stop-cocks and I painted them to match the pillars and --- Bob's Your Uncle --- there are the "stone" balls."

"You cunning devil," uttered the official," and I suppose Miss Brown knows nothing about that, does she? She thinks these are genuine granite?"

"You know what they say," said the Clerk, winking. "What you don't know does you no harm," and he went off, chuckling quietly to himself.

Miss Brown was devoted to her two large Airedale Terriers, Jake and Penny, and, as was very common in the country schools, brought them into the classroom daily, where they settled down under the teacher's desk during lessons then went out to play with the pupils during the intervals. The dogs, having been more or less brought up with the children, were extremely gentle and protective with them, obviously regarding themselves as their guardians. The kids loved the dogs, and could do anything with them for all that they were big, strong animals with a decided potential for aggression if aroused.

Miss Brown trusted them implicitly with the children's safety, and they all lived in their little school in one, big happy family.

In the teaching profession the sworn enemy is always the big, bad Inspector of Schools, who could, in those days, swoop down on an unsuspecting school unannounced, thus almost giving the unfortunate teacher a heart attack.

A certain Mr Greer, known and much disliked among the teachers, decided that, as the weather was good, he would go for an outing among the country schools in the area, as ever omitting to let the teachers know that he was coming. He loved startling everybody by suddenly bustling in at the school door and enjoying the look of horror on the teacher's face as she immediately wondered if all the jotters had been marked, and if he was going to inflict himself on them all day and criticise all she was doing, as was his reputation.

Mr Greer reached Miss Brown's school early one morning as the children were settling down to their arithmetic lesson and, as always, burst into the classroom without the common courtesy of first knocking at the door.

As he stepped into the classroom, startling everyone, Jake, the larger of the two Airedales, silently launched himself at the intruder and pinned him by the shoulders up against the door, where he was held by Jake's two huge paws, while the dog, standing on his hind legs and now snarling ferociously, slavered, with lips drawn back from gleaming white fangs, only centimetres from Mr Greer's terrified face.

Penny, the female dog, joined in the fray and stalked back and forth in front of him, stiff-legged, growling menacingly, and snapping viciously at his legs every time he tried to move a muscle.

"Get them off me!" howled the hapless Inspector.

The entire class was struck dumb and motionless with horror.

Miss Brown, who had been hovering about in a fever of shock, tried to call the dogs off, but they paid absolutely no attention to her whatsoever, and, in a desperate attempt to prevent a massacre taking place in front of their very eyes, she called out feebly, in a most inadequate response,

"Show no fear! Show no fear!"

This was of no help to the cowering Mr Greer who, far from showing no fear, was exhibiting sheer terror from top to shaking toe.

It was essential to rescue him before he died from heart failure, or from being horribly mauled.

"Jake, Penny --- DOWN!" shrieked Miss Brown, endeavouring to release the Inspector by hauling on Jake's collar.

Reluctantly the big animals gave up the attack and withdrew a little, still growling and exhibiting a strong inclination to go for the intruder yet again.

The unfortunate man slithered down the door and collapsed on to the floor, where he lay, gasping for breath, the colour coming back slowly into his pallid cheeks.

"Donald, go and get some water for Mr Greer," urged the teacher faintly as she tried to help him to get up on his feet again.

As if released from a holding spell the class came back to frantic life and rushed about, offering the victim a chair, offering him a glass of water, offering their teacher a glass of water, offering both Airedales a doggy treat in order to get them out of the room and into Miss Brown's car, and anxiously offering to call the doctor, or the ambulance, or the fire brigade or anybody else they could think of.

Naturally, highly coloured accounts of the incident flew like wildfire round the entire county. Mr Greer was prevailed upon by an anxious Education Office not to sue for damages. Teaching staff everywhere ostensibly tut-tutted at the awful thing that had nearly happened to Mr Greer while secretly smiling up their sleeves --- a case of schadenfreude if ever there was one!

And alas, Miss Brown's dogs were thereupon banned from the school for ever by the Director, much to the acute sorrow of Miss Brown, the pupils and the dogs.

"Serves him right," she confided angrily to a sympathetic colleague. "The dogs were only protecting the children. He should have had the good manners to knock before entering --- mannerless oaf that he is! I don't have the slightest sympathy for him!"

In the fulness of time more missives came round the schools from the Education Office banning dogs, cats, rabbits, mice, birds, tortoises, fish and every other living creature, except humans, from all school premises.

"For goodness sake," Miss Brown said tearfully to her good friend, the Clerk of Works, who had come rushing round immediately to offer a shoulder to cry on. "The whole thing is a complete over-reaction. As if a goldfish is likely to attack any visitor coming into the school!"

So the powerful, protective instinct of Jake and Penny was the reason for the fundamental change in education policy from that time onwards.

It is, however, good to relate that there was a happy ending to the tale of Miss Brown and the Clerk of Works.

A short time later he had turned up at the school one morning before the bell had been rung, and heard the sound of sobbing coming from the classroom. Anxiously, he knocked gently at the door and, getting no reply, cautiously opened it a crack and peered in. There was Miss Brown, standing crying in the middle of the room, her hanky pressed to her eyes. His first thought was that she was broken-hearted over the banishment of Jake and Penny, and he entered quietly, drew up a chair and sat her down in it, patting her shoulder kindly.

"What on earth's the matter?" he asked gently. "Is it the dogs?"

She looked up, surprised, for a short moment, then said, "No, no, Mr Ferguson. It's not the dogs. It's much worse than that."

The Clerk became very concerned. "Well, can you tell me what it is, dear Julia?" he asked, greatly daring.

Miss Brown broke out in another burst of weeping. "It's my birthday today. I'm forty!" she sobbed.

This galvanised the Clerk into long overdue action and the local teaching community was delighted to hear, shortly afterwards, of the engagement of Miss Brown, no longer sorrowing, but restored to her usual cheerful self, and her very favourite Clerk of Works.

The wedding was held in the local church and was attended by all the pupils and their parents, the entire teaching staff of the district and many of the Education Department staff, and of course, Jake and Penny, spruced up for the occasion with new collars decorated with tartan bows.

The only person noticeably missing was, of course, Mr Greer!

During her marriage to the Clerk of Works, Miss Brown, now Mrs Ferguson, remained devoted to her two big dogs and went everywhere in the car accompanied by their furry presence, treating them like cosseted children. The local folk were used to seeing her car driving through the village with Jake sitting aloofly in the front seat and Penny in the back, each dog securely fastened into its own individual, passenger seat belt.

This devotion to animals was also observed by Ronald when, as an official of the Ministry of Agriculture, he was travelling about Argyll, involved in a programme of widespread testing of sheep flocks for various diseases.

He had spent many days dealing with big flocks among the many farms and one morning found a note on his desk instructing him to go to a particular place to test a one-sheep "flock". After several frustrated attempts to find the address of the owner, and driving seemingly endlessly around the glens and braes of the county, he was on the point of giving up the quest when, on rounding a corner, he came upon a lady pushing a pram with one hand, and leading a sheep on a halter with the other. The animal was trotting along docilely at her heels like one of Miss Brown's dogs.

"Aha, at last," he thought. "Here's the mysterious one-sheep flock," and he wound down the car window, leaned out and inquired the lady's name.

Yes, she said, she was indeed the owner of the sheep, and Ronald checked the details on the paperwork. There, where the name of the breed should be entered was not the appropriate name, but the pet name of the animal --- Mint Sauce!

Tale no. 21: Inverness-shire and *The Rough Bounds*

"Is that the Primary Adviser?" said the abrupt voice at the end of the office phone.

Oh dear, I thought, this sounds like dissatisfied customer.

"Yes, it is," I answered. "Can I help you?"

"Well, I hope you can," snapped the voice. "This is Miss Nicolson at Isle of Bernera School. I am sick and tired of telling you folk in the office to send things to the right postal address. I've been waiting for these books for an age, and now they have gone to the wrong place.

This is not Bernera, North Uist. This is Bernera, Harris. Why on earth can't you get the postal address right?" and she slammed down the phone before I could say a word, while thinking, "Why did someone in this department not tell me the exact address for Bernera School?"

On arrival in Inverness I had been initiated into the complicated telephone system, but kept failing to reach my objectives.

One morning I tried to phone the school in Lochmaddy, North Uist. This was in the days when all the Inverness-shire schools were reached via the switchboard in the Education Office at 13 Ardross Street, Inverness.

I had asked for an outside line from the office switchboard, and gave the school's telephone number. I immediately heard the operator's voice. "You mean Miss Cameron at Lochmaddy School, don't you?"

"Well, yes," I replied, "but isn't that the right number?"

"Yes, but you don't use the number, you use the name," said the voice, patiently.

The whole business of trying to phone schools in the Western Isles was fraught with difficulty. Firstly, I had to get a line out of the building to the main Inverness exchange. This usually took some time as every Adviser seemed to be on the phone at the same time. Then I had to get another line out of Inverness exchange to the island exchange, followed by a third from the local exchange to the desired number itself.

It was all very time consuming and frustrating, especially when, once having got through to the North Uist exchange I was told,

"Oh, you can't get Miss Cameron at the school just now. She's not in. She's out feeding the hens. I can see her from the exchange window. Do you want to call back, or will I just run out and get her to go back into the school?"

I gave up at that point, put the phone down and sighed heavily, much to the amusement of May and Eileen, my Staff Tutors. They were well acquainted with the ways of the county schools and usually kept me informed about these little idiosyncracies, but hadn't got round to this particular one.

I was always very impressed about how the people who lived in these isolated parts of Scotland would strive to get a decent education for their children, no matter what the physical difficulties, and this made me think immediately of the Isle of Canna.

As phoning was so difficult I decided to get out of the office and just go in person to pay a long delayed visit to the little school on the island of Canna with its four pupils. There are actually two islands --- Canna and Sanday ---which were linked together, at that time, by sandbanks appearing only at low tide, though nowadays there is a road bridge. School had therefore to be held whenever the tide was suitable, as some of the pupils lived on the opposite island from the school. This sometimes meant a disrupted education for these pupils because, apart from the tides, the weather frequently was not good enough to send the children across to school.

In these days Canna belonged to Section 14 schools, along with those at Glen Kingie, Eilean Shona and the Isle of Muck. These were very isolated schools which couldn't attract a qualified teacher, so education was in the hands of "a responsible adult" --- usually someone in the local community --- who could follow a laid down scheme provided by the authority until such time as a teacher could be found, if ever.

Other Section 14 schools were usually in the more populated areas and could be described as Special Establishments. These were the Hospital School and the Occupational Centres, at Culduthel, Craig Phadrig School and the Nursery School at Balivanich on Benbecula.

I usually took my Labrador Roddy with me as, not only was he good company on the long drives out of Inverness, but the children all knew him and loved to have him in the classroom. I found that a shy or unhappy child, who wouldn't talk to me, would nearly always come out of his shell and talk to the dog, and in talking to the dog, might start talking to me as well.

As a former Head Teacher myself, I had occasionally led a sobbing child out of a stressful situation in the classroom, into the empty staffroom, got another child to bring in the dog, and then let nature take its course.

Roddy was always empathetic with the surrounding atmosphere and would quickly pick up on a child's distress. He would go over to the upset child, lay his head on the child's knee, and make little whining noises while offering a paw at the same time. This usually stopped the crying at once as the child became intrigued with the dog's behaviour and, instead of refusing to come to school at all, would then want to come in order to play with him.

I have seen a group of infants in the playground, completely surrounding Roddy, whose wagging tail was the only part of him to be seen above a surrounding sea of little people, all trying to pat him, pull his ears and climb on his back. He bore all this with total equanimity and was completely trustworthy with every child he ever met.

But he would occasionally let his joyful enthusiasm for people bring him into disrepute with authority.

One afternoon I was alone in the staffroom with the dog after school had gone home for the day, and heard footsteps on the stairs. I knew that Johnny, the local policeman, was intending to come in to discuss safety procedures on the road-crossing near the school and, as Roddy had crossed to the door and stood there, wagging his tail like mad, and making little whooping noises, I quickly opened the door to my visitor.

The dog joyously shot out to greet his friend --- he loved policemen for some reason --- and leaped upon him in welcome. The poor man staggered under the considerable weight of a fully grown Labrador and collapsed on to the floor, whereupon the dog stood on his chest and proceeded to lick his face with great enthusiasm, until I hauled him off and helped my visitor to his feet.

Naturally, I grovelled with apologies, which were gracefully accepted, and offered him a face towel and a conciliatory cup of coffee, which were also accepted.

But Roddy was not yet finished. As Johnny lifted the cup to his lips, the dog jumped up to show there were no hard feelings and tipped the entire, hot contents of the cup all over the front of Johnny's uniform. Frantically, I shoved Roddy out of the door, grabbed a dishtowel which I soaked in cold water, and sloshed the lot all over the steaming cloth --- and alas, all over Johnny's face, trousers and shoes as well.

Excitable welcome for Johnny

My aim was never all that good!

I then grabbed another dishtowel and tried to wipe the worst of the coffee and water off my visitor, who spluttered, "I should get danger money for coming into this school. I don't usually have this effect when I go out to discuss road safety on my patch!"

But now, as the Primary Adviser for Inverness-shire, I was no longer settled in one school, and had to go wherever the education authority wanted me to, and this meant the entire mainland county of Inverness-shire and all the Inner and Outer Hebridean islands except Lewis, which "belonged" to Ross-shire, and which I couldn't visit professionally. Inverness-shire was the largest education authority in Scotland at that time.

"Hands off my Lewis!" said Finlay, my colleague for Ross and Cromarty, but that didn't stop me visiting friends in Lewis outside official hours, and enjoying occasional forays into the pleasant town of Stornoway.

It was while there that Roddy got into another "situation". I had put him on a long, expanding lead while within the burgh boundaries and he had wandered off well ahead of me as we walked towards a small local post office. It was situated round a corner and he soon disappeared from my immediate view. I heard a bit of a commotion and just knew that it had something to do with my beloved dog.

Sure enough, on catching him up outside the post office, I found a dismayed little man helplessly trussed in the long lead as Roddy, with his usual enthusiasm for people, had circled round and round the unfortunate man --- his usual happy greeting --- woofing and wagging his tail, and of course trapping his victim in yards of expanding lead.

I had a sudden, impractical vision of myself running round and round the victim while trying to unwind seemingly endless yards of lead, or alternatively of making him spin around on the pavement in order to unwind himself.

But, after profound apologies on my part, I managed to get the lead loose enough to drop to the ground, and the victim was able to step directly out of its coils. He was magnanimous enough to assure me that no harm had been done, and that he could see the dog was just being friendly. But that was the end of the long lead in public areas or in towns. From then on it was used, strictly, in the open countryside only.

With relief I then returned to my own territory in the extensive County of Inverness, where I had to make contact with 134 schools, including tiny, one-teacher establishments; very remote schools with no qualified teacher --- just a "responsible adult"; special schools; full-sized big primaries in the towns and primaries attached to secondary schools.

There were 12 in Inverness burgh, 18 in Inverness district, 15 in Aird district, 26 in Lochaber district (including the islands of Eigg and Rum), 10 in Badenoch district, 20 in Skye, 9 in North Uist, 3 in Benbecula, 8 in South Uist, 5 in Barra, 4 in Section 14 schools (including the islands of Canna and Muck) and 4 in general others.

Quite a collection for one Primary Adviser and two Staff Tutors!

This was certainly the case on the A830 road from Fort William out to Mallaig, passing through the villages of Arisaig and Morar on the way.

12th century monks had settled in the little crofting township of Arisaig and called the entire area of Lochaber and Knoydart *Na Garbh Chrìochan,* The Rough Bounds, because of the wild nature of the country, and its remoteness.

One early spring evening I had arrived in the little Arisaig Inn on the shores of Loch nan Ceall, which was officially closed for the winter. I was given a room but had to have my meals in the front lobby as the rest of the building was unavailable. Fortunately there was a fireplace in the hall so at least it was slightly warm, though it tended to be very draughty and anything but comfortable.

Alas, the night was rendered hideous as a joiner, renewing woodwork somewhere in the upper part of the building, had left his radio on when he went home at the end of the day so, to my extreme exasperation, I had pop music resounding in my ears all night long.

At 2am, in desperation, I decided to get up and go looking for someone to stop the noise. After prowling around inside the establishment, without success, I then emerged on to the road in my dressing gown and slippers and searched the outside, in the blackness of the night, hoping that the local policeman wouldn't come along in his car and find a distracted waif wandering, in night attire, on the public highway like a lost soul.

I eventually realised that there was no one else in or around the inn but myself, so I wouldn't ever find the source of the noise and get it stopped. How I longed for 6am when the programmes stopped for a few hours and I could get a couple of hours' sleep (I hoped).

But there were compensations. At that time Arisaig had two primary schools --- Episcopal and Roman Catholic --- both the greatest of friends and constantly sharing outings and visits with one another --- really a delight to visit.

On a previous occasion it was just as well that I didn't have Roddy with me, as Miss Beecham (of the pharmaceutical firm) was visiting her neighbourhood school accompanied by her dog, which started up a fight in the classroom with the teacher's dog. There was quite a commotion, but both ladies were completely unfazed and carried on their conversation while efficiently separating the animals. The children didn't even seem to notice.

"Miss Smith's dog is a bit of a warrior," whispered Miss Beecham to me later.

"Miss Beecham's dog has a mind of his own," whispered Miss Smith to me when we met later in the village.

But, in spite of radio and dog hazards, the districts around Arisaig and Morar were a delight to visit, the scenery being breathtaking, especially the shell-white sandy beaches at Morar and the pale golden variety at Arisaig.

I often stood there on a glorious sunset evening looking out to the Hebridean islands of Eigg, Rum and Skye in a state of enchantment, lost in a romantic daydream of Prince Charles Edward Stuart's landing in Scotland on the 25th July 1745 in nearby Loch nan Uamh and his later escape to France after the disastrous battle of Culloden in February 1746, by means of a ship out of the same loch that he had sailed into, buoyant with hope and expectation, only nine months previously.

I especially remembered the loyal clansfolk who joined the Jacobite army during Charles's ill-fated bid for the throne of Britain --- later faithfully sheltering the fugitive prince in the dark days after Culloden in spite of the huge reward of £30,000 offered by the Government for his capture.

I thought, with pity in my heart, of the poor clansmen who were dragged into this catastrophe through no fault of their own, often very much against their will, and of the story of Cailean Beag, Little Colin, a poor crofter's lad who helped around the croft of his father Aonghas, by looking after their few cattle on the hills above the tiny clachan of Arisaig on Loch nan Ceall.

Cailean Beag saw, at first hand, the dramatic events which marked the end of the Prince's disastrous enterprise, and recounted to Aonghas, in breathless detail, all that he had seen one morning on the hill where their cattle were grazing.

"It's true, I tell you, Athair [Father]. *I was watching the beasts above our loch near the old shielings at Doire na Drise. It was well before the sun had come up, and I heard them before I saw them, so I ran and hid in the heather in case they were the saighdearan dearg".* [red-coats]

"Heard what? What, in the name of the Good Being are you talking about, a bhalaich? [laddie] *Slow down a bit and let's hear what you are on about."*

"I heard men on the hill near where I was. They were all around me on the Rumach Hill and the Torr Mor and the Cairn and the Druim an Dubh Leathaid and ---."

"Ist, ist, a Chailean. Slow down a bit and tell me what you saw --- very slowly!" said his father.

"I could see that the men on the hills were watching the loch and the two ships anchored near the shore."

"What ships?" interrupted Aonghas.

"I think they were French ships for I could see some of the sailors and our croitearan [crofters] *rowing in and out and bringing big barrels and casks back to the shore. The men on the beach were loading the barrels on to garrons and leading them away to the east, towards An Gearasdan."* [Fort William]

"Who were the men on the hills? Did any of them see you, and did you speak to any of them?" asked a now anxious father, for seeing what you were not meant to see could lead to disaster.

"No, Athair, but I could hear them talking together anns a'Ghaidhlig. [in Gaelic] *I think they were Domhnallaich* [MacDonalds] *for I caught a glimpse of their tartans among the trees. I managed to creep away quietly in case they would be angry that I had seen the big ships and all the stuff they were bringing ashore."*

"Good boy," approved Aonghas. *"Now, you and I will go out quietly and carefully and see if we can find out what's going on."*

They made for the shore and hid in the ring of trees surrounding the bay. The two French ships lay undisturbed at anchor while unloading took place, then Cailean Beag pulled at his father's sleeve.

"Look, Athair, I can see sails over the top of Rudha Arisaig [Arisaig Point]. *There are more ships coming into the loch.*

Others had obviously seen the approaching vessels too, for the next minute the hillside erupted with clansmen in the tartans of Clanranald MacDonald all rushing downhill, shouting warnings to the sailors and crofters in the small boats, and the big ships out on the water.

It was now safe for Cailean Beag and Aonghas to show themselves. These MacDonalds were their allies in the Jacobite cause, and the approaching ships turned out to be three Royal Navy sloops, smaller than the French ships but more than capable of blowing them out of the water with their plentiful cannons and musketry.

The two rushed down to the shore and helped the MacDonalds and the local crofters to bring the bulky loads ashore from the small boats, every man splashing out through the shallows, grabbing hold of a load, hoisting it on to willing shoulders, then scrambling frantically through the gentle surf and out on to the soft, pale sand which clogged their footsteps and slowed their progress up the beach to where the ponies waited patiently for their heavy burdens.

"Why are some of these casks so heavy, Athair?" gasped a breathless Cailean Beag as he struggled up the beach with his heavy load.

"They're full of armament --- bullets and gunpowder, and some are brandy casks," replied Aonghas, *"but the very heaviest ones are ---"* and he lowered his voice *"--- full of French gold to pay for the Prince's army. But keep that to yourself. I only found out when one of the cargo nets tore and some of the casks and barrels dropped and broke open on the deck of the La Bellone."*

Calum Beag squeaked in astonishment but, like all crofter's children, obeyed his father's instruction without question

And now, on 3rd May 1746, just over two weeks after the battle of Culloden, began the last pitched sea battle in British waters. The sloops stood in to the mouth of Loch nan Ceall and opened fire immediately, raking the stationary Frenchmen with cannon and musket fire. The latter had to remain at anchor and take this firestorm as they couldn't leave without unloading the last of the precious cargo, especially the gold.

They returned the fire as best they could, being at the distinct disadvantage of being unable to manoeuvre while being bottled up in the narrow confines of Loch nan Ceall.

Hours of unrelenting battle ensued with many casualties on both sides, the men in the small boats and onshore braving the hail of bullets while continuing to unload throughout the onslaught.

Cailean Beag loyally played his part in the struggle to get the precious cargo away and finally dragged himself, dazed and staggering with fatigue, up the beach to where the last of the garrons was being led hurriedly away towards the relative safety of Loch Arkaig where it was planned that the armament and gold would be secretly hidden until required by the remaining Jacobite forces.

As the long day dragged on eventually sheer war-weariness and fatigue brought the battle to an end and the sloops began to withdraw, firing as they went and still unloosing the occasional last deadly broadside on to the shore. The battered French ships finally completed their mission and, licking their many wounds, started getting up their anchors in preparation for sailing slowly away under seriously damaged sails and spars.

Cailean Beag looked around for his father, but couldn't see him in the immediate vicinity so, with growing anxiety, moved along the beach shouting his name. At last he saw Aonghas further along the pale golden sands of the bay and started out towards him, shouting and almost weeping with relief. His father waved, smiling happily at his son and stepping out eagerly towards him.

It was at that moment that a last, defiant, spiteful shell, from one of the sloops, hurtled over the waters of the loch and, bursting in mid air above the beach, caught Aonghas and three others in its indiscriminate blast. The four men dropped where they stood, and moved no more.

Cailean Beag was transfixed with horror for what seemed like an eternity, then ran screaming to where his father lay motionless in the beautiful golden sand, now streaked heavily with the lifeblood of so many casualties.

Cailean Beag knew, before he reached him, that Aonghas was dead. The utter stillness of his father's body told its own story, though there was not a single drop of blood to be seen anywhere upon him.

The poor lad broke his heart on that golden beach, holding his father's lifeless body in his arms and rocking him to and fro as he whispered Gaelic words of grief and blessing into his unheeding ear, until some crofter neighbours, taking pity on the stricken lad, gently took Aonghas from his grasp and, lifting Cailean Beag up and away from that fatal beach, got him back to the clachan and the loving ministrations of his elderly aunt, Iseabail, who was to cherish him as if he were her own son, from that day forward.

"Was it worth the dreadful sacrifice of all these lives?" asked Aunt Iseabail. *"The Prince has asked the world of us, and for what? Nothing but death, destruction, desolation and grinding poverty for us all from now onwards, at the hands of the saighdearan dearg."*

The tragedy was that the gold, having been carefully transported over the Lochaber mountains into the desolate empty spaces around Loch Arkaig, and hidden somewhere therein, was fought over and traitorously connived after, as hoards of gold usually are, and became known as the Loch Arkaig Treasure.

Incredibly, it was then lost and its hiding place forgotten. It would seem to be still lying undisturbed in that secret place, having done absolutely no good to anyone whatsoever.

Tale no. 22: "Lochaber No More"

My daydream of Arisaig and the last naval battle of May 1746, in little Loch nan Ceall, gradually faded away and I came back to the reality of the Arisaig of my current visit.

The clachan was never again visited by active battle, but during World War II Arisaig was taken over by the government to train agents for covert missions in Occupied France, and Arisaig House was used as a training school.

In the same way the Achnacarry estate, further to the east but still in Lochaber, and belonging to the clan chief, Donald Cameron of Lochiel, became the training ground for 25,000 commandos from 1942-45.

Commando Memorial

These areas were considered ideal for such training because of their extremely rough terrain and remoteness --- The Rough Bounds , *Na Garbh Chrìochan,* as named by the 12th century monks of Arisaig.

Meanwhile it was back into the car and along the A830 to visit the primary school in the fishing port of Mallaig at the end of the North Morar peninsula, at that time the busiest herring port in the British Isles. The road was still single-track in those days, requiring great concentration while driving, but was finally upgraded to double-track in 2008.

This was a pleasant experience and passed uneventually, without hazard.

As was usual in early spring the only hotel open in Mallaig was the Marine Hotel right down on the harbour. This was subject, day and night, to the endless clanking, screeching and banging of machinery on the fishing boats and ferries tied up at the quays, and in the processing plants.

I booked in, but again found it impossible to sleep right through the noisy night hours, and wondered if I would ever get a decent night's sleep in Lochaber. *Na Garbh Chrìochan* had an altogether different meaning, for me, apart from the simple geographical one!

But on Thursday morning I managed to gather myself together for the ferry crossing northwards from Mallaig, through the entrance to Loch Nevis, to the tiny clachan of Inverie on the almost deserted Knoydart peninsula. This has been accurately described as "Britain's last wilderness" and can be reached only by ferry out of Mallaig, or by a long, difficult walk in, over very rough ground, from the east. The entire peninsula was considered, in the 1990s, for use as a military training area. Fortunately this never happened.

Mallaig harbour

The sea was calm but there was a cold wind from the north as we started out on the long, slow sail out to Knoydart. Soon I was frozen, but hope to get warmed up during my visit to the little primary school.

To my relief the ferry eventually arrived off Inverie and drew in slowly towards the jetty --- but didn't actually stop or tie up. I watched, unbelieving, as a large mailbag was thrown ashore and deftly caught by an ancient person in dungarees, wellingtons and "bunnet", who then skilfully threw the outgoing mailbag right in to the well of the boat and exchanged a few words in Gaelic with our skipper.

With that the ferry was turned around in a big circle then brought back in towards the jetty, again very slowly, and a young, agile woman --- obviously, from her uniform, the District Nurse --- leaped fearlessly from the jetty into the boat without, apparently, batting an eyelid.

"What's going on here?" I asked, with a certain amount of trepidation. Was I expected to do a reciprocal leap from the boat on to the jetty? "Are we not going to land at Inverie?"

"Och, no," was the reply." We only stop on Mondays, Wednesdays and Saturdays. Were you wanting to go ashore?"

"Yes," I croaked, "I'm supposed to be visiting the school today."

"Well," said the skipper," you could go ashore, I suppose, but you'll be stuck here till Saturday and there is no hotel. Maybe you could be staying in the school."

This was obviously quite impractical. I would just have to go back to Mallaig right away. It was a well known hazard of Highland travel in those days that no one told you anything as they all expected you to know things without being told.

"Mo Chreach!" I thought. "All this way and I can't even get ashore!" and I subsided, miserable with cold and frustration, on the bench in front of the wheelhouse. The mate came round looking for fares. I struggled with frozen hands to get the required coins out of my bag and dropped the entire contents out all over the well.

Helplessly, I tried to chase the coins which had scattered widely around the deck, but my stiff fingers just wouldn't work, and after a few minutes the District Nurse asked if I needed any help.

"My hands are so cold I can't pick up these coins," I uttered unhappily.

She laughed and said, "Well, that's a new one on me. I've heard of many an excuse for not paying a fare, but cold hands is definitely a new one!" and she immediately paid the fare for me.

"Thanks so much," I said. "I'll pay you back as soon as we get to Mallaig, and my hands come back to life," and was extremely grateful when she kindly invited me to her house for a hot cup of tea and a thaw-out in her warm kitchen.

She was not from the Highlands and told me that she had been in Mallaig for a year but would be moving back to the Lowlands in the next few weeks as her contract was up.

"Nurses don't stay long in these outlying parts," she said. "It's a bit strenuous, especially in winter."

"I know exactly what you mean," I fervently replied.

This was not the first time I had set out to visit schools in various parts of the Highlands, and had not got there, but each time it rankled. I hated to be beaten.

The next day I had to return to my office in Inverness, so any further travel out to the west would have to wait for another day.

But soon the holidays were upon us, and I found myself, back on the road west to Skye, this time with members of my family and, of course, my Labrador, Roddy.

We enjoyed a sunny trip out to Mallaig where the car was put on the boat bound for Armadale on the Sleat peninsula of Skye. My aunt and mother found seats on the main deck while my uncle, Ronald, Roddy and I climbed up to the top deck in order to get the best views of the Sound of Sleat during the short crossing.

Unfortunately Roddy became very unsettled and flattened himself on the deck, back braced against a wooden raft and whining piteously all the way across.

"What's the matter with him?" I asked Ronald, who was in the Animal Health Division of the Ministry of Agriculture.

"I think the dog is unsettled by even this gentle swing of the ship and is trying to get down to a lower centre of gravity. He feels unsafe so high up on this ferry, even in an almost flat calm. He should be okay when we get ashore. Don't try to take him down to the car deck. It's too steep. We'll get Mum to just walk him off the gangway from the main deck."

This looked like a good idea so we all patted, and spoke comforting words to, our sad canine friend all the way across the Sound.

Everyone who passed was also full of compassion for the frightened animal and we had a stream of sympathetic passengers coming over to speak kindly to him, which confirmed my belief that the British are, fundamentally, animal lovers.

At Armadale pier the tide was low and the gangway very steep. My mother and aunt said they would have difficulty getting themselves off the ferry, never mind leading a scared dog off as well, so finally my brother hoisted a very heavy Labrador up in his arms and staggered down to the main deck where a kindly deckhand steadied him up the gangway with a brawny hand on his back.

"Whew," puffed Ronald. "Thank goodness we are coming back via the little ferry at Kyleakin. No high superstructure there."

As soon as he was put down on the nice, steady, dry land of Skye the dog recovered immediately and went off on a happy, sniffing expedition of this own.

We then set out for the north end of the island in order to visit my family's croft at Bornaskitaig, near Kilmuir, and decided to stay at the famous Flodigarry Inn on the north-eastern tip of the Trotternish peninsula.

The little clachan of Flodigarry was where the famous Flora MacDonald lived after Prince Charles Edward Stuart had escaped back to France.

We all knew the story, having often visited the grave next to Flora's, where my great-grandmother Catriona, is buried, but my English aunt didn't know much at all, so we set out to tell her Flora's story.

Flora was born in 1722 on the Outer Hebridean island of South Uist, but was on the neighbouring island of Benbecula when Prince Charles Edward Stuart was a fugitive fleeing for his life after the disaster of Culloden in 1746 and was almost trapped on that island.

Flora was persuaded, reluctantly to begin with, to help the Prince avoid being captured by the locally stationed Hanoverian Government militia, and was introduced to him. A plan was then hatched to get him safely away from the Outer Isles and back to the mainland where, it was hoped, he would escape aboard a French ship.

She obtained a pass for herself and her maid Betty Burke, to leave Benbecula for the island of Skye, but it was Charles, disguised very unconvincingly as Betty, who actually left with Flora and a manservant on 27th June 1746.

They were rowed across to Skye by six MacDonald oarsmen but, although the party successfully escaped to the island, and Charles was quickly passed on to Portree then the island of Raasay, someone had overheard the chattered conversation of the rowers and Flora was arrested for aiding the Prince's escape.

She was firstly imprisoned at Dunstaffnage Castle near Oban, and later taken to the Tower of London where she remained until the Act of Indemnity of 1747 was passed. She was then quickly released, having become renowned as a charming heroine in the polite society of London.

Her great bravery and loyalty were much admired, although she had been a true Jacobite, and many felt a great deal of sympathy for a young lady of such loyalty and good manners, who had been so closely involved in the romantic adventurings of the Prince while on the run.

She returned to Skye and in 1750, aged 28, she married Alan MacDonald, son of MacDonald of Kingsburgh, in the northern peninsula of Trotternish, and it was at this point that they went to live at Flodigarry, another MacDonald estate, on the north-east side of the peninsula.

Then Flora and family emigrated to America in 1774 where Alan was captured and imprisoned during the American War of Independence. So Flora had to return alone to Scotland in 1779 where she lived at Dunvegan with a daughter, until Alan's release in 1784. At this point they were finally able to return to the main family estate at Kingsburgh.

They lived there until Flora's death in 1790, at the age of 68.

My aunt patiently took all this in and said she was looking forward to our stay in Flodigarry Hotel, just yards from Flora's former home.

The hotel was in local ownership at the time, and was quaintly run, the arriving guests being told to go and choose their own rooms, none of which had keys for the doors. Guests found this disconcerting and many of them wedged pieces of furniture under their door handles to "repel boarders" in the night.

My uncle, however, was in his element, being back on his favourite island where he had spent part of his childhood, and we found him, that first night, sitting at our table in the dining room at 11pm, telling the waitresses, in fluent Gaelic, that he was waiting for his breakfast. They giggled, and from then on, waited upon him hand and foot. He was, as we say, "not so daft!"

He always loved playing tricks and, several days later, when the entire party was out fishing off Uig in a small rowing boat, he got hold of my aunt's line, underneath the boat, without her seeing him, and tugged it hard. She shrieked, convinced that she had caught a whale at the very least, and was tempted to push her mischievous husband overboard when she discovered who was on the other end of her line.

Then we set off round the northern tip of Skye for Kilmuir cemetery and Flora MacDonald's grave.

There is a tall stone cross there, with the admiring words of Dr Samuel Johnson engraved upon its face:

[hers] *is a name that will be mentioned in history, and, if courage and fidelity be virtues, mentioned with honour.*

We feel honoured that our great-grandmother lies in the adjoining grave. What better place could such a humble lady have than to be alongside such a heroic lady!

Our travels then took us over to the ancient castle of the Clan MacLeod at Dunvegan, spectacularly situated on its basalt eminence high above Loch Dunvegan, and where we came across a land controversy in full swing at the very doors of the castle itself.

"Dé tha dol?" (What's going on?") demanded Donald, our irrepressible uncle, on overhearing a bad-tempered spat between two Gaels standing at the entrance to the castle. They turned out to be a MacLeod and a MacDonald, both natives of Skye, and evidently engaged in their own personal clan warfare.

"It must be obvious, even to a MacDonald," growled the MacLeod, "that our chief urgently needs funds to preserve the castle. The roof is leaking so badly that guests have to put up umbrellas in the bedrooms! You can't keep an 800 year old structure without needing repairs from time to time, and this costs money --- a lot of money!"

"Of course I can see that," spluttered the MacDonald angrily, "but your chief, John MacLeod, has no right whatever to offer the Black Cuillin Mountains for sale to any bidder, no matter what nationality. These are the heritage lands of Scotland, and no mere clan chief can just declare ownership and sell them at will."

He was referring to the fact that John MacLeod of MacLeod, 29th chief of Clan MacLeod, had caused outrage by offering the charismatic mountain range for sale on the open market, in the year 2000, for £10 million.

MacLeod loudly declared, "Mere clan chief, indeed! I'll have you know that John MacLeod is one of the foremost, and most respected, of the clan chiefs of Scotland. This castle is in immediate need of far-reaching repairs, and the money will go to maintaining the family seat and providing a Clan Centre which all MacLeods, and other people, can visit, whether it suits you MacDonalds or not!

You MacDonalds were always jealous of our land-owning in Skye from the very beginning, and wanted to own the whole island yourselves."

"But the mountains are not his to sell!" insisted the increasingly incensed MacDonald.

Our Donald --- who was a member of the Clan MacPhee, which is not one of the "big guns" among the Highland clans --- took several steps backward. This was becoming a very bad-tempered argument indeed.

"Of course they are," shouted MacLeod, getting distinctly red in the face. "They are part of the clan lands granted by the Crown to us in 1611, so our chief can sell them and any other land if he feels like it!"

This controversy was no longer limited to the island of Skye but had attracted adverse criticism from the world-wide diaspora of clans and other interested parties. It was generally felt that the Cuillin were already in public ownership, and that MacLeod had neither the moral nor the legal right to sell.

But MacLeod had not finished his strop:

"The Charter of Dunvegan of 1611 definitely grants the Barony of Dunvegan to the MacLeods, when its ownership was returned from the Crown to the clan chiefs, so you can't dispute that fact. It's written in the law, and not even you MacDonalds are above the law," spat the incensed MacLeod.

MacDonald obviously felt that he was in danger of losing the argument, and marshalled the last of his forces:

"We'll just see about that," he snapped. "Several organisations have requested the Crown Estate Commissioners to investigate the whole matter --- extent of land holdings as well as legality, of this so-called deed of Ownership.

For goodness' sake, it goes back to an ante-diluvian grant which was probably given verbally and has no written charter associated with it. How out-of-date can you get? Anyway," he added, with the air of one producing his trump card, "Land Reform Scotland, as well as the Scottish Office, among other interested parties, have all requested legal clarification in this matter."

The protagonists had now run out of steam as well as arguments, and each stumped off in opposite directions, muttering furious Gaelic oaths which turned Donald's face pale.

"Thank Heaven they weren't armed," he breathed. "That's how wars begin."

So we entered the famous castle in thoughtful mood, but enjoyed the experience nonetheless, especially as the Chief, John MacLeod, was prevailed upon to sing to the assembled tourists in his very pleasing, trained operatic voice.

This spat, that we had observed, was a far cry from open clan warfare, but the argument rumbled on, and we heard later that the whole matter was regarded, legally, as a real "hot potato".

However, on the 19th July 2000, cautious legal opinion found that there was a definite recorded title in favour of the MacLeods which included the Cuillin range and therefore, that John MacLeod had the right to sell the mountains, and furthermore, that the Crown Commissioners would not mount a legal challenge against the chief, as "a legal challenge would have little prospect of success."

According to the law John MacLeod needed to prove a recorded title capable of including the Black Cuillin, and possession for more than twenty years.

And he did.

The Cuillin were then put on the market, but there were no firm offers, so they were taken off the market in 2003.

Finally, in 2006, a consortium offered to buy the castle and the Black Cuillin. In return they promised to repair and restore the castle, and build a Visitor Centre.

This was acceptable as the dignity of Clan MacLeod was upheld and the chief retained the right of residency.

"Well," said Donald," wouldn't it be interesting to find out just how many of these ancient deeds are valid and acceptable in present-day Scotland?"

Tale no. 23: The Vengeance of Clan Campbell

"Here, hold it for a minute while I get you some butter," said the farmer.

I was puzzled by his request until I realised the "it" referred to his baby daughter, and I have to say I was quite scandalised by this seemingly heartless way of referring to his child.

However, it became increasingly obvious that he doted on the little one, and the eccentric nickname had occurred originally because neither he, nor his wife, could agree on a suitable name for their new arrival. Eventually a grandmother had to be summoned to provide names popular in the family from way back, and little Jane finally got her proper name.

Rab, the farmer, ran a most successful dairy farm on the small Hebridean island of Colonsay, a former territorial possession of the Clan MacPhee, until the murder and mayhem of the 17th century, known to history as the *linn nan creach* --- the century of forays --- lost them their chief, their ancestral lands and their independence in one devastating go.

In the days when I visited the island it was in the hands of a private owner with decided views on his rights over his tenantry, a fact which very often led to tensions between himself and the sitting tenants on this island. This was, alas, a fairly common occurrence on other islands in the Hebrides, and the mainland as well.

Rab was just such a tenant, and was in the midst of a long running dispute with the owner over access rights to the farm.

"How on earth does he expect me to live and work on this land when he challenges my right of access into the farm?" demanded Rab, and I couldn't blame him. There were tales of other folk, some of them long term inhabitants of the island, who were similarly in the midst of various, acrimonious disputes with the landlord.

Colonsay was not a happy island.

Other Highland areas, mainland as well as island, had gone through similar experiences, and many had achieved a satisfactory conclusion in the form of a "buy-out", which put the tenants in charge of their own destinies --- but with all the subsequent, unexpected responsibilities which that entailed.

In some cases the transferred ownership turned out to be anything but the Shangri La which many tenants had envisaged, and disputes still arose among the groups and individuals who had a vested interest.

Meanwhile I handed little Jane back to her father and he handed me a present of a large, newly made, pat of the most beautiful fresh butter, from his own dairy, that I have ever tasted.

Ronald, who was with the Animal Health Division of the Ministry of Agriculture, then indicated that he would like to get on with the job of inspecting Rab's dairy herd which was, apparently, grazing in a field on the other side of the island.

"I'm up to the eyes this morning," said Rab,"so just you take the Landrover and drive round to the field and you'll see my dozen Ayrshires in there. It'll be a nice trip this morning, now the sea mist has lifted."

Driving farm vehicles was a common feature of travel for Ministry of Agriculture personnel on the islands, particularly the small ones. The roads were narrow, single-tracked, often badly surfaced, and the regulations about MOTs, road tax, insurance and such-like annoying matters were as nebulous as the sea mist, so visiting officials were frequently requested to be their own taxi drivers in a variety of clapped-out farm vehicles, held together by faith, hope and binder twine.

I climbed into the passenger seat --- no seat belts, of course --- noticing with interest that there was a large hole in the vehicle's floor between the driver and passenger seats. The uneven surface of Colonsay could be clearly seen through the gap, but we set off anyway, and bumped our careful way along the rutted surface of the "main road".

It was just our luck that the biggest rut on Colonsay was right in the middle of our path, and recent heavy rain had turned it into a junior loch of unknown depth, which couldn't be avoided. Inevitably we bumped heavily into it, and were immediately soaked by the cataract of dirty water which shot up through the gaping space in the floor, while a loud bang echoed from the rear of the vehicle.

"That'll be the suspension finally gone," said Ronald gloomily. "Rab will really have to get another car very soon. This one is an utter wreck."

It seemed like an age before we found the field with the dozen Ayrshire cows grazing unconcernedly, and Ronald soon completed his inspection of the double ear-tags and general condition of the animals. We then had to find other farms and crofts on his list and this took forever as farmers seemed to have bits of land in various places over the island, not all in one place, as in most farms.

He also wanted to see official documents such as Cattle Passports and Movement Books which the Ministry insisted every keeper of animals must produce on request from its Animal Health Officers, on every farm and croft on the mainland as well as the islands.

Ronald issued groaning, from many a farmhouse after trying, unsuccessfully, to extract some of these documents from casual-minded persons.

One dear old soul scratched his head musingly when asked for a document;

"Oh, yes, the Movement Book. Now, I know I had it last year when you came but the dog got it after you left and I haven't seen it since. I'll just have to ask my brother if he knows where it is. You'll have a dram while you're waiting?"

"No thank you, Mr MacGillivray," said Ronald patiently. "Could you please just ask your brother for the book now while I'm here?"

"Well, I don't rightly know where he is at the moment. Are you sure you won't just have a dram while you're waiting" --- and Mr MacGillivray stared unseeingly into the distance while scratching his head thoughtfully. "Wait you now, he'll may be out on the hill looking at the ewes or no, I think he said he might go over to MacNicol's croft this morning to help round up his sheep for market. But then he might have changed his mind and gone to pick up some cattle feed from Mrs Beaton. She's very good that way --- generous in letting us have some feed when we are running short ---" and Mr MacGillivray rambled on vaguely. "Are you sure now, you won't take a dram while you're here?"

If Ronald had accepted all the proffered drams on his way round the island he would have been drunk and incapable in a very short time.

"I'll be back next month, Mr MacGillivray," sighed Ronald. "Would you please make sure you've got the Movement Book ready for me when I come?"

"Certainly, certainly," the unfailingly polite Mr MacGillivray assured him." I'll ask my brother about it when he comes in, don't you worry."

"It's impossible to be annoyed with them when they're always so polite," said Ronald.

He then told me about his last visit to one of the islands in search of public waste disposal facilities, in other words, the local dump, where the Hebridean trait of disarming politeness was also much in evidence.

The dump was a high-fenced enclosure with a gate in one side into which local household refuse was deposited every week. It was a hazard to grazing animals if someone left the gate open, or the fence was damaged in any way, as the beasts were inclined to eat plastic, waste meat products and other unsavoury materials which were commonly found in these places.

It was part of Ronald's job to inspect these small, local dumps and report any faults which might harm livestock, so that the local authorities could arrange for speedy repairs.

He was approaching the enclosure about 11 o'clock one morning and saw the refuse lorry parked just outside the perimeter, near the gate, which lay wide open. Inside the cab were two men peaceably eating their "pieces" (sandwiches) --- and drinking tea from their flasks.

Ronald thought he'd better check the entire perimeter before speaking to the men, so quickly walked around the length of the fence, discovering that the fourth side was missing entirely and, by the look of things, had been missing for some time. This was now a three-sided dump, wide open to wandering livestock, and a potential menace to their health and safety. In fact, he had to chase out a sheep which had wandered in and might have already eaten something harmful. He had no way of telling.

He hurried back to the lorry. The two worthies looked out at him, smiling and incurious. Ronald approached the open window of the cab.

"I'm from the Ministry," he said. There was no need to specify which Ministry as everyone knew it was the Ministry of Agriculture, "and I am concerned about the state of this dump."

The men gazed inquiringly at him, good-natured smiles still in place.

"You know that cows, pigs and sheep might get into the dump and eat harmful materials?" stated Ronald. "In fact, I have just chased out a sheep a minute ago. Goodness knows whether it has eaten something bad or not."

The men looked politely concerned.

"Is that a fact?" they tutted, shaking their heads sympathetically. "That will never do at all, at all."

A flask of tea was then hospitably held out of the cab window to The Man From The Ministry who, even more politely, declined the offer.

The Man from the Ministry

"Did you not see that the dump was not secure and that the fourth side was completely missing? This should have been reported to the Council," persisted Ronald.

"Och well, we might have noticed that there was a bit of fence missing, but we always make sure we shut the gate," was the response. "Don't you be worrying yourself now. We'll see to it that the gate is shut alright before we leave. The animals won't get in through this gate, at all."

The small matter of the missing fourth side seemed not to have entered their consciousness in any way. Ronald gave up and went away, followed by earnest assurances from the worthies that he was not to worry as they would be sure to shut the gate before they went away.

He knew that he would have to report the missing fence himself.

Unfortunately, not all stories, whether ancient or modern from the islands reflect this gentler and more humorous side of island life and the beautiful isle of Mull has its own particular tales of plotting, violence and skulduggery, particularly in clan times.

One concerns the rivalry which existed between the clan chiefs, Lachlan MacLean of Duart, who resided in Duart Castle which overlooks the Sound of Mull, and Archibald, 4th Earl of Argyll, who resided in his imposing castle at Inveraray on the banks of Loch Fyne.

There are at least two versions of this story but both refer to the events of 1527. In one version the lady involved is Catherine, sister of the Earl, and in the other she is Elizabeth, daughter of the Earl, but in other respects the stories mainly coincide.

The lady, described here as Elizabeth, beloved daughter of Archibald, 4th Earl of Argyll, was brought up in Inveraray Castle and, as was common among the aristocracy of the Highlands in those days, was married off to another Highland chief, Lachlan MacLean of Duart, of the Clan MacLean of Mull.

Inveraray Castle

This marriage was very much against her will and was simply a dynastic arrangement by the chiefs in the hope of future peaceful co-existence and cooperation between the two clans.

MacLean was gratified by his marriage alliance to the great MacCailean Mòr, head of the prestigious Clan Campbell, and the Earl was happy enough to have a new ally adjacent to his western lands, as a buffer against possible incursions by other clans.

After the marriage Elizabeth was ordered, by her new husband, to cut all ties with her family in Inveraray, but made the best of her unhappy situation by busying herself with the poor MacLean clansfolk, so much so that she became loved and revered by the simple crofters but, alas, became the object of suspicion and resentment among other small-minded and surly folk who started a whispering campaign against her.

One day Elizabeth was startled and delighted to overhear, from her devoted MacLean folk, that her brother, Lord Lorn, and her old sweetheart, Sir Malise Graham, had arrived incognito in Duart to find out why she had apparently cut off all communication with her old home.

There was a joyful, though secret, meeting of the three and the men told her that the Earl, her father, now deeply regretted the marriage alliance with MacLean, and urged her, if she was unhappy, to return with them to Inveraray at once.

She tearfully told them that she could not leave Mull as she now had a little son who would one day become the chief of Clan MacLean.

Lord Lorn and Sir Malise Graham had to leave, full of regrets, but recognising that her love for her baby son overwhelmed all considerations of her own personal happiness.

Unfortunately, on the way back to their boat, they were spotted by Duncan, the cowherd, who resented Elizabeth because she had upbraided him for mistreating a calf.

He went straight to Allan MacLean of Lochtarish, and told him what he had seen, and of his suspicions that the two strangers had come from Campbell territory.

The whispering campaign among the troublemakers now grew steadily, and soon the spiteful story was put about that Elizabeth was really a Campbell spy, planted by her father in order to pass on information to him about MacLean business.

The scandal-mongers worked themselves up into a white heat and confronted their chief about his choice of a wife, and the danger in which she was placing the entire MacLean clan. They issued an ultimatum --- he must choose between his wife, or his position as Chief of Clan MacLean.

MacLean was a coward at heart and, rather than risk his status as Chief, told them to do what they liked with Elizabeth, as long as he himself knew nothing about it, and off he went hunting for several days.

The unhappy Elizabeth was then abducted, carried down to the shore, thrown into a small boat and rowed out into the Sound of Mull. On arrival at a half-tide rock at the south end of the island of Lismore she was dragged out and abandoned there at low tide.

The captors then rowed away, callously leaving her to drown --- as they thought. No more would she endanger the MacLean clansfolk and the castle, no matter how powerful her father, the Earl.

The tide had been ebbing when Elizabeth was stranded on the rock, and she spent a bleak night of utter despair, clinging to a mooring stake driven in to the top of the rock, waiting and watching as the tide inevitably turned and began its inexorable rise towards the summit.

The sea gradually rose past her feet, legs and was up to her waist when she almost succumbed to despair and cold. She was only semi-conscious and in another few minutes would have either died of exposure or been swept away by the tide.

She was scarcely aware of the rescue when it belatedly came.

Lorn and Graham had been alerted by a superstitious Campbell fisherman who fearfully insisted that, while out fishing in the Sound during the night, he had heard cries as from a lost soul and had seen some sort of ghost-like white thing on the rock.

The Campbells had their suspicions that MacLean might have tried to get rid of his wife, so all three jumped into a boat and rowed quickly out to the rock where they found the half-drowned girl, just alive and no more. She was swiftly lifted into the boat and taken to the safety of the Campbell shore.

The following day she was returned to her father's stronghold of Inveraray Castle, where the chief was informed of the treacherous deed.

It was a truly enraged Earl who soon received a letter from Duart announcing the tragic death of Elizabeth as the result of a "serious illness". The supposedly grieving husband proposed to visit Inveraray in order to express his condolences, and pay his respects, to the Earl in person.

This being the heart of the Highlands, the furious Earl carefully laid his plans to exact a most bitter revenge on the treacherous MacLean.

He ordered Sir Malise to take two riding-horses out of Inveraray, and to ride westwards towards the coasts of Loch Linnhe and Morvern, then across to Mull.

Meanwhile, back at Inveraray Castle, Lachlan MacLean of Duart and Allan MacLean of Lochtarish appeared in the guise of the bereaved and broken-hearted relatives who had arrived to tell of the sad death of poor Elizabeth.

They were met by a grim-faced Earl and Lord Lorn, who listened in silence to this tale, but seemed strangely reconciled to their loss. The Earl told the MacLeans that, although they were all obviously distraught about his daughter's tragic end, they had been preparing for a great celebration when the sad news arrived and, as all Campbell chieftains were present in the castle, they would just go ahead with the planned feast.

An invitation was then extended to the MacLeans to join in as there was to be a new mistress arriving at the castle that very night.

Rather taken aback, but willing to do anything to appease the Earl, the scoundrel MacLean agreed to share in the welcome to the new mistress, perhaps regretting getting rid of a wife whose father held such virtually regal state in Inveraray.

Into the great hall of the castle that evening came the Earl with a beautifully dressed and veiled lady on his arm, the chieftains crowded round and the banquet began.

MacLean, eager to please, sprang to his feet and proposed a toast to the new mistress, saying that, if her face was as lovely as her gown and her jewels the Earl would be a happy man indeed.

The cold-eyed Earl replied that her face and her soul were easily as lovely, but that it was a pity this had not been appreciated by those who should have been her nearest and dearest!

MacLean was beginning to feel the hairs rising on the back of his neck, especially when the lady, at a sign from the Earl, finally threw back her veil, revealing Elizabeth's face to her husband.

A deathly silence followed, then the chieftains raised their glasses and roared out their approval.

The MacLeans were trapped.

"This is the new mistress of Inveraray," shouted the Earl, *"whose sudden death from illness you mourned so sadly. Now, drink her*

health before you and I, MacLean, go out on to the castle green and settle this for good with our swords."

The intense sword fight which ensued could only have one ending, and at the end the Lord of Duart lay dead on the green.

Allan MacLean of Lochtarish, expecting a similar fate, nevertheless mocked the Earl for having regained his daughter, but lost her baby son.

"Look behind you," grated the Campbell," *and just see if I have lost anyone!"*

Lochtarish looked round just in time to see two riding-horses enter the castle green. Sir Malise climbed down from his horse, took the baby, Roderick, from his nurse and placed him gently into the arms of his ecstatic mother.

Tale no. 24: Murder, Mayhem and Mystery

"A mhàthair, a mhàthair, what will I do --- what will I do? Oh, help me, mo mhàthair, help me, help me!" and young Marsaili fell across the threshold, and collapsed, wailing, into her mother's arms.

"Ist, ist, what ails you, my child?" exclaimed her frightened mother. It wasn't usual for her brave daughter to be in such a hysterical state.

"I've killed him --- but I didn't mean to --- and he's just lying out there where everyone will see him --- and they'll come for us --- and we will be blamed for his death --- " and Marsaili became incoherent, babbling on incomprehensibly into her mother's shoulder, while pulling in agitation at her sleeves.

Annag held her distraught daughter close and rocked her to and fro, whispering soft, calming words until the girl was able to speak without sobbing uncontrollably. Marsaili finally sniffed back her tears, wiped her eyes with the back of her hands, and began to tell her mother the whole, appalling story:

"I took Maili away up on to the shieling in Salachan Glen, just as you told me, so she could graze on the nice fresh grass up there, and she wandered about happily while I sat on a hillock and watched her. Everything was fine until about midday when I went to put the halter on her and bring her back down to the infield, and then --- and then --- " and Marsaili burst out weeping again, seemingly unable to bring herself to describe what had happened next, while wringing her thin hands together continuously.

"A Mharsaili, you must tell me what happened," said Annag urgently. *"Was it something to do with the soldiers, or the factor, or what on earth was it? You must tell me. You are really frightening me!"*

Marsaili made a great effort to speak coherently and eventually the whole dreadful story tumbled from her numbed lips, bit by stammering bit:

"We were at that place where you can see right across Loch Linnhe to Sgeir nan Gillean. It's a bit rough and Maili jerked on the halter so that I stumbled over a tussock, and just at that moment ---"

and the girl hesitated, obviously reluctant to relive the terrifying events of the morning.

Annag, reluctant to force her daughter to go on, just stared at her with wide-open eyes in her pallid face until Marsaili managed to pull herself together enough to continue and, standing stiffly in front of her mother, at last told her the rest of the tale, like an automaton, without expression or emotion.

"There was a gunshot and my poor Maili fell down dead with a bullet through her throat. And there was all that blood and if Maili had not made me stumble it would have been me that was lying dead there on the hill. I'm the one that should be dead, not our poor little cow."

Annag pulled her apron over her face in her distress, and let out a moan before realising that Marsaili had more to say. She spoke hoarsely. *"Go on, mo ghaoil, you must tell me it all."*

"I stood there, holding Maili's halter, not knowing what to do next, and then one of the hateful saighdearan dearg [redcoats] *sprang out of the bracken and bounded down the hill towards me. His gun was still smoking and I thought he was going to raise it and shoot me there and then. But he didn't. He seemed to be alone and there weren't any other soldiers with him."*

Marsaili's voice faltered, but she recovered herself and went on, *"I couldn't move with fright and he came right up to me, pointing the gun at my head, laughing at me and kicking poor Maili. How I hated him and wished him dead!"* and the tears coursed down the girl's face as she recounted the events of the next few minutes in that place of horror.

"The next minute the beast of a soldier threw down his gun and seized me in his filthy grasp. I knew what he intended, but I was full of rage for what he had done to my little Maili, and how he was enjoying it, so I found the strength to twist out of his reach, kick his shins as hard as I could, which made him yell out and fall over. While he was trying to get up I looked around for something to hit him with --- but, a mhàthair, I didn't mean to kill him, I really didn't --- I didn't ---"

"Yes, a nighean, of course you didn't," soothed her mother. *"Go on, go on!"*

Hesitantly now, Marsaili continued, *"Then I lifted the gun myself. I caught it up by the barrel."*

Her mother gasped in horror for taking a King's soldier's gun, in the year 1752, would lead to severe reprisals against her family.

"What did you do?" she asked hoarsely.

"I didn't know how to fire it, but I was so angry that I held it tightly by the barrel and swung it high and wide before I --- I brought it down, as hard as I could, on the back of his head. I heard a crack and --- and the soldier never got up. He just lay there, breathing like someone snoring heavily and his face a purple colour." Marsaili now couldn't get her words out fast enough, and it all came pouring out of her like a river:

"I stood looking at him lying there in the heather and him not moving or saying a thing and after a minute he stopped snoring and was quiet. I knew then that I had killed him."

And she stopped her flood of words as if a tap had been turned off, and stood there, shaking and silent, in a kind of trance, until her mother rose swiftly, took her gently by the arm and said, *"Now a Mharsaili, we must get to him before the other soldiers find him. We must bury him and hide the gun. We must hide Maili. Right now we have to get Ruaridh back from the shore and tell him everything."*

Marsaili was in such a state of shock that she would have agreed to anything her mother said, so the pair of them threw their shawls over their heads and, after checking that there was no one lurking about outside the door, ran swiftly and furtively down to the rocky beach where Ruaridh was gathering up seaweed as a fertiliser to spread on their stony little fields, and forking it on to the pony cart.

He looked up in puzzlement as his sister and his mother came hurrying in such an obviously distressed state along the beach towards him.

"What is the matter?" he asked. *"You look as if you have seen a ghost, the pair of you,"* and was alarmed when his sister burst into tears at his words. He listened intently, and with growing alarm as they jerked out the story between them.

"So you see, Ruaridh," said his mother, *"We've got to get to that man and his gun before the rest of the troop find him. We must bury them both, or we're all dead."*

"And this is the aftermath of Prince Charlie's wonderful dream," said Ruaridh bitterly. *"All we have been left with after the fiasco of Culloden has been starvation, shootings, robbery, burnings and bitter division among the clans. What a legacy he has given us!"* and Ruaridh spat out his words with barely controlled anger. Then he recollected what the two women had told him and the dangerous plight they were now in.

"Come, both of you. Show me where the saighdear dearg is lying. Quickly now! We must hide all evidence of his death right away."

A heavy shower of rain fell as the three ran from the beach and up on to the hillside where the redcoat still lay beside his gun, and Maili's pathetic little body lay sprawled a few yards away.

"A Mharsaili, you'll need to go and get the pony and cart from the shore. That's the only way we can get Maili away from here. Hurry now!"

And the strong young crofter hoisted the inert redcoat up and over his shoulder while Annag picked up the gun and hid it under her shawl. Fortunately the heavy rain shower had more or less obliterated all traces of blood from the ground.

Marsaili, now filled with a sense of urgency, scrambled down to the beach, seized the pony's bridle and led him carefully up the steep track to the scene of the crime. Fortunately, nobody came while they struggled to attach the cow, with ropes, on to the back of the cart and dragged her slowly back to the house. Marsaili managed to lead the pony and cart while keeping her eyes averted from the heavy burden draped over her brother's shoulder.

The gun was temporarily hidden in the thatch of the roof, the dead soldier was thrust behind the pile of peats outside the crofthouse and poor Maili was left in the small byre attached to the house. As it was full daylight they didn't dare try to bury the evidence in case they were seen. They planned to dispose of the corpse when darkness fell, and so they waited all day in a frenzy of fear, but no one came.

"That soldier must have been a deserter," said Ruaridh, *"otherwise we'd have had the entire garrison about our ears by this time. We can't risk anyone seeing us burying him so, a mhàthair, will you sew a large bag big enough to cover this wretch and will you, a Mharsaili, gather some boulders to weigh down the sack. We'll get rid of him in the loch."*

When darkness had fallen the large, heavy sack was carried down to the beach on the pony's back, along with the gun, also in a weighted canvas, and both were transferred into their small fishing boat.

In a glimmer of moonshine the women stood watching on the shore as Ruaridh rowed far out into Loch Linnhe as far from their croft as possible, to where the loch was deepest. His muffled oars made very little splashing in the ruffled surface of the water, which also helped to hide the faint splash as, first the redcoat, and then his gun, were carefully slid over the gunwale and sank, without any commotion, below the surface of the big sea loch.

For days afterwards they waited in a fever of anxiety for the arrival of any soldiers, but none came, It seemed that he must have, indeed, been a deserter, probably on the hunt for what loot he could steal, as did many of the government troops, for there were no searches in their vicinity and gradually they dared to relax a little, though Marsaili became silent and withdrawn as time went by.

She was unable to get the awful experience out of her mind and, although completely innocent of deliberate murder, constantly relived, in her mind, the manner of his violent death.

Strangely enough, the catastrophic battle of Culloden of 1746 resulted in remarkably few reprisals by the Highlanders against the undoubted brutality of the Hanoverian troops --- surprising in such a warlike race --- but probably as a direct result of deliberate starvation, grinding poverty, the wholesale destruction of property, and the utter humiliation of defeat, so resistance was mainly a matter of isolated incidents of revenge and opportunism --- Marsaili's actions were the unplanned result of her revulsion over the redcoat's bestial behaviour.

Other incidents are well documented, and for quite some time after the battle, travellers through the Highlands would ask for, and receive, military escorts to protect them against robbery and revenge attacks from the clansmen.

I recollected this true incident while driving out of the town of Kinlochleven at the head of beautiful Loch Leven. As the Primary Adviser for Inverness-shire and the Western Isles (except Lewis) my furthest south school was in Kinlochleven. This was a strange arrangement for the northern half of the town was in Inverness-shire, and therefore on my "patch", while the southern half belonged to Argyll and I couldn't visit schools there.

As I had intended to go on to Oban for an education meeting with Argyll colleagues I now drove westwards along the lochside, through the glaciated valley of Glencoe, sombre today in a pervasive mist. Inevitably I thought of the dreadful events of 13th February 1692, now very well documented, when the sept of the MacIain MacDonalds was set upon, in the dead of night, by two companies of government troops under the command of Robert Campbell of

GlenLyon, after giving traditional Highland hospitality to the soldiers for ten days.

Thirty-eight men, women and children were massacred by the redcoats and many others, escaping into the freezing mountain passes of the glen, perished from exposure, wounds and starvation in the days that followed.

The story is long and complicated, and not, as so many imagine, the usual clan spat between MacDonalds and Campbells. The giving of hospitality was almost a sacred rite, and that it should have been violated in this murderous way was regarded among Highlanders, as unforgivable.

As it was, the British government, including King William himself, was aware of the general intention to attack --- though Robert Campbell of GlenLyon carried out his orders with unseemly ferocity and was guilty of slaughter under trust.

This amounted to treason by the government against the people.

An inquiry was eventually constituted but no one ever stood trial --- this being the biggest crime of all in the whole sorry affair.

It occurred to me that this entire district, from Glencoe south, had the unenviable reputation of being Murder Mile, or rather, Miles, for the incident of Marsaili and the redcoat happened just a few miles south of the entrance to Glencoe, although sixty years later.

The year 1752 saw, in that same district, another equally infamous murder, but with a resultant mystery, for the murderer was never apprehended, although his name was known to certain people and secretly passed down through generations of the Stewart clan for 260 years.

This was the notorious Appin Murder, regarded as the last true Scottish mystery. The famous Scottish writer, Robert Louis Stevenson, based his enthralling story, *Kidnapped,* on true historical facts, except for the fictional character of the youthful David Balfour.

The Highlands were still in the grip of Hanoverian revenge after the failure of the second Jacobite Rising of the year 1745 when Prince Charles Edward Stewart/Stuart made his ill-advised bid for the throne of Britain.

Although the clans were devastated during the battle at Culloden Moor in 1746, and its appalling aftermath, the government in England still lived in fearful apprehension of another uprising in the Highlands. After all, Prince Charles's army had reached as far south as Derby, causing terror in London and the panic-stricken flight of the royal family to France.

He could well have gone on and reached the capital, but unfortunately Charles listened to his incompetent advisers, and decided to retreat from Derby, as winter was fast approaching. Many of his Highlanders were deserting in order to rush back to the Highlands to save the vital harvest crops and, much to Charles's disappointment, the majority of the so-called "English Jacobites" took cold feet and didn't turn up at all.

So the ostensibly victorious Jacobite army turned back from Derby and fought a running rearguard action right up through England, southern Scotland and back to the Highlands where the whole disastrous enterprise had begun.

The catastrophic, thirty-five-minute pitched battle on the morning of 16th April, 1746, saw the cream of the clans fall dead and dying under Cumberland's cannonfire on Culloden Moor near Inverness, and the beginning of the end of the Clan System for ever.

The battle was swiftly followed by vicious reprisals, including a deliberate policy of mass starvation, and the enforced exile of many clansfolk to the new American colonies.

Six years later the government was sending out its tax collectors to collect ever more exorbitant rents from the defeated Jacobite clans, and in the area of Appin this meant the Stewarts, who struggled to pay these crippling rents while still secretly also sending their former rent money to their exiled chiefs abroad.

The tax collectors were usually from clans which had not come out in favour of Prince Charles, and in Argyll, were nearly always Campbells. Those who could not pay the punitive rents were evicted and faced destitution.

The situation was seriously aggravated as the Stewarts watched their old enemies, the Campbells, supporters of the Hanoverians, rapaciously taking over the lands they had held for centuries.

Colin Campbell, the red-haired laird of the small estate of Glenure, and known as the Red Fox, was appointed by the government to set and collect rents from the defeated Stewarts on the Ardsheal estate, some of whom were to be evicted for non-payment, and replaced by Campbells.

He was factor of several estates forfeited from Jacobite clansmen. Naturally there was seething resentment throughout Appin against the reviled Campbells.

In the afternoon of 14th May 1752, Glenure and three companions set out down Loch Linnhe side and rode slowly through the edge of the Wood of Lettermore.

Suddenly a single shot rang out and Glenure fell from the saddle, mortally wounded by two bullets in the back. His nephew, one of his companions, could later say only that he saw a figure in a dark coat and carrying a gun, running away along the hillside.

This single shot set in motion a chain of events which led to what can only be described as judicial murder by the state.

The king was informed, and the government in Edinburgh and London, apparently afraid that this was the first shot of yet another Jacobite Rising, gave orders that the perpetrators were to be apprehended and treated with the full vigour of the law.

Thus began a manhunt which spread all over the country, even as far as the Firth of Forth where ships, sailing for France and the Low Countries, were stopped and searched --- to no avail.

The man seen on the hillside by Campbell's nephew, was believed to be the clan courier, Alan Breac Stewart, who became the prime suspect for a while, but successfully eluded capture and completely disappeared.

Therefore a scapegoat had to be found, and an example had to be made, *pour encourager les autres,* and so fabricated evidence was provided by a pitiless Campbell court, implicating James Stewart of the Glen, the most prominent Stewart in the district, and a completely innocent man. There followed a complete travesty of a trial held in the Campbell stronghold of Inveraray, with a jury of fifteen, eleven of whom were Campbells, and presided over by the Lord Justice General, the 3rd Duke of Argyll himself, and all of them complicit in the atrocious deceit. Of course, James was found guilty though there was not a credible shred of evidence against him, and he had produced a solid alibi.

He was almost rushed to the gallows with unseemly haste, and his body left hanging in the gibbet at Ballachulish until it disintegrated, proclaiming, to any who might be tempted to instigate further murder or rebellion, that the severest measures would undoubtedly follow by an unforgiving state.

This was a black day for Scottish justice and has never been forgotten.

No one was ever charged with the murder but Clan Stewart of Appin apparently knew who had committed the deed. They kept this to themselves, the name being passed down through the generations in the strictest secrecy, until very recently.

In 2001 an elderly lady, Anda Penman, a descendant of the Stewarts of Appin, decided to end the secrecy and name the murderer.

She declared that the attack was planned by four young Stewart lairds and that the gun was fired by the best shot of the four --- Donald Stewart of Ballachulish ---- he who had to be held down in a house in Ballachulish when the verdict was given, in order to prevent him rushing forward to admit to the crime and save the innocent James's life.

Anda died soon afterwards and no Stewart has yet spoken out, corroborating her account, but the story goes that James's bones were collected very much later and given a decent burial --- by a certain Donald Stewart of Ballachulish.

Tale no. 25: Eriskay Idyll

We had a calm crossing on Caledonian MacBrayne's comfortable car ferry *Hebrides,* from Uig in Skye to Lochmaddy in the Outer Hebridean island of North Uist, from where I would drive over causeway and bridge to Benbecula and South Uist. Then I would sail southwards across the Sound of Eriskay to the little island of Eriskay --- *Eric's Isle,* in Viking parlance.

My faithful hound, Roddy, sprawled comfortably along the back seat of the car. He was a big, cream-coloured Labrador and I took him with me whenever possible as he was so good at breaking the ice in school situations when the pupils were too shy, or too nervous, to speak to me. Most children fell for the appeal of the dog's happy personality and unfailing gentleness, so he was a decided asset to me as Primary Education Adviser of the most extensive county in Scotland, comprising the entire mainland of Inverness-shire, and the Outer Hebrides from Harris to Barra, along with the Inner Hebrides of Skye and the Small Isles (Canna, Rum and Eigg) --- quite a "patch".

I took him out of the car during the crossing and we wandered out on to the main deck where relaxed passengers were strolling about, gazing happily at the entrancing island scenery, taking lots of photographs and sunning themselves in every corner of the open deck.

"Hello, there," said a voice and I turned to see Finlay MacDonald smiling and waving at me from the upper deck.

"Hello, Finlay," I called. "What are you doing on the Lochmaddy ferry?"

Finlay didn't answer immediately but made for the companionway and descended to the main deck. He came over to where we were standing and lowered his voice.

"Unfortunately it's not a happy journey that I'm on." he said, his soft island voice sounding rather sad.

"My old Uncle Seumas has passed away and I'm on my way to his funeral on Eriskay. You'll maybe remember that my mother comes from the island. She is not well enough to come herself so I am representing our part of the family at the funeral. But what are you and the dog doing out on the island ferry?"

I explained our proposed schools visit and mentioned that we would be on Eriskay, possibly at the same time as himself.

We spent the rest of the journey chatting sociably and passed a companionable hour or two until the ferry turned in to Lochmaddy pier, where we both went to our respective cars in preparation for disembarking, and promised to look out for one another on Eriskay.

As always, when visiting the Western Isles, I stayed out on the islands for at least a week at a time, or preferably, a fortnight, as taking a car out from Uig in Skye was so expensive for the education budget that I had to justify my journey by covering as many schools as humanly possible so, while out there, I visited every one of my primary schools, from North Uist, through Benbecula, to South Uist, Eriskay and south to Barra.

Only one of my total of thirty-four Outer Isles schools was on the island of Eriskay, which lies to the south of South Uist and which, in the days before the advent of the big causeway in 2001, could only be reached by a small, open motor-boat from Ludag in South Uist or by an infrequent big ship.

Getting ashore from the motor-boat was a considerable problem as there were only two options --- the pier, or the rocks!

If the first option was chosen I would have to clamber up the steep, wet, weed-covered and very slippery iron ladder clamped to the side of Eriskay pier, obviously even more hazardous when the tide was out and about twenty feet of ladder was exposed. It was like trying to climb the Eiffel Tower, and I decided it was definitely not on, burdened as I was by briefcase, handbag and dog.

It would have to be the second choice --- the rocks!

This meant that I would not have to climb the terrifying ladder, but instead had to balance precariously on the boat's gunwale as it was manoeuvred in towards the shore, then trust to fate and make a leap for dry land.

"Remember now, and chump when I say chump!" said Fergus the boatman in a tone which allowed for no argument.

"Okay," I said, while wavering about in the bows, trying to clutch my belongings high in my arms out of reach of the spray, and not lose my balance and topple into the sea.

"Chump!" yelled Fergus, and I leaped for the shore, missing dry land by several inches and deluging my shoes with sea water. I then squelched, with considerable difficulty, up the pebbly beach to the shore pathway.

"Och, you'll be fine, chust fine," yelled the unsympathetic Fergus, as he pushed Roddy overboard and turned the ferry away.

"What a disgraceful state for the Primary Adviser to be in when visiting schools," I muttered while emptying sea water out of my shoes, but Roddy had swiftly adapted to being thrown into the sea and was enjoying himself swimming around, until I sternly ordered him ashore and dared him to shake himself dry all over me.

Actually we had managed quite well. My colleague May, had opted for the ladder on her last visit, and it was a sad and bedraggled soul who finally appeared at the school door, clothes covered in green slime, with tights hanging in ribbons around her legs, and nearly in tears from the dreadful attack of vertigo she had suffered during the long ascent of the ladder.

"Really, being asked to go to Eriskay is a form of torture," she complained to me.

"Actually, it's an initiation ceremony for all new education staff when they join the county," I said, but May was not amused.

The little primary school had thirteen pupils, most of whom had learned to handle boats almost as soon as they could walk. There were few metalled roads on the island at that time --- some were just rough tracks, so each family had, not a car, but a fishing boat at the end of the garden.

Mr MacLeod, the Head Teacher, was a pleasant, but highly strung young man, who was inclined to stutter a great deal, especially when excited. He also had rather loose dentures, and his mischievous pupils loved to set him up and see who could get his dentures to wobble first. Then the teeth seemed to take on a life of their own, completely independent of their wearer, and slipped on and off his gums the more worked up he became. The poor man would then have hurriedly to shut his mouth in order to press his teeth back into their appointed place again.

I was always welcomed into the classroom, mainly because I was the person who brought Roddy to the school --- I had no illusions!

The diminutive Eilidh, a Primary 1 pupil, toddled out to the front of the class, holding up her tiny hand.

"Yes, wh – what is it, Eilidh?" asked Mr MacLeod gently, the very little ones being his especial favourites.

She gazed up at the two of us, round-eyed, like someone staring up at two tall trees, and stuck a finger in her mouth.

"Sh-- she's a wee bit shy," explained Mr MacLeod, and asked again what she wanted.

The cherubic Eilidh, removing the finger to reveal a gap where her two front teeth should be, lisped, "My Uncle Finway ith at the houth and evewyone ith vewy cwoth with him," and she took a deep breath, with the air of someone about to impart momentous news.

"Y –, yes?" prompted her teacher.

Eilidh's big blue eyes opened wider and she continued slowly, "He ith here for Gwandpa MacDonawd's funewal, but he didn't know," and she stopped again.

It dawned on me that she was talking about my companion of the ferry, and I listened with interest.

The endlessly patient Mr MacLeod asked her what Uncle Finlay didn't know.

"He wath athleep in hith bed and he wath thnowing, but he didn't know," went on the little one, "tho Awec had to go and tew him," she said.

"T – , tell him wh – what?" asked the teacher.

Eilidh looked at us solemnly, for quite some time, in unnerving silence.

"Gwandpa MacDonawd ith dead," she finally announced to us all, then turned and went back to her seat, leaving us completely in the dark about why everyone was angry with Uncle Finlay. Between Mr MacLeod's stammer and Eilidh's lisp we could get no more information on this riveting subject.

Discussions about everyone's relatives were common enough on a small island like Eriskay as everyone shared in both the joys and the sorrows of fellow islanders.

Meanwhile the pupils vied with one another to get the dog to sit beside them and give them a paw. All except one boy, Rory Morrison, who was very sly and pulled Roddy's tail when he thought no one was looking.

Mr MacLeod was now talking earnestly to me but, like all good teachers, watching the class out of the corner of his eye. He saw Rory pulling the dog's tail and frowned at him, before continuing his smiling conversation with me.

The bold Rory paid no attention. Mr MacLeod stopped smiling at me and said, threateningly, "R - R -Rory, stop that!" and resumed his conversation.

But the bad Rory then pulled Roddy's tail so hard that he yelped. The rest of the class, outraged, set upon him and soon he was engulfed in a struggling mass of bodies, like a rugby scrum at Murrayfield.

Mr MacLeod gasped, his face scarlet with anger.

"S-s--s--top that at o-o-once," he yelled. "S-s--sit down everyone!" but battle continued.

Mr MacLeod opened his mouth to shout even louder, "S-s-s --" and, to my horror, his upper dentures flew out of his mouth, describing a perfect arc through the air.

That certainly stopped the fight in its tracks, and we all watched, spellbound, as Mr MacLeod, with the speed born of desperation, shot out an arm, caught the dentures in full flight and restored them to his mouth in one, smooth, flowing movement.

He then finished his sentence as if nothing had happened, "S-s-s-it down, all of you and leave poor R-r-r-oddy alone."

The children, struck dumb by their teacher's acrobatic teeth, obeyed in stunned silence, but very soon young shoulders were seen to be shaking in silent laughter.

What a tale to tell their parents that evening!

I nearly choked trying to keep a straight face and pretend I had noticed nothing out of the ordinary.

As for the dog, he just wagged his tail hard against Rory's legs until it was the boy's turn to yelp, and then he gave poor Mr MacLeod a paw.

School business was eventually done and I said farewell to the children of Eriskay Primary School and the hapless Mr MacLeod.

Back we went to Lochmaddy to catch the ferry and, as we had an hour or two to wait, I put Roddy on the lead and let him out of the car. We would have a walk around the village before the long sail back to Uig.

It was while we were strolling along the sea front that, without warning, the black-suited figure of a diver in full gear rose suddenly out of the sea in front of us and started to move shorewards. My big, brave Labrador took one look at this strange being emerging from the deep, set up a frantic yelping, and lunged away from me, tail between legs, in a blind panic and yanking the lead out of my hands. He tore along the roadway with me running after him, shouting in vain for him to stop. I didn't catch him until about a mile down the road and finally cornered the terrified animal in the hotel doorway. It was some time before he stopped shaking, and I patted him and uttered soothing words until he dared to come out of the hotel on his newly attached lead.

An American tourist, watching the proceedings with interest from the hotel steps drawled, "That sure is a fine dawg you got there, ma'am, but you don't want a lead, you want a saddle!"

On the ferry that evening I spied Finlay in the ship's cafeteria and went over to speak to him.

"How did you get on at the funeral, Finlay?" I asked. "I'm sure they were all pleased to see you there. Your little niece, Eilidh, at the school, was telling us about your visit."

I didn't mention that she had told us how "cwoth" everyone was with him, hoping he would spill the beans himself.

"Well, it was all a wee bit unfortunate," he replied, looking fixedly at the cafeteria floor, and repeated, "Yes, a wee bit unfortunate," and he rubbed his chin, leaving me wondering why members of that family seemed determined to avoid answering direct questions, and started sentences which suddenly stopped in mid air, so to speak.

"You see," he said after a few minutes' silence, "there is no funeral director on the island, so the families have to see to their funerals themselves --- do everything themselves, I mean. I had forgotten that. "Well ---." He soon got into his stride and went on quite briskly, "We had a great wake the night before the funeral. The craic [conversation] was good and the whisky was flowing. Seumas would have been delighted with it all, and him being praised by all the family and the neighbours too. It must have been about two in the morning before we all got to our beds, and I fell into a deep sleep.

The next thing I know is that my cousin, Alec, is shaking me and shouting in my ear to get up and get a move on. "There is no time for you to be eating your breakfast this morning," he said.

I thought why, in the name of the Good Being, is Alec in such a hurry, and the funeral is not till the afternoon anyway? So I turned over and ignored him. He's probably got a hangover and isn't too clear about what he is saying, I thought.

Alec grabbed my shoulder and shook me awake. "Get up, get up!" he shouted.

"Why?" I shouted back, really annoyed now that he was keeping on at me.

"Because you'll have to dig the grave!" he said.

I shot up in bed. Now he really had my full attention.

"What? Are you telling me that Seumas is to be buried this afternoon and there is no grave ready for him?"

"That is exactly what I'm telling you. You are the nearest male relative and it is your duty to see to it."

After that everything was a complete blur. I fell out of bed, threw on my clothes and tumbled down the stair to the kitchen where all the neighbour women were staring at me in disapproval.

"You should have been up and out to dig the grave long since, Fhionnlaigh," said Aunt Jeannie. "Surely I didn't have to tell you!"

Fionnlagh, panic-stricken grave digger

So I got no tea or anything else and Alec hustled me over to the graveyard where he and another lad had started breaking open the ground. What a morning we had of it! I never was at a funeral like it, nor ever wish to be again. Fancy being asked to a relative's funeral and then having to dig the grave yourself!

We dug like fury and I thought my back was going to break, but we got finished in the nick of time. Then I had to rush back to the house and get into my good suit before the four of us carried Uncle Seumas into the graveyard to where the minister was waiting.

"I am sorry to see, Fhionnlaigh, that you have forgotten our island ways, now that you have been so long in the city," says the minister." You nearly didn't get poor Seumas to his grave in time," and he goes off shaking his head.

"There's gratitude for you!" says I to myself.

I was completely jiggered afterwards, I can tell you, and things weren't any better back at the house where Aunt Jeannie and the other mourners were waiting with the funeral tea.

"My word, Fhionnlaigh, but you have got soft since you left the island and went to the city," she said, disapprovingly, and the others, all standing around like a row of crows, nodded in agreement.

I couldn't even get a nice wee game of golf on the course that Alec and some of the other lads had laid out since I was last on the island. The land didn't belong to them so someone went and built a house on the second tee, and that was the end of the golf course.

Talk about being frozen out! I tell you I couldn't get off the island fast enough, and there'll probably be a family feud from now on, for ever. I'm right glad to be going back to Glasgow where you don't have to dig your uncle's grave after being asked to his funeral" --- and poor Finlay sank back into the comfort of the *Hebrides's* bar and sought solace in a large dram.

Looking out at the rock-strewn coastline of Eriskay I remembered the true story of the sinking of *SS Politician* on a reef off the island during the dark days of 1941. Many ships met with a similar fate during World War II, but only this one carried a cargo of such notable interest to the folk of Eriskay.

The ship's main cargo was whisky, destined for America. It must have seemed like destiny to the whisky-starved population that she went on to the rocks more or less on their doorstep, and it became a frantic race between the men of Eriskay and the Customs officers as to who would get to the cargo first.

But, as well as whisky, the *Politician* was carrying the modern equivalent of several million pounds worth of paper currency to the West Indies and the United States. At first the Crown Agents were unconcerned as they thought the notes would be washed away or ruined by the sea, but by 1958 notes had turned up in banks in Britain, Ireland, Canada, the USA, Malta, Switzerland and Jamaica and thousands of others were never accounted for.

Altogether a bad day for HM Customs and Excise!

At this point, enter author, Sir Compton MacKenzie, who saw the comedy potential of this event and promptly wrote his unforgettable book, *Whisky Galore,* the story being set on the mythical island of Todday where the locals took advantage of the unexpected windfall, snatched the precious cargo from its watery grave and hid it out of sight of the "grasping" Customs officer, Mr Farquharson.

The novel was shot as a film on the nearby island of Barra and released in 1949 by Ealing Film Studios. It has since enjoyed remarkable status as, possibly, Scotland's finest comedy film.

The story goes that the inhabitants of Todday are seeing out the war without being much affected by rationing, until the desperate day arrives in 1943 when there is no whisky left and the bar owner can see no more arriving on the island in the foreseeable future. Consternation and deep depression all round!

Then, late one foggy night, the *SS Cabinet Minister,* ie the *SS Politician,* hits the rocks offshore and begins to sink. The Biffer and Sammy McCodrun hear her alarm sounding and row out to discover, from the crew, that her cargo is 50,000 cases of export whisky --- the best --- destined for America!

The pompous Englishman, Captain Waggett of the island Home Guard, takes it upon himself to organise a guard on the ship in case of smuggling by the locals, but not before the latter have been alerted by The Biffer and Sammy, and all meet down at the shore in the dead of the night, where they set out in their boats to the crippled ship in order to "liberate" its highly desirable cargo.

The sympathetic (although English), Sergeant Odd, engaged to Peggy Macroon, the postmaster's daughter, manages to get himself "tied up" so that the men can get out to the ship without being arrested.

Much whisky is salvaged and taken to a secret cave out of the way of the Customs or Captain Waggett, and Peggy and her sister, Catriona --- also engaged to be married, to the local schoolmaster ---

have a glorious joint *reiteach,* or engagement party, at the post office where many drams are enjoyed by the entire local population until, from his bedroom window, an elderly resident sees the furtive arrival of the Customs launch in the bay and warns the party-goers --- just in time.

The subsequent, frantic efforts of the islanders to hide the illicit whisky in the most unusual places is one of the most hilarious and unforgettable scenes in the entire story, as is the arrival of Farquharson and Waggett at the door of the post office at two in the morning, demanding immediate entry in the hope of catching out Joseph Macroon and discovering any illicit whisky on the premises.

An apparently sleepy Peggy opens the door in answer to Farquharson's insistent knocking, looks out innocently, as if butter wouldn't melt in her mouth, and states the obvious, "Oh, it's yourself, Mr Waggett. The post office is closed!"

In spite of their best efforts, Farquharson and his excisemen can find no trace of the smuggled whisky and are forced to retreat, frustrated and empty handed.

But Captain Waggett, in the meantime, desires the captain of the inter-island steamer, to take back to Obaig some ammunition cases containing bullets which won't fit his rifles. What he doesn't know is that six bottles of prime whisky have been secreted in the cases. Waggett is soon summoned to the mainland to explain himself to the Customs authorities, leaving the field open to the islanders to resume their interrupted *reiteach,* and enjoy many happy years of whisky drinking,

It seems that, to this very day, the odd bottle of whisky is still turning up in unexpected places on Eriskay!

Tale no. 26: Into Every Life a Little Rain Must Fall

Hector stood, alone and drenched, in the middle of Kintyre Park, as the downpour darkened his already sodden kilt with water, and ran down his stockinged legs, filling his brogues through their open-laced uppers. His Glengarry drooped wetly over his downcast head, the rain trickled down his face and even ran in rivulets down the pipe which he held upside down between clenched teeth, and dripped into his already saturated brogues.

He appeared to be in silent communication with the rain gods as they hurled down their fiercest deluge on his lonely presence. Everyone else had run for cover but he had stood his ground, at least for a while, as if to show that not even the most persistent cloudburst could drive the Headmaster of Kinloch School from his rightful place on the sports field.

The park squelched under the onslaught of the sheets of drenching rain descending from leaden skies. This was the annual Sports Day for Millknowe and Dalintober Schools, which together comprised Kinloch Primary School, the biggest primary school not only in Campbeltown but in the entire Kintyre peninsula, and was regarded as an important event in the school's social calendar.

The forecast had threatened rain but we had gone ahead with the sports anyway as June could be an unchancy month in the west of Scotland and, with a bit of luck, we might beat the jinx and, hopefully, enjoy a sunny afternoon of races, ice-creams and parental satisfaction.

Alas, we had got it all wrong and although the early races were run in warm sunshine, all too soon dark clouds built up and the miserable downpour ensued. Those lucky enough to have already taken part in their competitions scattered for the exits and home as soon as the first heavy drops fell but I alas, was delegated to oversee the finishing line of the sprint races right up to the end of the afternoon, and couldn't leave my post without incurring the wrath of both parents and runners. So there we were, pretending to be enjoying the final races while the rain beat down inexorably on children and adults alike.

This was bad enough but I had to deal with the inevitable parental disagreement over my decision as to who had actually won a race, argued hotly in front of what was left of the assembled crowd. Such was my miserable, rain-saturated state that I argued back just as hotly in a desperate attempt to bring the whole sorry event to an immediate end, and escape to the welcoming warmth and reviving hot coffee of Togneri's attractive cafe in the middle of town.

I looked appealingly in Hector's direction, and he must have seen the desperation in my face for he, reluctantly, plodded his way back to the loudspeakers and made the gloomy announcement, to a field now largely devoid of human life, that the sports would have to be abandoned immediately because of the inclement weather.

Thankfully, I escaped from the finishing line and, collecting one or two other similarly suffering teachers, headed for Main Street, a nice, warm, dry cafe and the reviving qualities of piping hot coffee.

Obviously, everybody groused a bit about the vagaries of the weather and being forced to take part in all sorts of events at all times of day and night, regardless of physical and mental comfort. This was part and parcel of school life, but we always recovered quickly and got on philosophically with the daily happenings of life in Millknowe and Dalintober.

In fact, my days there were some of the happiest of my entire teaching career and life produced only infinitesimal amounts of "rain" during these years. I have to thank Hector MacNeill and his colleague, Bill Beveridge, for all they did to make it so.

I was later encouraged, by both of these kind men, to seek a post of Head Teacher myself and, having done so, spent many happy years in senior posts in Highland schools.

But it is inevitable that, when the status of promoted post has been achieved, the smooth course of living begins to change and, at that point in one's life, "a little rain must fall".

For me this first happened when I applied for the Education Adviser's post in the largest county in Scotland and a "little rain" began to fall almost at the interview itself where three of us were on the selected short list.

"Would you just come this way, Miss," said the polite steward and I stood up nervously, ready to follow him to whatever fate awaited me on the other side of that big wooden door at the head of a small flight of stairs in the County Buildings in Inverness.

I said a quick goodbye to the other two applicants, one male and one female, who were waiting, as I had been, to be interviewed by the entire Education Committee of the County Council and to hear the results of the votes of all Council members who had turned up on that day.

The steward reached past me, opened the door and ushered me into an intimidatingly large open space, which I immediately recognised as the stage of the main auditorium in the County Buildings. I gazed in horror at the sea of official faces, along with those of any interested member of the public, which confronted me. I certainly had not expected my job interview to take place on a public stage in an auditorium, in front of Everyman and his Wife, and probably would have politely declined the interview if I had known in advance what to expect.

But there I was --- trapped like the proverbial rabbit in the headlights --- and, short of making a quick run for it, I couldn't escape, so resignedly I took the proffered chair and turned my unwilling attention on the six, solemn-faced, Very Important Persons who sat in an imposing semi-circle around a large table, a long distance away, it seemed, on the other side of the stage. Strangely, the Director of Education himself was not present.

Now I understood, literally, what actors mean when they talk about the horrors of stage fright and I felt my jaw muscles tighten up as I strove to take in the questions being fired at me, then give a considered and thoughtful answer in a steady and audible voice. The questioning voices droned on and on as the long minutes slowly passed.

The Education Committee had the first go, then questions were invited from the floor of the house. Would this dreadful experience ever end, I wondered, and at this point I had the unnerving experience of seeming to float several feet in the air above my quaking person and look down on myself from above. Later I had no idea what questions were asked, nor what answers I managed to give, and even today the whole experience dissolves into a vague miasma.

Eventually official smiles and nods from the Committee advised me that the ordeal was at last over, but I was then ushered down off the stage and made to walk up the central passage of the hall between the mass of members, no doubt so that the folk could see in close up the victim they had just interviewed.

As I passed the middle row a white-haired, elderly man shot up from his seat, waving at me and shouting, " Bornaskitaig!" and in my shaky state I vaguely remembered informing the Committee that my folk came from Bornaskitaig in north Skye. He was the committee member from the island. My island comnnection had, apparently, gone down well with the various Skye members, and no doubt did me some good when it came to the voting.

At last I was ushered into a small waiting room and sank down, trembling with nervous reaction, on to a hard, plastic chair, of which there were three in the room.

Apparently I had to wait, in a state of suspended animation, until the other two applicants had been interviewed, after which all three of us would be informed as to the result of the voting.

After my intensive, hour-long interview this was definitely prolonging the agony and, I felt, was rather cruel to the applicants. However, that was the way things were done in these days and anyway the dreaded interview was now behind me.

The second applicant eventually arrived back in the room, like myself, in a decidedly shaken state, but we managed to converse a little and it turned out that she was already a Staff Tutor (of whom there were two in this county) and was now energetically seeking the promoted post of Primary Adviser.

It seemed that she was a great friend of the then Director of Education and it was obvious that she really expected to get the post on the strength of this connection. However, we had to wait until the third trembling applicant arrived back on the plastic chairs before the dignified arrival of an official who instructed me to follow him back on to the stage as the Education Committee wanted to speak to me again.

Apparently it was a good sign to be asked back on to the stage, so it looked as if my interview had been successful. At any rate the other two stood up to congratulate me and we all shook hands before I was led back into the meeting where a beaming committee informed me that I was now the County Primary Adviser if I would, in fact, accept the post.

In a rather dazed state I politely accepted the position, and, in the course of time, made my move back to the land of my fathers.

It was when entering my new office for the first time that I discovered that one of my two Staff Tutors was none other than the female applicant I had met at the interview --- the one who knew the

Director of Education and was sure that she would get the job on the strength of it.

If only I had known!

Then began an overtly unsubtle campaign of undermining my authority and making barbed comments either directly in my hearing or, more often, to those of her very many acquaintances involved in some way in the education system. She told me to my face that my interview had been much easier than hers because she had been kept longer than I had, and hers had been so much more difficult, mine having been unjustifiably easy!

How she came by this imagined "information" I could not say, but comments were continually made about how things would have turned out differently if the Director had been present on the Committee during the interviews. He, it seemed, had been otherwise engaged in hospital after a serious road accident.

Frequently I was not given exact information about the whereabouts of certain rural schools, and arrived back at the office in a state of extreme exasperation having traipsed about the countryside in an unsuccessful bid to find some of them, thus annoying the Head Teachers waiting to meet me. Also, important information about meetings and courses was sometimes so vague that I arrived at venues unprepared for important discussions and conferences.

This was my first experience of blatant enmity from a member of staff and I took it very badly as I had arrived in post full of hopes and expectations of goodwill and cooperation.

As if things were not bad enough someone ran into my parked car during my first night in my new digs, and drove off without leaving a note or any form of contact. The whole side of the car was knocked in, but this time I was actually given the right information as to where to find a good (and expensive) panel-beater!

I formed a very bad impression of the stifling parochialism often to be found in local officialdom. The common attitude was, "You are an intruding incomer and not one of us. You are of little importance here, whereas I am very important and I know all the right people. My family has been here for generations and we know everyone who is anyone in this county, whereas you are an interloper and know nothing. I should be in charge, not you ---" and so on, and so on ---.

Here I have to make an exception of the many large town schools, as well as small, rural and island schools (with one notable exception) where I was welcomed with warmth and kindness and many of whose staff are my friends to this day.

This was the first time I had actually experienced the disadvantages of a promoted post --- unexpectedly, as my first promotion had been a happy and fulfilling experience.

But by far the worst experience came years later, and could be accurately described, not so much as "a little rain", but as "a full scale deluge". And again the green-eyed monster, jealousy, was the undoubted cause. By this time I was a very experienced teacher in primary, secondary and tertiary education and had amassed a great deal of practical experience in the running of schools and the Advisory service.

My main critic had her Primary Certificate, a vicious tongue and that was all.

In her overweening self-regard she had never bothered to sacrifice part of her summer holidays in order to take extra qualifications at Teacher Training College, as had all my Campbeltown colleagues (in their own time and often at their own expense!). Her actual words, spoken in my hearing were, "No one can tell me anything about teaching!" I found this insufferably arrogant.

My very presence in that community was an affront to her. She made it known that she should have had the post of Head Teacher regardless of the fact of being completely unqualified for the job and having taught only at the lower end of a primary school during her entire teaching career, which was, in any case, years shorter than mine.

The comments of a retired teacher, who was not local were, "If I had known you were going to apply for this post I would have advised you not to touch it with a barge-pole. That woman is poisonous with jealousy over your success with the school."

Inevitably a whispering campaign against me grew until it reached a boiling point of unbelievable spitefulness when my personal, private life was the subject of speculation and vicious gossip --- a real witch-hunt such as one sees, too often, in the pages of the gutter press. What they didn't know they simply made up. My good name and career were put in jeopardy. That was, in my eyes, unforgivable! Naturally I reported the matter to the lawyers of the

Head Teachers' Association of Scotland who gave sound advice and told me not to give up, but to carry the fight into court. I seriously contemplated this course of action, but instead I became seriously ill.

I lay the blame for this directly at the door of those who made my life such an utter misery, including certain members of the education establishment.

This was one of the blackest times of my entire life, and I find it difficult to contemplate forgiveness for the despicable people who deliberately set out to destroy my life, good name and living because of their own pettiness and inadequate personal lives.

As a result I swore never to enter another classroom again in my lifetime, but in fact I was requested to do so, and did, and had several wonderful years in an inspirational School for Special Needs, and then as a language teacher of twenty different nationalities in a college of Higher Education.

These experiences undoubtedly "restored my faith in human nature".

Nowadays my teaching is done via the publishing of books for schools and universities --- mostly on my favourite subject of Scottish history. This has been the joy of my life.

In addition, I have had the continued pleasure of meeting many of my former pupils and foreign students on a regular basis, and of enjoying their friendship over many years.

As for my beloved family --- they are my true and everlasting Treasure on Earth.

Tale no. 27: Sgeulachdan ---- Little Stories

Snatches of overheard conversations

Shepherd's Delight

Shona, daughter of a local hill shepherd:- *Mummy and I had to go out last night before Daddy got in from the hill. She left a note to say that his dinner was in the fridge, and he was just to heat it up because we would be late back.*

Her friend, Janie:-*That was a good idea.*

Shona:-*No, it wasn't because when Mummy and I got back home we found Daddy hadn't eaten his dinner at all because it was still in the fridge. But Daddy said that he definitely had eaten his dinner. He said that he had eaten the meat in the blue dish, and Mummy said, "Oh, dear, you have eaten the dog's dinner instead of your own."*

Janie:- *That was terrible, wasn't it?*

Shona:- *Yes, and then Daddy's face turned really green!*

Just after Christmas

Mary Anne, forester's daughter:- *We had an awful Christmas. Mummy put the turkey in the oven and then went out into the back garden. She started talking to Mrs Black over the fence, and they went on talking and talking and she forgot all about the turkey till Daddy came in the front door and found the whole place full of smoke and started shouting for Mummy.*

She came running in and found the turkey was burned to a cinder, so Daddy and Mummy started shouting at one another and we didn't get any dinner. We just had a cheese sandwich. It was awful.

We had a really awful Christmas!

Horse sense

Some crofters are on their minibus on the Ullapool to Stornoway ferry. Sorley, the driver, spots a car with a trailer full of what look like small, shaggy dogs. Intrigued, he gets out and asks the car driver what breed they are.

"*Falabellas,*" is the reply.

"*I've never heard of these dogs before,*" says Sorley.

"They aren't dogs, they're horses," says the car driver, *"and I'm hoping to sell them when I get home."*

"You're kidding me --- I've never seen horses that size --- ever! They're about the size of a dog."

"They're real horses, I tell you, and they can live for over forty years," says the driver.

Sorley is amazed, and goes back to the minibus to tell the others.

"I think I'll buy one for my wee granddaughter," he says.

Then another man decides to do the same, and another, and so on until they end up with six little Falabella horses.

How to get them home?

Sorley has an idea:

"There is plenty of room in the minibus. We'll just take out the back seats and put the wee horses inside."

The others think this is a very good idea as the animals wouldn't take up much room. Then an argument takes place about whether they should put the seat belts on them.

"How do you put a seat belt on a horse?" asks one.

A very serious discussion then ensues until they finally come up with a solution.

"We'll just sit on our seats and hold the wee horses on our knees," says Sorley," *but, as I am driving, one of you will need to hold my horse as well as your own until we get home."*

Problem solved!

A little local difficulty

Susie, to her friend, Alice:- *The teacher was very late for school this morning.*

Alice:- *Why was that?*

Susie:- *She was driving up the road to school when she saw a big horse galloping along the road towards her.*

Alice:- *My goodness, what happened?*

Susie:- *She had to pull into the lay-by and get out of the car to try to stop the horse in case it caused an accident.*

Alice:- *She was awfully brave to do that.*

Susie:- *Yes, but you know how she likes animals, and she didn't want the horse to get hurt.*

Alice:- *Did she manage to stop the horse?*

Susie:- *Yes, but she had to grab it by its mane because it didn't have a bridle on. Then she led it into the lay-by beside her car but she had to hold on to it until someone came along and she got them to go down to the police station to get the policeman.*
Alice:- *Gosh, that was exciting. Did they get the horse back to its owner?*
Susie:- *Oh yes, it was Mrs Barbour's horse and she said it was a new horse and it was unhappy at being in a new place and so it jumped out of the field and tried to go back to its old home.*

The teacher said that when she decided to become a teacher she never thought catching runaway horses would be part of the job, and you just never know what you're going to have to cope with next!

Horses again

In fact the teacher soon had to contend with yet another unexpected, horse-centred occurrence.

She commented that, far from being a quiet and peaceful place, the countryside was one of the noisiest places she had ever lived in.

Young birds chirped and cheeped merrily from the break of day in the bright, spring mornings, the lambs in the fields bleated continually to the ewes and the young calves bawled piteously when separated from their mothers for the first time after being let out into the fields on a May morning, while the local shepherd's collies started up barking and howling when waiting to be let out of the barn next to the schoolhouse. The village coal dump was also next to the schoolhouse and very early mornings were rendered hideous with the racket of coal being shovelled up on to the ancient crate of a lorry which started up in a cloud of black smoke, clattering and banging as it drew away.

At daybreak the local hens started cackling and crowing, in noisy opposition to the local bird life and, as if all this wasn't enough, the farmer had turned out a herd of trekking ponies into the field by the school, where they kicked up their heels and thundered about, neighing in happy enjoyment of the new grass.

Her Labrador Roddy, being a young puppy, thought every person and every animal was his best friend.

The youthful Roddy climbed out of a window in the schoolhouse and scampered happily into the field of ponies, no doubt wishing to play with them and also hone his juvenile herding skills. This was a big mistake. The ponies did not like being herded and turned on him, kicking and neighing angrily.

The Janitor:- *You'll have to come at once, Miss. The dog's being attacked by the horses.*

Miss:- *Heavens above! How on earth did he get in among them? I'm coming!*

With the speed of desperation she leaped over the fence into the field and found her "bold" puppy collapsed in a terrified, furry heap while the ponies galloped around him, threatening him continually with teeth and hoofs.

Miss:- *Roddy come!*

Roddy was in no position to come, so stayed, cowering, where he was.

Miss, to ponies:- *Shoo, the lot of you, frightening a wee puppy like that! Roddy, come on now, my wee laddie. I'll chase the bad horses away from you, a ghraidh!*

And, fearlessly, she chased off the wild gang, grabbed Roddy by his collar and hauled a very chastened little puppy back to the safety of the house, where both collapsed, shaken and trembling.

Miss, in total mood reversal:- *You bad wee brat! You've just taken years off my life! Why can't you stay where you're put?*

Miss, later, to janitor:- *And this is what you mean by the peace and quiet of the countryside?*

Margaret, the gamekeeper's daughter, to friend Jill:-

I was late for the school car this morning, and the driver was annoyed at being held up.

Jill:- *Why, what did you do?*

Margaret:-*Well, I got up and went into the bathroom to have my bath, but I couldn't get into the bath.*

Jill:- *Why not?*

Margaret:- *Because there were three wee brown animals in the bath and they kept crawling about.*

A saucer-eyed Jill:- What were they?

Margaret:- *Well, Daddy found a vixen's litter on the hill and the mother was lying dead beside them, so he brought them home and put them in the bath.*

Jill:- *When do you think you'll be able to get a bath?*

Margaret:- *When Mummy gets annoyed with Daddy and makes him take them out of the bath, I suppose.*

Jill:- *Well, you can come and get a bath any time in my house, if you like.*

Angus, on arriving home after school:-

There was an awful commotion in the class this afternoon.

Mum:- *What happened?*

Angus:- *You know how all the schools were told they weren't to have animals in the classroom any more, after Miss Brown's dogs attacked the Inspector?*

Mum:- *Surely Roddy isn't big enough or wild enough to attack anybody?*

Angus:- *Oh, it wasn't Roddy. It was wee Breac, Jenny's cat.*

Mum:- *You're never telling me that Breac attacked someone!*

Angus:- *No, no! You know how all the classroom windows are opened by clicking the catch and pulling them inwards --- well, one of our windows is loose and opens very easily. Wee Breac knows this and she always sits on the sill just there and looks in at us. If we don't let her in quickly enough she opens the window with her paw, all by herself, and then she climbs in and sits on our desks or the floor.*

Mum:- *But I thought you weren't allowed to have animals in the classroom any more?*

Angus:- *Yes, Miss told Breac that she wasn't allowed in again, but Breac didn't believe her and climbed back into the room whenever she wanted. Breac actually came in and sat on the teacher's lap while she was hearing the reading, and Miss didn't shoo her away.*

Mum:- *Yes, I know Miss likes animals, but what caused the commotion?*

Angus:- *Breac went and sat on the carpet near the door and while she was there the door suddenly opened and in came this big, scowling man, without knocking, and he just fell over the cat and she spat at him and scratched him and then ran away, miaowing.*

Mum:- *Now I see why there was a commotion. What happened next?*

Angus:- *The man said he was an Education Officer and he was annoyed that the cat was in the classroom. Miss asked him to come to the staffroom and get his hand fixed, so he went out but he was scowling even more and muttering away. Miss tried to make a joke of it and said that we had told Breac she wasn't allowed back into the school but she didn't listen. The man didn't even smile.*

He was a right sour puss!

English Language Class

Lana, from Ukraine:- *I know I have not passed English exam.*

Teacher:- *Why ever not, Lana?*

Lana:- *You know how worried we were about finding Anniesland College where we sit exam, and not being late?*

Teacher:- *Yes, but you left in good time and we gave you lots of directions.*

Lana:- *Of course, but when we were crossing road to go into college worst thing happened.*

Teacher, very alarmed:- *What on earth ----?*

Lana:- *Black cat ran across road right in front of me and now I know I don't pass exam. This is very bad luck!*

Teacher, relieved:- *No, no, Lana. You have got it all wrong. Black cats bring good luck in this country. You are sure to have passed your exam.*

Irina, a few days before her wedding to her Scottish fiancé:- *I got awful fright like that about bad luck. Only it is about day of my wedding.*

The class:- *Oh, Irina, what happened?*

Irina:- *Jim and I were talking about flowers for wedding. Jim said he will send bouquet for me on wedding morning, and what flowers do I like best? I say, roses, so he says, "I will send you the biggest and most beautiful bouquet of yellow roses, to match your beautiful hair."*

I am horrified. Yellow flowers in my country mean friendship is over! I cry.

Jim does not understand.

I say, "Why do you not want to marry me now?"

Jim says, "But I do want to marry you."

The class:- *What happened?*

Irina, turning to me with a beatific smile:- *I phone teacher, and she tells me that yellow flowers are beautiful for bride, so Jim and I are happy again!*

The class:- *And we all wish you and Jim best of luck!*

*(I never could get some of the Europeans to say "a" and "the",
no matter how hard I tried.)*

*Six days later we all trooped into the church for the wedding and
gave a happily smiling Irina, who was carrying a huge bouquet of
glorious yellow roses, a silver horseshoe --- just to guarantee her
good luck!*

Chaos at Cowal

Robbie, member of the Combined Schools' Pipe Band:- *There we
were, marching up Argyll Street along with all the other bands at the
Cowal Games, on a great sunny morning. I was in the first line of
the pipers, with the drummers marching up behind us. All the way
through Dunoon the folk were crowding the pavements and cheering
us, especially when we played The Black Bear!*

*All the pipers were concentrating hard on the piping and the
marching. We wanted to look good and not let our supporters down,
for this was our first time at the Cowal Games.*

*Every so often we were stopped while the police sorted out all the
bands gathering at the far end of Argyll Street, so we had to watch
that we kept our places and didn't get out of line with one another.*

*Most of our band had never even seen the Games before and were
quite excited about being out in public like this. They were really
pleased that so many of our supporters were cheering us on from the
buildings and pavements on either side of Argyll Street.*

*Then all of us pipers saw that the police had stopped the band in
front so we started to slow down, but decided just to go on playing in
the street until the jam was sorted out.*

*Unfortunately, the drummers had caught sight of a gang of our
schoolmates waving and shouting at us from the pavement and took
their eyes off the pipers for a couple of minutes. So they didn't notice
that we had stopped, and they kept on marching --- straight into us.
The whole band concertina-ed into itself and we had drummers
crashing into pipers all over the place!*

*It took us ages to get ourselves sorted out again while the
spectators clapped and cheered as if we had done it all on purpose.*

Our Pipe Major was going mad!

However, it seems that the band, in spite of this bad beginning,
did very well in competition and covered themselves in glory, no

doubt having been threatened, by their irate Pipe Major, with all kinds of horrible fates if they disappointed while on the field.

David, to his friend Rab:-

We had a terrible time at the weekend and Mum isn't speaking to Dad any more.
Rab, rather uninterested:- *How come?*
David:- *You know my Dad loves his game of golf and the golf club were all going down to Machrihanish to play in a competition last Saturday?*
Rab:- *Right. What about it?*
David:- *They had a great game and won a cup, so afterwards they all went into the clubhouse and had a few drams --- more than a few, really, then, late at night everyone climbed back on to the hire bus and set off back to Oban. But because it was now dark and they were all a bit tiddly no one noticed that my Dad was missing.*
Rab, now fully interested:- *Where was he?*
David:- *He had slipped down behind a settee and was busy snoring his head off until, in the middle of the night he woke up fuddled in the empty clubhouse and realised that they had all gone away without him. He was a bit annoyed, but decided just to walk back to Oban --- a hundred miles away!*
Rab:- *He must have been crazy!*
David:- *No, just drunk. Do you know he walked right through all the defences, including Alsatian dogs and high fences around the NATO Air Base at Machrihanish, and nobody saw him.*
Rab:- *So much for international security!*
David, in full flow:- *Then he saw a big vehicle in the dark a few yards in front of him. "Great," says he, "I've caught up with the Oban bus at last," and he climbs in, goes up to the back seat, dumps his clubs, and falls into a deep sleep. Much later he wakes up, hears the engine roaring and thinks, "That's a terrible noisy engine," and feels the need of a cigarette.*
 Rab is now leaning forward, his attention fully engaged.
David:- *So Dad clambers out of the back seat and staggers down to the driver."Do you have a light?" he asks politely.*
"Certainly sir," replies the driver, offering his lighter," and may I ask who you are?"

Dad replies, "One of the golf team. Isn't this the hire bus?"

The driver now looks thunderous, and suddenly the last shreds of mist clear from Dad's brain as he realises that he is now standing on the flight deck of a military plane and the "driver" is, in fact, the captain of a big Hercules aircraft which has just taken off on a secret mission into an English air base.

Security is now completely blown.

The captain is absolutely mad and he barks at Dad:-"This most certainly is not the ----- hire bus!

Do you realise you are on a NATO aircraft? I saw you asleep back there and thought you were a VIP, with full security clearance, hitching a lift with us down to play golf on an English course, so I didn't wake you up."

Rab:- *Geez! What happened to your Dad?*

David- *They thought he was a spy or a terrorist, so they signalled the control tower for emergency landing clearance, banked that great big plane right round and came back down on to the runway.*

Poor Dad was arrested right away and dragged off to Campbeltown jail where he was questioned up and down for hours.

Eventually Mum arrived and everything got straightened out, but she was hopping mad with him and called him all sorts of names. You should have heard her!

So now they are not speaking.

Tale no. 28: From the Sublime to the Ridiculous

or, Things that you wish had never happened

Sublimely beautiful though Norse longships were, their appearance on the Scottish and Irish coastlands struck terror into the hearts of the Celtic populations living in these areas.

It is impossible to imagine anything at all amusing about the incursions of the Vikings, but even they occasionally became involved in unexpected situations, leading to a severe loss of Norse dignity!

In Norway the Viking era was known as the time of great "ship delight" when the ship was universally regarded almost as a living being of imagined spiritual presence, and signifying prestige, power and beauty.

The Dragon, or Great Ship, of which only 16 were built between 995 and 1262-3, was the equivalent of the modern battleship, and was extremely expensive to build, man and maintain. In addition, it was not all that good in a sea battle, as it was easily blown broadside on when the wind hit its high sides, unless it first got in close to its enemy, grappled it, then pulled it in ready to be boarded and dealt with.

Otherwise the smaller Twenty-Five longship, with twenty-five pairs of oars --- the equivalent of the modern destroyer --- was much faster and more manoeuvrable in a sea fight, but the Dragons continued to be built by kings or chiefs as symbols of their perceived importance.

In Norway, from the 1160s to about 1240, there were seemingly endless power struggles and, during these years, many of the Dragons were built, including the first *Mariasuden,* the battleship of King Sverre, who recognised that ships were the only way in which a king could gain, and keep control of, his country.

So, in 1181, after a serious naval defeat at Nidaros, he decided to build a Dragon in order to declare publicly, to all who would dare to question it, that he was the undoubted overlord and king of Norway. This was to become the *Mariasuden I* which was laid down at Nidaros during the winter of 1182-3.

The measure of a ship was how many "rooms" she had ie. spaces between the cross-beams, each room corresponding to a pair of oars (These ships were constructed for both rowing and sailing).

6 of the 16 Dragons were of 30 rooms, about 52 metres long --- a fairly average size, and the *Mariasuden* was one of these. Sverre also ordered a number of other ships to be built at that time, mainly of 20-30 rooms.

During the months while the nine initial rounds of his Dragon's planking were being laid in, King Sverre had spent the winter away at Møre, thus being unable to oversee the construction of his new ship and, being rightly considered a non-seaman in anybody's book, did not anticipate what size she would be when completed.

Conversation among the townsfolk of Nidaros where King Sverre's ship was being built|:-

Bjorn, to his neighbour:- *It's now nearly spring and that ship of the king's will have to be launched soon if she is to get into the water in time for the summer expedition.*

Arne:- *But how is she going to get down to the water? She is being built so far from the sea.*

Dag:- *King Sverre knows damn all about shipbuilding, insisting that the ship should be built so far inland for security, and away up at the top of the town. He must be mad!*

Bjorn:- *It's you who are mad, saying such a thing about the king. Shut your trap for Odin's sake, unless you want to end up as a galley slave.*

Bjorn's wife, Audr:- *Dag is right. Why on earth is the ship lying on the stocks above the town and so far from the water's edge?*

Vivi:- *Look at that great long slipway --- it goes right down in among all our houses. If the ship is launched from away up there how is it going to get down through all our houses, without damaging them, that's what I want to know.*

Master Shipwright:- *You folks are quite right. I have argued with the king till I'm blue in the face, but will he listen to me? No, he will not! I am the most important person on this build but he is the most stubborn man I have ever met, and knows nothing --- absolutely nothing whatever --- about building a ship, far less a Dragon.*

Dag:- *Wait till you see, he'll have to demolish some houses in order to get the ship down to the water. It's an utter disgrace! That man has over-reached himself in his arrogance --- as if none of us, or our houses, mattered a bit.*

Master Shipwright:- *I foresee only disaster for this ship.*

Arne:-*Why? What do you think will happen?*

Master Shipwright:- *When the king got back here he saw the size of the ship and completely lost his rag. He shouted at me that the ship was far too small and commanded me to cut her in two and insert extra six metres of planking into her keel.*

Arne:- *A "pieced" ship! You can't do that. She'll be forever weak all through her hull.*

Master Shipwright:- *I know that. I tried to make him see sense, but he just wouldn't listen and threatened to replace me --- me, the king's personal shipbuilder --- with some other shipwright! I am mad about it, I can tell you! I've said it once and I'll say it again --- truly I foresee disaster for this ship.*

The townsfolk went away, muttering angrily, but King Sverre got his way. The *Mariasuden* was lengthened, against the Master Shipwright's advice, and finally completed. Local seamen gave their considered opinion that as she was a *samskaret,* or pieced ship, she would never be any good.

She had been cut far too much, both along the keel and, as a result, also in her strakes, with the joints far too close together in a bunch amidships. When the terrific stresses of water and wind hit her she would be weak and vulnerable throughout her hull.

However, the day came for her launching. Many gathered to observe the event, and many cursed the king for demolishing their homes in order to clear a path for the launching.

It seemed, indeed, that the fates were on their side for, as the big ship began to slide down the slipway, the air was suddenly rent with the shrieks and groans of over-strained planking and the sound of splintering timber. Clouds of sawdust and wood chips burst forth into the air. Then the entire hull gave way at the seams and the unlucky vessel collapsed into a heap of expensive matchwood!

Bjorn:- *Did you see the king? He was in a right royal rage. I never saw a man actually dance with rage before.*

Vivi:- *Yes, and he tore off his hat and jumped up and down on it. I was afraid for the Master Shipwright, and none of it was his fault. He warned the king about what would happen. If I hadn't been so angry I would have laughed. It serves him right!*

Arne:- *But what will happen now? All that money and timber wasted!*

But Sverre had not yet given up on his ship and had the bits of her put together again, finally going so far as to give her an ornate Ship's Blessing. This was a fairly common occurrence, both to give the ship her name and to commit her safety to whatever gods were in vogue at the time.

But *Mariasuden* was not worthy of the designation of Dragon, simply because of her extreme piecing. As a result her crew of experienced sailors --- and like all sailors, very superstitious --- had no confidence in her at all, especially when they discovered that Sverre, having finally admitted to himself that just perhaps his Dragon ship was none too safe, had smuggled aboard two heavy chests, later discovered to be full of rivets, in case anything gave way while at sea!

She actually took part in a sea battle in Norefjord and managed to give a reasonable account of herself, but the crew said that she would have been far more effective if the king had listened to his Master Shipwright and she had been properly built from the start, with no piecing.

Sverre must have had his own private doubts about her and possibly admitted to himself that he had pushed his luck far enough, for he then ordered her into Bergen harbour where she was beached and had a roof built over her.

That was the end of her sailing career --- only a few short weeks after she had been launched in Nidaros in 1184 --- a tragically short career for any ship, never mind a Dragon.

But, in 1185 Bergen was attacked and it was decided to try to relaunch the *Mariasuden*.

All able-bodied citizens were press-ganged into trying to push her into the water but, by this time, she had completely settled and would not give an inch. Later, more desperate attempts were made to shift her and very slowly she slightly unstuck herself from the strand, but the strain proved too much for her pieced and weakened hull, and she began shuddering and shaking so violently that her prow snapped off, causing a fatal collapse of her clinker planking.

This signalled the end for the poor *Mariasuden*. Sverre bowed to the inevitable loss of face and ordered her to be destroyed. So she was immediately set on fire and burned right out.

King Sverre goes down in the history of seafaring as an incompetent, arrogant man --- most definitely no sailor --- most unusual in a Viking king --- who made an utter fool of himself over this ship.

"There are none so blind as those who [absolutely] will not see.
It would all have been so ridiculous if it hadn't been so tragic.

Strangely enough, during the well-documented Norwegian expedition of 1263, when King Hakon IV led his battle fleet through Scottish west coast waters, more opportunities for disastrous loss of Norse dignity occurred.

Hakon ordered the building, at Bergen, of the biggest Dragon ship to be built in medieval Norway, over the winter of 1262-63, and named her *Kristsuden*. She was a huge ship of 37 rooms and very large in proportion. She was specifically intended to be his flagship during the Scottish expedition. (It was the *Kristsuden* which was to carry Hakon's body from Orkney back to Norway in 1264)

It is widely held, even by his detractors, that Hakon's punitive expedition was competent enough on the administrative side, ie before the fleet set sail --- but militarily it was a dog's breakfast, with no planned strategy, and the so-called battle of Largs was not so much a battle as a series of incompetent blunders for which King Hakon himself must personally bear responsibility.

The illness which killed him a couple of months later in Orkney was undeniably psychological in origin and led to his ultimate physical collapse.

The reason for Hakon's attack was that the Scots had *"made great dispeace"* among the Hebrides, which Norse kings regarded as their personal territory. He mustered a great many ships (exact numbers unknown) with a suitably large force of fighting men, and set out to take back the Hebrides, by force, if necessary and possibly gain even more territory in Scotland.

Having sailed openly down the western coasts of Scotland, where Islay and Kintyre quickly submitted to him, the king turned his fleet into the Firth of Clyde and anchored *"in Arran Sound"*, greatly alarming King Alexander III of Scotland who sent a series of Dominican monks back and forth between himself and Hakon in an attempt to establish terms of peace between them.

But Hakon, sure that he had the upper hand, boldly made a list of all the west coast islands that he claimed were his, and now claimed the Clyde islands of Arran, Bute and the Cumbraes as well.

King Alexander was having none of it.

After considerable, unsuccessful to-ing and fro-ing between the kings, peace negotiations fell through, neither side trusting the other, but the Scots had deliberately played a delaying game in order to await the hoped for equinoctial gales when the Norse fleet would be at a definite disadvantage lying at anchor in the open waters of the lower firth.

Hakon then sailed his ships close to the Ayrshire shore, into the shelter of the Cumbrae islands where his men started agitating because of the growing shortage of rations. Plunder was called for.

The Scots were now seen to be gathering onshore in large numbers but, it was at this point that Hakon decided that a show of strength was necessary across Scotland and hit on the novel idea of sending away forty of his ships up to Loch Long where they were portaged overland to Loch Lomond --- just when they were about to be needed in battle!

From Loch Lomond the Vikings scattered across the breadth of Scotland, looting and burning as they went, miles and miles from the Ayrshire coast and completely out of touch with the main force.

Sending part of his army away when just about to go into battle was, to say the least of it, an unusual stratagem by any war leader! (cf. Colonel Custer at the battle of the Little Bighorn)

By Michaelmas Day, Saturday 29th September, the main Norwegian force observed the Scots massing inland close to the Ayrshire coast. This dealt the final blow to all peace negotiations, so the Norse withdrew to their ships to get ready to attack.

This was just as well for, on the following Monday, the expected gales suddenly blew up with astounding ferocity and ten of the Norse ships, among them some longships and a merchant ship, were driven ashore. All day long, far from abating, the storm grew so bad that some crews lowered their masts, having lost all control of their sails, while other vessels drifted away helplessly, their sails blown to shreds.

King Hakon's ship, *Kristsuden,* put out seven anchors and a sheet anchor, but they did not stop her dragging, though fortunately they gripped later. The superstitious crewmen swore that witchcraft was behind all this violence of the sea.

To add insult to injury a merchant ship, having lost her anchors, drifted backwards into the king's ship, getting tangled up in her cables and ripping the elaborate nostrils off the dragon figurehead.

Then the merchant ship drifted aft alongside the king's ship until her anchor caught in its cables and started to drag it backwards too.

Chaos ensued as the crews realised that the merchant ship was in the process of pulling loose the royal ship's anchors. In desperation Hakon ordered the cables of the merchant ship to be cut, causing her to be driven on to the shore. Fortunately *Kristsuden*'s anchors now held and she lay without sails or awnings (the only form of shelter even on a big longship) until morning. In all, she had eight anchors out.

At this point the distraught Hakon went ashore in desperation, in order to pray for his ship's safety and found himself in the company of the crewmen who had survived the wrecked ships and were now stranded on the shore, dangerously at the mercy of any marauding Scots. The entire company was trapped ashore all night while the unceasing storm beat about their heads.

More distress ensued when the Norsemen discovered that the Scots had sneaked up under cover of darkness and were plundering their stranded merchant ship. Inevitably a fight ensued between the Scots and the angry Vikings but, strangely enough, only a few were killed though many were wounded.

Towards daybreak the storm abated a little allowing the Norse to recapture their merchant ship, and clothe and arm themselves with whatever the Scots had left aboard her.

During the morning the Norse commanders saw a large force of Scots approaching and thought it was the Scottish king with his army, so they insisted that Hakon, who was showing signs of serious, but unspecified, illness, be rowed back to the *Kristsuden,* out of harm's way.

He went reluctantly, thus remaining safely on board while the fighting took place --- hardly the inspiring act of a leader of men!

Was Hakon already feeling the early effects of the fever which would later overwhelm him in Orkney?

And perhaps, at that point, the king was beginning to regret ever setting out on this ill-fated adventure in the first place.

By this time there were from 800 to 900 Norsemen on the Ayrshire shore, about 200 of whom had climbed a steep shingle mound in order to get a good view of the enemy, the rest remaining below on the beach. (The crews on the Loch Long adventure remained, of course, out of touch exactly when they were most needed).

The Scottish king was seen to be advancing with a huge army which threatened to surround the Norse on the mound, so the latter had to make a tactical withdrawal and get quickly back down to the beach to join their main force.

This gave rise to another rather farcical situation, though obviously no one saw it at the time.

When descending a shingle mound you should never run, as the pebbles underfoot will undoubtedly act like ball-bearings and carry you away in an avalanche of sliding stones.

Inevitably, during the rush to get down to the beach, the shingle gave way under the Norsemen's feet and they came tumbling downhill ever and ever faster, in an uncontrollable landslide, trying in vain to keep their feet on the treacherous scree, colliding violently with one another, landing in struggling heaps on the shore below, and crashing in among their waiting countrymen who, alas, thought that they were trying to flee from the enemy and rushed to join them in a headlong flight to the ships.

Now followed an undignified scramble down the shore to where their small boats lay at the water's edge, waiting to take them off to the longships. In the ensuing chaos many boats sank and several men were drowned.

Later however, the Norse finally managed to rally, having been sent ashore again by their commanders when the situation became less chaotic, and now it was the Scots' turn to climb up on to the mound, firing arrows and throwing stones at the enemy. The Norse advanced boldly at last and the Scots were forced to withdraw.

To and fro all day went attack and counter-attack until it seems that battle weariness prevailed and, with the day nearly over, the Norse returned to their ships for the night, coming ashore in the morning only to recover their dead.

Hakon's war weariness must have set in for he ordered the wrecked ships to be burned, and decided to set sail for the Hebrides where he could lick his wounds. No doubt he felt that all the odds were stacked against him, especially as the Scots, in the minds of his superstitious seamen, had certainly used witchcraft to defeat his invasion.

This was to be his last voyage.

Neither side won in this series of uncoordinated skirmishes later to be dignified with the name of the Battle of Largs.

As a final blow, while the Norwegians weighed anchor and got slowly under way out of the Firth of Clyde who should at last arrive but the forty ships Hakon had sent to Loch Long --- much too late to be of any assistance!

Shortly after arriving in Orkney Hakon's illness overwhelmed him and he died there.

Surely the most appropriate comment, and last word on the subject, comes from a certain well known Ayrshire man:

The best laid plans o' mice and men gang aft agley.
Robert Burns

Tale no. 29: The Dinosaur, the Crofter and Ostaig's Big Barn

I opened the door and came face to face with the dinosaur. Utterly shocked, I stood transfixed, and for a minute we stared at one another while it fixed me with a glassy stare.

I recoiled in horrified surprise but almost immediately realised that it was not alive. It was made of papier maché with eyes made of two large marbles stuck into the sides of its head.

I had walked in to the big classroom in Kilmuir Primary School, in the district of Trotternish in north Skye,where I was visiting in my capacity as Primary Education Adviser for Inverness-shire County Council, and was amazed at the size of the beast which took up the entire central length of the room, so that to get from one side to the other you had to walk right round the massive creature without, of course, standing on its rather frail feet or on its enormously long tail.

I wondered why the class had encumbered itself with this major obstacle and was told that it had not been planned to be that big but, like Topsy, had just "growed".

The circumnavigation of the dinosaur must have increased the walking distance in the classroom quite considerably --- one way of getting exercise when the weather was too bad to go out during playtime and lunchtime.

Like all children the Kilmuir pupils were fascinated by all things "dinosaur" and told me, at great length about all the different kinds of the creatures, including the ones found on Skye itself.

Donald John rapidly appointed himself as my mentor and guide in this matter.

"Yes, Skye is known as Dinosaur Island because of all the dinosaurs we have here," he announced seriously and, rapidly warming to his subject, continued, "My grandpa and my brother and me were all down on the beach and saw the footprints at An Corran --- that's at Staffin, you know," he declared importantly.

But Mairi Ann was not to be kept out of the discussion and, to Donald John's acute annoyance, butted in, "Yes, we all know about the footprints in the rocks that you can see after a big storm when the sea sweeps all the sand away and ---" she rushed out the words then was forced to hesitate briefly in order to draw breath.

Seeing his opportunity Donald John plunged in during the hiatus.

"They are 165 million years old. Miss told us that was the mid-Jurassic Age and our dinosaurs were called Stegosaurus and Ce---" and he trailed off in frustration.

Mairi Ann triumphantly jumped into the empty space, "It was Cet-i-o-saurus," she enunciated loudly and carefully.

"Miss", also known as Miss MacDonald, then informed me that I could see some of the actual bones in the Staffin Museum at Ellishader.

But Donald John had not yet finished, "Our dinosaurs were her-di-vores," he finished uncertainly.

"Her-bi-vores," crowed his rival, Mairi Ann, in a flash.

Donald John glared at her for stealing his thunder. No doubt the rivalry would be continued outside in the playground at the interval.

The subject was satisfactorily ended by one of the little Pr.1 pupils who trotted out to me, holding up her stuffed toy for me to see. Naturally it was a dinosaur but nobody could decide upon which one it was.

"What kind of a dinosaur is that?" asked her teacher.

The little one had the last word. "It's a Topsy," she replied. End of discussion!

It was always such a joy to visit Kilmuir School as my own folk had all gone to that very school since the establishment of public schools in every parish.

My grandfather was not altogether sure this was such a blessing.

"We arrived in the school on our very first day, at the age of five," he said, "and were immediately told by the teacher that we must not speak Gaelic, only English, or we would be punished. [This was part of a policy of deliberate eradication of the Celtic languages by governments in Scotland, Ireland and Wales in the early 20th century.] The trouble was, we could only speak Gaelic as we had no English at all, so were continually being punished. No wonder we didn't like school!"

Kilmuir dinosaur

This universal attitude hastened the near eclipse of the Gaelic language in all the Gaelic-speaking areas, and now there is a desperate and belated attempt to restore this ancient and beautiful language to its rightful place among the indigenous languages of the British Isles --- the P Celtic, or Brittonic group comprising Welsh, Cornish, (and originally Breton/Breizh, which is no longer associated with Britain), and the Q Celtic, or Goidelic group comprising Manx, Scottish and Irish Gaelic.

English does not come into any of these groups being one of the incomer Germanic languages belatedly entering the islands of Britain with the Angles, Saxons and Jutes from the near continent, at a much later stage.

But I was not thinking of this as I happily accepted the kindly invitation from the Kilmuir School staff to stay and have a supper with them in the schoolhouse after school had closed for the day.

What a spread --- home-made "everything", apart from tea and sugar.

There were home baked scones, pancakes, bread and oatcakes, spread with their own churned, fresh butter; crowdie and Dunlop type cheeses; local honey; home-made jams made from raspberries, gooseberries and rhubarb and ginger; jellies and jams made from rowans, rose-hips, blackcurrants and sloeberries and lightly delicate puddings of carrageen and cranachan.

Even the hams, venison and cold salmon were local produce.

The only uncomfortable bit about it all was having to turn down invitations to have, "just a wee bit more of this ---"when I was feeling that I would not be able to eat another crumb for at least a week.

The really special thing for me was, when visiting Kilmuir often in years to come, the former pupils all remembered me and made themselves known, even when grown into big, brawny lads and pretty young women.

"I remember you looking shocked when you opened the classroom door and found yourself nose to nose with our dinosaur," sad a fully grown Donald John to me, grinning at the memory.

I suppose that all this could be construed as parochialism, and so it is, in a good way, as it is all part of the caring, crofting community which holds its people and its memories dear.

This had been the case since time immemorial and was exemplified when, in 1877, the rents of the crofts on the Kilmuir estate were doubled without warning. The factor had difficulty in collecting the rents as many were unable, as well as unwilling, to pay what they rightly regarded as extortionate increases.

The usual blackmail ensued with the estate threatening eviction and the withholding of necessary seed supplies, unless rents were paid in full.

So, of course, the rents had to be paid, and were, but with growing resentment to the point that, in 1880, at Staffin, over on the used to wake me up, and continue for ages while I tried, in vain, to get back to sleep. Many a time I sneaked out of the house in the dawn light and tiptoed down the garden towards the source of the endless ratcheting noise. Just when I thought I was about to come upon the nuisance and drive it away it would fall silent and remain so until I gave up and retreated to the house again, whereupon it would start croaking all over again. I lost hours of valuable sleep over that corncrake.

A family of screeching owls lived in the horse-chestnut trees at the side of the house, and they, too, added to the clamour of early summer mornings, along with the bawling of the poor little calves in the nearby fields when separated from their mothers for the first time --- Oh, the peace and quiet of the countryside!

Another noisy, but faintly comical feathered friend was a large herring gull whom we named, George. He had alarmed us on his first visit by battering with his beak on the kitchen window and staring in boldly at us when we tried to get him to fly away. His object, of course, was food, and we made the mistake of throwing some to him, mainly to save the window from demolition by bird. This encouraged him no end, and he continued to demand food, with menaces, by assaulting the unfortunate window for many years, but inevitably we got quite fond of him. Fortunately, he never managed to break it.

Quieter inhabitants of our countryside were the otters in the Conaglen, the blue hares in Kerran Glen and stoats and weasels all around. I was thrilled one icy December morning to come upon a stoat in his winter ermine coat undulating across the road in front of me. He was absolutely beautiful.

Cattle, of course, fall into both categories of noisiness. Normally they are quietly grazing the lush Kintyre grass and pay no attention to anybody passing their field, but occasionally we were made very aware of a bovine presence in the shape of the next-door Ayrshire bull of bad reputation. This animal would rush to the fence and roar out a deafening challenge to anyone who dared to walk past his field. How our mild-mannered farmer neighbour managed this ravening beast was a mystery.

One Sunday morning, as my father was well into his sermon, our ears were assaulted by a loud, intrusive noise --- the Ayrshire bull was in the field opposite the church and had started up in serious opposition to my father, who had to keep steadily raising his voice in order to be heard. Soon the bull got well into his stride vocally, and it quickly became bull versus minister. Our farming congregation were starting to look around at one another, no doubt wondering which party would win the contest. My father struggled valiantly against this unexpected rival, but after some time gave up the unequal competition and gazed fixedly at the owner of the bull who was sitting near the front of the church. There was an embarrassed silence then our friend and neighbour was forced to get up out of his pew and, keeping his head down, scuttled hurriedly out of the church. The bellowing continued for a short time until, at last, blessed silence descended. Presumably the offender was banished to a far-distant field, for my father resumed his sermon in his normal voice, to everyone's relief.

It seemed particularly relevant that the next hymn on the list that morning was All Creatures Great and Small.

Tale no. 5: Those Who Go Down to the Sea in Ships

Spring was the season for taking the boats out of the water and getting them ready for the busy weeks ahead. But early in the year there was always one of Archie's boats still in the water from the previous year --- the service launch for Sanda Farm and the lighthouse.

This time it was the *Rex* which had been afloat all winter and we expected to have to do a lot of work on her. Archie had decided that she badly needed a new keel strip, which meant that she would have to be turned over on a nice level piece of ground. We couldn't put her in the Lifeboat shed as it was already full of boats and gear so, after hauling her out at Dunaverty jetty, we transported her up to the machair in front of Archie's house. There her engine and all moveable parts were taken out and she was turned over and laid on heavy trestles. The hull was okay but the keel strip had been damaged, no doubt when she grounded so often on a rough shingle shore. This was a two-person job and Archie had booked me to come and help as I was definitely more agile than he when it came to climbing up on to the keel of the upturned *Rex*.

It was a gorgeous morning and the larks were singing as they soared up and beyond the machair, and the oyster-catchers and sand-pipers ran calling along the golden beaches. There was a noticeable warmth in the early spring sunshine, the wind had died down to almost dead calm and the sky was filled with mackerel clouds, heralding a spell of good weather --- perfect for boat repairing.

I balanced on the boat's broad hull as we started the slow business of prising off the damaged metal strip, and pulling out the screws holding it to the keelson. When everything had been loosened I carefully slid down on to the grass and we gently lifted the strip off the hull. Any damage to the wood was immediately repaired and the area prepared.

The next bit was the tricky part where two people were needed, so I had to get back up on to the upturned boat, holding the stern end of the shiny new keel strip while Archie took the bow end. Between the two of us we carefully placed it in position while the new screws were inserted through the metal and into the hull, with me holding the strip in place as Archie attached them tightly to the keelson.

While we had the boat upturned in this position we decided to start on the painting of her hull --- always a tedious business because, like all our boats, except *Catriona,* she was clinker built and the undersides of her overlapping timbers were awkward to get at when she was upright. These increased the boat's buoyancy, so it was important to get a good coat of preservative and paint on to them. At Dunaverty we called these overlaps "the landings", and, when a few of us were painting, both John and Archie would always call out to us, "No holidays on the landings, now!" --- a "holiday" being a missed bit.

With two of us at work we soon had the entire underside of the hull well covered with marine paint enhanced with a good dollop of linseed oil. The boat was left until everything had completely dried then we began the difficult business of righting her, replacing the engine and all other parts, to Archie's satisfaction.

At last she was ready and it was a spic-and-span *Rex* which Archie eventually took out to test the engine and lay his lobster creels.

It was hard work to get all six boats repaired and spruced up each spring, but what satisfaction it gave us to see our small fleet in good order, knowing that we had done our best to make them safe for use in the often dangerous waters of the Mull of Kintyre.

The fact that we often had a great deal of pleasure and laughter around Dunaverty, and made many friends among the summer holiday-makers, was an added bonus.

One summer morning John and I took my boat *Catriona* out to "look the net". We rowed out of the Conaglen River into Brunerican Bay where the big stake net was anchored, and carefully searched the skirts and bag of the net for any signs of salmon. We had been pushed for time on leaving the shore and had forgotten to bring along with us one of the wooden fish boxes for stowing any possible catch. It isn't advisable to lay fish directly on to the bottom boards of any boat as the fish scales quickly dry on to them and are a nightmare to scrub off.

Having pulled ourselves out along the leader rope to the bag of the net we peered down into the clear water and saw only one big, beautiful salmon caught by the gills and flapping in a panic as he tried to get away.

We soon released him and lifted him into the boat, then realised that we had nowhere to stow the fish.

Catriona carried the usual baler, mooring line and other small gear. And today, fortunately, we had put a bucket containing bits and pieces in the bow. This would have to do, we decided, though it was a big salmon and just a medium-sized bucket. After a short deliberation we found that the only way to get the fish into the bucket was by placing it in head-downwards as it was too big to lie on its side in the usual fashion. There was a considerable amount of tail hanging out of the bucket but it would have to do.

Off we went shorewards when Kenneth Nicolson, a Glasgow dentist on holiday at Southend, hailed us from the beach.

"Any fish?" he yelled.

"Aye," shouted John, "a nice big one --- about fifteen pounds."

We pulled past the high rocks at the mouth of the river, briefly out of sight of Kenneth, and could hardly believe our eyes when our "dead" salmon suddenly started quivering, gently at first, then violently from head to powerful tail, until with one massive, muscular convulsion, it hurtled, tail first, upwards and outwards, all in the same smooth movement, out of the bucket, over the boat's prow, and into its natural element with a resounding splash.

As we gazed around futilely, looking for something to catch it with, it floundered and sank towards the sandy bottom --- but only for a minute. Then it seemed to regain its natural incredible strength and shot off towards the open sea, never to be seen again by John or me.

In astounded silence we drew into the shore and grounded the boat.

John picked up the empty bucket and climbed over the side.

"Where's the fish?" demanded Kenneth.

John and I looked at each other helplessly --- Kenneth would never believe our tale of the one that got away!

But, inevitably, as around all the sea-coasts of Britain, there were the dark times when tragedy struck the fishing communities, and Kintyre was no exception.

My colleague, Bill Beveridge, and I had wandered one lunchtime down to the New Quay in Campbeltown where the recently arrived motor yacht, *Quesada,* was moored, and attracting a great deal of attention.

"Quesada" at New Quay, Campbeltown

Built in 1937 in Southampton by the British Power Boat Company, as a minesweeper of double diagonal, hard chine wooden construction, with twin motors, she was 58.4 feet long and weighed 43.11 gross tons. In 1939 she had been fitted with three powerful Napier engines for her conversion to a high speed motor torpedo boat.

Later still, in the 1950s, after her wartime service, she became a pleasure craft with only two Dorman engines. In 1966 she arrived in Campbeltown and was involved in various peacetime activities, including holiday charter work, which meant that she was classed as a yacht, with the appropriate safety equipment for that class.

As we walked along the pier Bill admired her lines and asked me what I thought, obviously expecting an enthusiastic reaction.

He was rather taken aback at my adverse comments and seemed to think I was being needlessly critical. I looked at the boxy hull, high superstructure and almost flat-bottomed build and pointed out that she no longer had the powerful engines of the naval torpedo boat, which had enabled her to plane safely at high speed. I thought the lack of power would cause her to wallow at the reduced speeds necessary in the frequently high winds and rough seas around Kintyre. In addition, her high sides would catch the wind, like sails, and make her difficult to control. I also knew that on a recent trip to

Northen Ireland the helmsman hadn't liked the way she handled and thought she lacked sufficient power.

Altogether I was not impressed with the boat in her new capacity as a cruiser, and said so. Bill obviously disagreed, but we left it at that.

I would like to have had the opinion of our headmaster, Hector MacNeill, who had been on the bridge of the warship *Hotspur* at the dreadful battle of Narvik, and also at Matapan during the Second World War, and knew what he was talking about when it came to ships and boats.

On the morning of Monday 23rd May I was rushing about the kitchen as usual, getting ready to leave for school, and switched on the radio to get the news and weather forecast.

My blood ran cold when I heard the news reader make the sombre announcement that the motor yacht, *Quesada*, had sunk off Davaar Island, near the entrance to Campbeltown Loch, with the loss of eight lives. There were ten survivors. With utter dread I shouted to my father to come and listen for himself, as I knew that two of our Southend farmers had been on the boat. I drove off to school in a state of great anxiety, and found, it seemed, that the whole of Campbeltown was in a fever of distressed speculation as to what had happened, who had been lost and the condition of those who had been saved.

I just looked at Bill as I met him in the school hall, and he shook his head sadly, but said nothing.

Eventually the whole bleak story came out, at first in bits and pieces, and subsequently in full, during the disaster inquiry held in the town before Sheriff-Substitute Donald J. MacDiarmid.

At Southend we were greatly relieved to hear that our two farmers were among those saved, but shared the grief of those who had lost dear ones whom we knew, as is the way in small communities.

The boat, with eighteen persons aboard, was originally to have sailed to Northern Ireland but, because of an adverse weather report, had instead sailed from Campbeltown at 7.45 am on Sunday 22nd May, to cruise to Lochranza, Isle of Arran. The journey to Lochranza was uneventful, apart from a minor fault in the port engine, which was quickly put right, so it was agreed that they should sail on to Rothesay, Isle of Bute, where they went ashore for over two hours.

All went well and the boat left there, on its return journey, at about 5pm, arriving at Tighnabruaich in the Kyles of Bute about 6pm.

Quesada left there at 8.30pm for the return to Campbeltown and her passage was smooth and uneventful until she reached Skipness, at the north end of Kintyre, where the wind began to freshen to Force 6, gusting to Force 8, and continued all the way down Kilbrannan Sound. By the time she was off Carradale the wind had risen appreciably and, when she was approaching Campbeltown Loch, it had reached full gale Force 8 from the north-west. But still there was no immediate cause for concern.

Thus far she was safely on a weather shore and, according to the official Wreck Report, *while there was some movement and slapping of the vessel as she listed over with the wind, she proceeded steadily on her course, being well handled by the experienced veteran fisherman Archie Stewart.*

But, about a quarter of a mile north of Davaar Lighthouse, the boat refused to take the starboard helm and her port engine failed, so that instead of entering the loch, she wallowed, on her starboard engine only, to the east of Davaar Island, to all intents and purposes out of control on an inadequate single engine in the force of the gale.

About ten minutes after the port engine had stopped the starboard engine failed also.

Quesada was now noticeably down by the stern and drifting helplessly downwind to approximately four and a half miles south-east of Davaar Island.

No-one aboard was able to restore engine power so, at just after 0045 on Monday 23rd, a May Day signal was sent and received by Kildonan coastguards on Arran. Hand flares were also set off but, as she was behind the bulk of Davaar, nobody in Campbeltown saw them until she had drifted some way clear of the island, by which time four men, subsequently lost, had cast off in a liferaft and tried to reach the shore.

Meanwhile, such life-saving equipment as there was available, was being issued, but not everyone received a lifejacket. According to the official Wreck Report:

There can be no doubt that the lifesaving equipment on board was inadequate and did not conform to the regulations.

It later transpired that, at that point, no-one ashore actually knew where the *Quesada* actually was.

The coastguard station at Southend was now contacted by anxious relatives and, the Wreck Report states:

--- at 2323 hours {on Sunday 22nd May} the coastguards at Southend sent a signal to Portpatrick station asking for a broadcast. This message was immediately put on the air by Portpatrick coastguard station asking for information as to the whereabouts of Quesada. The result was negative.

By now many people ashore were becoming seriously concerned about the non-arrival of the boat and the sighting of some flares, so Campbeltown lifeboat was asked to go out and make a search. The first maroon calling the crew was fired at 0100 hours on Monday 23rd and, amazingly, it took only twelve minutes for the lifeboat to sail, in spite of the fact that some crew members had to be fetched by car.

Meanwhile the crew of the fishing boat *Moira*, tied up at the New Quay, were asleep or nearly so, on board in preparation for an early start on Monday morning.

The Wreck Report goes on:

Within a few minutes of the flare being seen south of Davaar these men were off in the Moira on a mission of rescue. Neil Speed was in command of his own boat (Moira), ably assisted by James Meenan (Stella Maris) who directed operations. On the way out of the loch lengths of rope were cut in preparation for the rescue work. The skill, cool courage, intelligence and character shown by these men, which resulted in the saving of ten lives in a full gale, from a sinking vessel, with spindrift making vision impossible, and in confused seas, is deserving of the highest praise and commendation. Neil Speed's skilful handling of the Moira alongside the sinking Quesada, with James Meenan's direction of operations, are in the highest and best traditions of the sea.

Quesada sank at about 0200 hours on Monday 23rd May.

Moira returned to port with the survivors, but went out again and continued the search until the following afternoon, along with the lifeboat and the other Campbeltown fishing boats, Stella Maris, Mary McLean, Golden Hind, Little Flower, Boy Danny and Regina Maris. No further survivors were found.

Although the ship was said to have been well maintained she did not have the necessary lifesaving appliances as required by law, and there were no notices showing what equipment was available and how to use it. She was also deficient in the protection of deck openings, strength of doorways, height of sills and coamings, and in watertight bulkheads.

The primary cause of the disaster, especially the sudden loss of both engines, with catastrophic results, has never been established, but the obvious secondary cause was the flooding of the engine room.

Mr Walter Weyndling, an experienced ship surveyor and a dedicated investigator into the tragedy, put forward his theories as to what had caused her to sink, as follows:

1. A weakness in her port exhaust pipe with consequent fracture allowing an inflow of water sufficient to flood both port and starboard engines in the time which elapsed;
2. structural damage to the bottom;
3. failure of the engine room WC discharge;
4. failure of the propeller bracket;
5. failure of the port engine exhaust.

He gave the first as the most likely cause of the flooding, but it was impossible to establish this with any certainty, --- *in the absence of the hull itself.*

The final comments by the enquiry were sincere appreciation of the quick-thinking, quick-acting fishermen at Campbeltown who sailed, within a few minutes of the flares being seen, in the fishing boat *Moira*, along with the crew of the lifeboat, all of whom continued the search all night and morning, until the following afternoon.

The Report ends:

The actions of all concerned are worthy of commendation.

The loss of the *Quesada* was deeply felt in Kintyre, used though the area was used to tragedies at sea, and it seemed that everyone was in mourning.

Since official records were first kept at least four hundred named ships are reported to have been wrecked off the coasts of Kintyre, many around the Mull itself and the island of Sanda, and this does not count smaller vessels, like the *Quesada*. Not for nothing is the area known as *the killing ground*, though this label refers mainly to the deep water of the North Channel between the Mull of Kintyre and the coast of Antrim where German U-boats lay in wait to torpedo ships coming in from the Atlantic during World War II.

I could well empathise with the relatives of all who sailed in the *Quesada* on that fateful voyage, for, just a few years earlier, I had known the heart-stopping fear of waiting for news of a family member involved in a shipwreck.

It was a Saturday in early October and my mother, who had been visiting friends on the little island of Gigha, off the west coast of Kintyre, was due to return to West Loch Tarbert on the MV *Lochiel.*

This ship was an important part of MacBrayne's fleet, as she was the first of two mailboats ordered in 1938, built in 1939 and the fourth vessel of that name. She sailed mainly on the Islay service, calling at Port Askaig and Port Ellen, and also the islands of Colonsay, Jura and Gigha, where my mother had boarded her.

As at the time of the *Quesada* disaster I was alone at home in the kitchen and had casually put on the radio, expecting to hear a Scottish music programme. I remember the mind-numbing horror when I heard the announcer's voice say:

We interrupt this programme to report the sinking of the MV *Lochiel* in West Loch Tarbert, Argyll. No casualties have been reported, and a telephone number was given for anxious relatives to contact MacBrayne's office in Tarbert.

My father was, at that moment, driving to Glasgow and, obviously, could not be contacted --- no mobile phones in these days --- and Ronald was out somewhere in the district. I felt utterly alone, helpless and in a state of incipient panic, as in my frozen state of suspended reality, I hadn't managed to get the telephone number of the shipping office in Tarbert given by the BBC.

Who should I phone, MacBrayne's, or the BBC, and anyway how would I get the telephone numbers, as we had only a local directory, and there were no Yellow Pages?

I remember being in such a complete daze that for several minutes I just stood staring at the radio, not doing anything and not knowing what to do.

Eventually I managed to get myself back into some semblance of control and went to get the telephone directory. I was feverishly scrabbling through the pages, looking for MacBrayne's number, and jumped when the phone rang suddenly in the silence of the house. In that heart-stopping moment I dropped the directory and grabbed the phone, dreading to hear bad news but desperate to get any news at all.

The relief was overwhelming as I heard my mother's calm voice assuring me that she was safe, and had never been in any actual danger as the ship hadn't sunk in deep water, and would I please come and get her at the West Loch pier.

Wouldn't I just!

Babbling to myself between joy and tears I scrambled into the car and, holding myself back from driving like a fiend, safely covered the forty-eight mile length of Kintyre to the West Loch where I found that the survivors had been safely deposited on the pier and were all milling around among their almost hysterical relatives.

I saw my mother standing alone a little apart from the others, obviously watching for my arrival.

On the journey home I kept sneaking quick looks at her and thinking how this event might have ended in disaster for my family. We could have so easily lost her. What a tiny distance there is between normality and catastrophe.

She seemed quite glad to tell me about what had happened to the ship, and I was pleased that she didn't want to keep it all tightly locked up in her mind.

The *Lochiel*, with over a hundred passengers and a flock of seventy-five sheep on board, had proceeded as normal on the last lap of her voyage from the island of Gigha to West Loch Tarbert --- a seemingly uneventful journey. My mother was in the main saloon, thinking about gathering her belongings together as they neared the entrance to the loch when the ship, quite undramatically, ground to a stop and rolled slightly over to port. She had hit Sgeir Mhein -- submerged rocks in the mouth of the loch. There was no panic, though apparently water was swilling around in the engine room, but soon the engines started again and the ship sailed on for a mile or two until they finally stopped for good as the seawater overwhelmed them.

In a blessedly calm sea the *Lochiel* drifted gently on to a mud bank just north-east of Eilean da Gallagain in the West Loch and settled upright on her keel.

It soon became obvious that she would sink no further, and the main deck remained above water. The crew gave out lifejackets, launched the two lifeboats, one with an outboard engine and the other with oars only, and started to ferry the passengers ashore. The engine gave out almost immediately, so both boats proceeded under oars until everyone was safely ashore, both crew and passengers helping in the operation.

Meanwhile, the barman, up to his oxters in water, proceeded to salvage the contents of the bar and handed out bottles to all who would take them, although the water was above their waists by this time!

The poor sheep were pushed out of the cargo doors by the crew and left to save themselves by swimming ashore. Some managed to do this, but some swam around helplessly in circles and some, alas, drowned as their saturated, heavy fleeces pulled them down. A number were saved by compassionate passengers who managed to grab them by the horns or fleeces and tow them ashore behind the lifeboats.

Fortunately now the *Lochiel* settled on the sea-bed and so was able, in the course of time, to be raised by the salvage tug *Plantagenet*. She was repaired but did not return to service until the following March when she was sold to an Isle of Man company, then to three other owners in succession until she was finally scrapped in 1991 at Bristol --- a sad end for a well-liked and familiar ship in west coast waters.

Fortunately I had happier memories of the *Lochiel* which, although not what you would describe as a good-looking ship, had her very own old-fashioned charm.

One winter's day, when she was relieving the *Lochfyne*, which usually sailed the Clyde to Loch Fyne route, I sailed in her to Tarbert, east Loch Fyne, where I used to catch the service bus to Campbeltown on my way home to Southend.

I went aboard her at Dunoon and, after clambering over the usual assorted deck cargo scattered about the main deck, including a little calf, I entered the saloon to find that I was the only passenger aboard.

I sank happily into a pale-coloured settee in front of a glowing heater, and waited for the arrival of the steward bearing a tray with coffee pot, milk jug, sugar bowl and a plate of biscuits --- such luxury! In these days many of the passenger ships still had their own silverware, tastefully displayed in glass-fronted cabinets from the time when such items were part of the original fittings of ships of that era. So did the *Lochiel*, whose saloon could almost be described as quite elegant.

I especially remember that journey as there had been quite a snowfall that morning and sailing through the Kyles of Bute resembled a voyage in fairyland with the forests, islands and rocky mainland covered in what looked like a dusting of icing sugar. We slowed down, as always, on leaving Tighnabruaich, in order to pass safely between the Burnt Islands where rare white heather grows.

Some of this had been collected and sent out to Africa where a friend of mine was being married. She later told me that the heather had been used to decorate the tables at the reception, but she had not got one single piece of it back as all her sentimental, homesick Scottish friends, knowing exactly where it had come from, had taken it as a souvenir for themselves.

I noted the well-known landmark of the "Maids of Bute" --- two long boulders set on their ends at the edge of the water and painted, supposedly, to resemble two girls standing on the shoreline. This requires a considerable stretch of the imagination!

Soon we were out again in the main channel of Loch Fyne and approaching the wooden bulk of Tarbert pier. Every time I sailed this route I thought of the fabulous history of the area, particularly the famous tale of how the notorious King Magnus Bareleg of Norway tricked his way into acquiring the entire Kintyre peninsula in the eleventh century.

It was a fact that the kings of Scotland, having no fleets to speak of, were forced to recognise the power of Norwegian royal fleets in these days. The Scots knew that they had no power or control over their own western islands in particular so, by default, had allowed these, as well as the northern islands, to lapse into Norse control.

Magnus already had control of most of the islands and now cast covetous eyes over the mainland itself. He looked at the fertile lands of Kintyre and liked what he saw, declaring:

Kintyre is a great island, and better than the best island in the Hebrides, excepting Man.

So, in a treaty of 1098, King Edgar of Scotland, had to bow to the inevitable. He declared that he was willing to share control of all the western islands round which Magnus could sail a ship with her rudder in place, as long as he did not plunder the kingdom itself. In this way he hoped to keep Magnus in the islands only, and away from Scottish mainland territories.

The *Heimskringla, King Magnus Bareleg's Saga*, describes how Magnus, in typically bold Norse fashion, carried out a well thought out stratagem, sailed up the widest part of the lower Firth of Clyde, into the great sea loch of Loch Fyne then turned westwards into East Loch Tarbert, where he:

--- *caused his men to draw a skiff across the isthmus of Kintyre, and to set the rudder in place: the king himself sat in the afterdeck, and held the helm. And thus he took possession of the land that lay to the larboard.*

Kintyre remained classed as an island, by the Scottish government, until the beginning of the 17th century, and Magnus continued his land-grabbing by sailing, during that winter, through all the west coast firths and around the islands, claiming them in his own name. The Norwegian grip on Scotland was now considerable. This situation was to continue for centuries and was the cause of almost continual strife between Scotland and Norway until that final, official Norse withdrawal in 1469 when the last island --- Shetland --- was sold to the Scottish Crown for eight thousand florins.

On a recent visit to the Port Charlotte museum on the island of Islay, I had the flashback experience of reading an account of the sinking of the *Lochiel*, described in full. The ship had, of course, begun her fateful voyage from that island. The awful reminder of my paralysing fear flooded back into my mind with appalling clarity, and yet, I reminded myself, our folk were the fortunate ones --- they were saved, when so many on the over four hundred Kintyre wrecks were not.

O hear us when we cry to thee
For those in peril on the sea

Tale no. 6: Locals, Lobsters and Langoustines

There was absolutely no doubt that the main sport in the Kintyre village of Southend, apart of course from football --- mainly a spectator sport --- was golf, and this was not just a game for men. The ladies were equally enthusiastic. It seemed that I was the only person in the community who did not play golf, and I determined to do something about it. My father possessed a bag of elderly clubs and had been known to venture out on to Dunaverty course when parish duties, and weather, allowed. Early one brilliant July morning he suggested that we should sally forth as a family unit and try a round while the course was quiet. I had definite reservations about this but realised that practice was the only way in which I would make any progress at "the golf".

Off we drove to the course where we parked the car on the beaten earth of the main parking area outside the small wooden building which was the clubhouse. Nowadays there is a more impressive building where you can actually have a meal and enjoy social activities, but things were simpler then.

The golf course is actually part of the farmlands of Machribeg, and among the many hazards were the cattle which grazed at will on the machair.

After the usual changing of shoes and paying of fees we went out, myself rather self-consciously, on to the first tee, where I gave the usual beginner's demonstration of how to beat up the turf by missing the ball entirely, then hitting it wide among the inoffensive cattle which scattered, mooing plaintively.

My mother swung the club as if it was a hockey stick and showed me up by occasionally managing to swipe the ball --- though it usually travelled only a few feet then trickled to a stop. My father valiantly attempted to tutor us by advising on correct stance, position of the head while swinging the club, etcetera, and we crashed around the first five holes with little success. By this time we were exhausted with the effort of concentration, and having to retrieve the balls from rabbit holes, the long grass of the rough and the River Conaglen. I'm sorry to say that I gave up the struggle at this point.

"This is supposed to be enjoyable," I complained to whoever would listen."I'm obviously not cut out for golf. It's just a good walk spoiled."

The real reason for my decision to give up on the game was that the fifth tee was situated above the river, and I could see my boat at her mooring right below me.

"Catriona" and *"the punt"* in Conaglen River

Abandoning my parents and the golf, I ran down the steep bank, got into the boat and escaped out into Brunerican Bay.

But how foolish of me to imagine that there would be no-one to see my efforts at that hour of the morning.

Of course, Angus MacVicar, himself an excellent golfer, had seen us on our maiden voyage round the course, and lost no time in commenting gleefully when we met later that day:

"Oh yes," he said, "I saw you out on the course this morning. My, that's a great swing you've got. What a pity you can't hit the ball!"

I was invited to join in several games with some of the local girls who kindly decided to take me under their wing, but I became known as a rotten partner as my concentration failed me completely when we reached the fifth tee and I looked down longingly at my boat moored in the River Conaglen below.

But I did remain a sort of detached member of the Ladies' club and, on one never to be forgotten occasion, helped to paint their very small clubhouse --- really just a glorified shed. As usual it had been raining and the ground outside was saturated with water, turning the Ladies' parking area into a quagmire. Unfortunately most of our cars had been parked there and were now sitting in a sea of glutinous mud.

Eventually we finished painting and made our way out through the long, wet grass to the cars, exclaiming in dismay as we saw how much water had fallen since we had arrived.

One of the girls, with difficulty, squelched through the bog and clambered into her car. She started up the engine but couldn't move the vehicle, so deeply had its wheels sunk, so the rest of us got in behind and started to push.

Suddenly the wheels spun, sending a thick shower of drenching mud all over our faces, but we persevered and the car actually started to move forward under its own engine power. Unfortunately, one of our number hadn't stopped pushing fast enough and, as the car lurched forward, she fell flat on her face in the mud and lay there inert, as we --- lamentably--- fell about laughing at our unfortunate friend, face down and helpless in the soggy morass. She couldn't manage to get up by herself so we, laughing hysterically, had to pick her up and try to wipe her face clean enough for speech and vision to be restored. Unfortunately there was no way in which we could de-cake her mud-clogged clothes so she was wrapped in a travelling rug and placed gently in the back of her own car like a large, wet parcel while someone drove her home.

It looked for all the world like a scene from a Laurel and Hardy film. If we had tried to do it we couldn't have achieved a more spectacular effect, and it was a crowd of very undignified, and unlady-like "ladies" who left Dunaverty Ladies' Golf Club that afternoon. We thanked Providence that none of the men had seen us, or we'd never have heard the end of it.

Several of my school colleagues played golf regularly, mostly on the prestigious championship course at Machrihanish and, with their energetic encouragement I, and a teacher friend, decided to go out there and get some lessons from the club professional.

We were somewhat diffident about being allowed to walk on this hallowed turf, but duly sallied forth, were given a lesson and good advice from the professional, and told to go off into a quiet area and practise what we had been taught. Obediently we did so, giggling far too much, especially at some of our more unsuccessful efforts. Inevitably, lack of serious concentration made us careless, and my friend who, for some unaccountable reason, was wearing nylon gloves, took a tremendous swing at the ball which soared off spectacularly into the rough --- closely followed by the golf club, and the gloves. Choking with laughter, we scrabbled about in the long grass for some time before recovering the lost items, but I'm afraid that was the end of our practice session and we slunk away, hoping that none of the serious golfers on the nearby tee had observed our disgraceful performance on this prestigious course.

We thought we would definitely be asked to leave and didn't dare to go back for any more lessons. After very little thought, and with great relief, I finally decided that "the golf" was not for me.

My next foray into the sporting world of the countryside was angling --- after all, we were allowed to fish that part of the Conaglen which ran through the manse glebe. A youthful Angus MacVicar and his brothers had once, spectacularly, taken a large salmon, by very questionable means, out of the river in order to provide for a visit from the Moderator of the Church of Scotland --- the dog having illicitly eaten the roast originally planned for dinner and caused a major panic in the household just before the Moderator's arrival.

It was arranged for Dod Knox, the gamekeeper at The Point, further up the Conaglen from the manse, to give me some tuition in the finer points of casting. He was a very patient tutor but I'm afraid I was a sad disappointment to him. I just couldn't get the fly to land in the river. Instead, I regularly hooked the foliage of the trees behind me.

"It's all in the wrists," he kept instructing me." Just flick the line over that nice little eddy there, and let then let it float back. You can practise down the river on your own stretch in the glebe." The glebe stretch abounded with trees on either side!

Dod, alas, spent a considerable amount of time clambering into trees and bushes in order to untangle my errant line but, having done his best to instruct me, finally gave up on his very worst pupil. However, in the goodness of his heart he lent me a rod, no doubt feeling it was a small price to pay for getting rid of me, then took me in to see his wife with instructions for her to give me tea and send me home. So much for my new hobby of fly-fishing.

So it was back to the shore and the beloved boats for me.

My family had frequent contact with the island of Sanda, my father through his parish work, and myself and Ronald through John and

Archie Cameron, the local fishermen. We often met Jean and Jim Russell who owned the island farm, and admired their fortitude in living and working in often difficult conditions, as everything had to be laboriously carried in and out by boat, even in unchancy weather.

Then there was always the danger of accident in such an isolated place --- Jean herself was once thrown by cow whose horns had not been removed. Fortunately, if such a word can be used, the animal came up behind her and the spread of its horns was wide enough to catch Jean under each arm, and not through the flesh of her back. Luckily she was not badly hurt as there were no life-saving helicopters in these days and the lifeboat would have taken quite a while to come round from Campbeltown. Such delays could easily have cost people their lives.

Archie Cameron transported food and other supplies for humans and animals alike, in *Zena, Rex* and *Ace,* while "the school run" took on a whole different meaning when applied to Sanda.

The Russell boys had to sail the two miles across the Sound of Sanda to get to primary and secondary schools on the mainland, and sometimes had to help in the exhausting process of moving live sheep and cattle from the farm to the mainland in the very tubby and ungainly boat kept at Sanda for that purpose only. However they seemed to thrive on the experience.

One of Archie's many duties was that of taking the Sanda lighthouse keepers on for their six-week spell of duty, and off for their three weeks' break at the end of it, but the regulations stipulated that he should always be accompanied by a crew member in case of accidents.

He phoned me one morning out of the blue.

"Hughie can't make the lighthouse run today --- he's not well. Could you come instead, as crew?"

Hughie Stewart, at this time, was over eighty years of age, but wouldn't miss the Sanda run, no matter what.

How-an-ever, as they say in Kintyre, it seemed that Hughie was temporarily laid low with a bout of 'flu, and Archie was forced to get second best, ie. me.

I duly arrived at Dunaverty jetty, where Archie was preparing *Zena,* the brown varnished open launch, for the two-mile sail across the Sound of Sanda.

"It's looking a bit rough the day," he said. "We'll need to put a bit of ballast in her, for over the Bow Reef."

So ballast was placed in the bottom of the boat, tarpaulins were stowed handily for protecting us all in case the sea came over the sides, and we awaited the arrival of Calum, the ongoing keeper.

As it was just before New Year the keeper was, quite naturally, a bit depressed at having to leave family and friends at Scotland's most festive season, to go on to a remote island at the south end of Kintyre. The fact that he would, in all likelihood, have a very sociable and festive time with Jean and Jim, was no consolation to him and he carried with him a large carpet bag which clanked suspiciously whenever he moved.

We got aboard and set off out of Dunaverty in a very choppy sea, then went hard-a-port round Dunaverty Rock, and straight over the infamous Bow Reef. *Zena* lurched heavily as a big wave caught her, causing Calum to cannon into me, and sending me up against the tiller. Fortunately Archie was made of sterner stuff, and retained his grip on it, standing there like Old Father Time, unmoved by weather or unsteady passengers, and contemptuous of tarpaulins.

Archie and friends in *"Zena"*

Calum and I sorted ourselves out and cowered behind a tarpaulin, which really wasn't much use at keeping us dry, as sea spray was coming over from all sides. With one hand attempting to hold the tarpaulin over his head Calum rummaged noisily with the other in his carpet bag, and eventually emerged waving a bottle of The Famous Grouse.

"To keep the cold out," he explained. "Just you hold that while I find the glasses," and he dived again into the depths of the carpet bag, to emerge clutching a handful of glasses.

Archie and I immediately intimated that there was no way we could sample the Grouse while on duty, but Calum was not deterred, and instructed me to hold his glass steady while he attempted to pour a dram into it. This was not an easy task, and while *Zena* plunged over the waves like startled whale, more whisky was poured on to the bottom boards than into the glass. In addition, the whisky that actually made it into the glass was immediately deluged by the sea water spraying liberally over the gunwales.

Undeterred, Calum managed to get a "small sensation" to stay in his glass at last, and, looking fondly at me while offering the toast, "Och, you are a good sea-woman!" he swallowed it down, spluttering as the whisky-flavoured sea water hit his tonsils. That was enough even for Calum, and no more good whisky was sacrificed to the sea gods.

Half an hour later we moored the drenched *Zena* at Sanda jetty, and squelched and clanked (Calum) our way up to the blessed sanctuary of Jim and Jean's farmhouse.

Kind-hearted Jean had made us wonderful hot tea and scones, and told us that the outgoing keeper had just arrived and was waiting to greet Calum, his relief, before leaving for Dunaverty with us.

We were ushered into the warm, fire-lit sitting room, and Jean and I sat together on the settee near the window, beside Jean's potted geranium.

Before going over to the lighthouse Calum insisted on all present having a dram of his Famous Grouse for the New Year, and swallowed his --- minus the sea water this time --- in a state of deep melancholy, while Sandy, the outgoing keeper, was in a state of high, in anticipation of spending the next three weeks with his family.

Jean, like myself, an unenthusiatic whisky drinker, managed to distract all the men while I quickly flipped both drams into the geranium.

"My, I can see you ladies like your dram!" said Sandy, impressed with the speed with which we had dispatched the whisky. "Here, have one on me," and, despite our protestations that we weren't really whisky drinkers (which he quite obviously didn't believe), he poured out another generous dram into our glasses.

Jean and I sat nursing our newly filled glasses, wondering how to get rid of the whisky this time.

Then Jean "remembered" something very important which she just had to show me, in the kitchen.

"Bring your glass along with you," she said, winking at me, "as this might take a wee while."

Thankfully I shot off in her wake and we left the men to their celebrations, while we escaped to the whisky-free kitchen.

"I think we may have killed my geranium, "said Jean sadly.

At last we said a fond farewell to Calum, Jean and Jim, and wished them a Happy New Year, before collecting a very merry Sandy, escorting him carefully down to the jetty and placing him in the boat for the return trip.

Zena bumped and bounced her way back to Dunaverty, with Sandy singing The Road To The Isles at the top of his voice, while hanging on to the engine casing for dear life. Soon Dunaverty jetty came into view and we tied up there before thankfully handing Sandy over, in one piece, to his devoted family waiting on the beach.

Soon after that we were intrigued to hear that the BBC, with whom Angus MacVicar had close contacts, was going to come to Southend to make a documentary film about our remote community, and we were warned to expect to be asked to join in our various activities for the cameras. The next Sunday, at church, Jean, Angus's wife, whispered to me:

"Come down to Dunaverty early this afternoon and be ready to take out the boats for the BBC to film."

"What are we to do?" I asked, but she was very vague about the whole thing, so I arrived at the jetty just a little bit apprehensive. Archie was already there and, as he had been asked to take the *Zena* out and be filmed taking lobsters out of all the creels in the bay, he and I hatched a cunning plan.

"Come on, quick," he whispered. "We'll need to get round the creels and put a live lobster in each of them, or these blasted cameras'll have us trailing round the bay all day long. They seem to have got the idea that you always find a lobster every time you lift a creel!" We knew, from grim experience that it was very possible to go round all the creels and find absolutely nothing in any of them,

77

apart from the odd crab. The BBC had a totally exaggerated idea of the practicalities of lobster fishing.

Fortunately Angus had been let into the plot and agreed to distract the production team long enough for us to carry out our dastardly plan. No doubt the lobsters, if they could talk, would be utterly confused about being put back into the water instead of, as usual, being taken out.

At last we were ready to be filmed and brought *Zena* into the jetty in order to get last minute instructions from the director. Off we were sent round the bay and carried out our instructions to lift the creels and take out lobsters. We did so quite smugly, knowing full well that there would definitely be one in each creel, so no time would be wasted on lifting empty ones. Strangely, we didn't have a cameraman in the boat with us, but could see the cameras pointed in our direction, to Archie's discomfort.

"The boat is just rolling about in this swell. She'll look like a log in the water," he lamented.

When we got back to shore, to our astonishment, the director asked us to tie the boat up to her mooring, but keep the engine running in neutral while we opened up the creels and took the lobsters out. After that we were to put bands on their claws, as usual, order to prevent them damaging each other, or us.

The sound engineer then held his microphone down at the stern beside the puttering exhaust to give the impression of the boat moving at sea, while the cameras were angled to show us working, and the sea beyond, but not any of the jetty. The whole thing had been artificially manipulated, we felt, but the BBC men seemed quite satisfied.

The entire community was involved one way or another, and we were told to expect the film to be shown on BBC television in the May of that year. Alas, a certain politician decided to devalue the pound right on the evening in May when the documentary was to be shown, so it had to be postponed for some time.

The film was finally to be shown on a Saturday evening in September.

In the meantime I overstrained my wrist while manoeuvring a boat down the ramp from the lifeboat shed, and my right arm was swathed in a thick, crepe bandage from fingers to elbow. Inevitably my pupils in Millknowe School had all watched on that Saturday night, and on the Monday morning were waiting excitedly to see their teacher, who had appeared in the unusual role of film actor.

It seemed they especially liked the scene where Archie and I were lifting the lobsters out of the creels and getting the bands quickly on to the wildly waving claws before they clamped on to our wrists. Naturally my pupils were goggle-eyed when I walked into the classroom, my wrist swathed in the bandage.

Of course they put their own interpretation on events and spread it about that I was wearing that big, thick bandage --- because one of the lobsters had got me!

I heard about this story and decided to give it a touch of reality.

The next morning, complaining about how uncomfortable my arm was I began, very slowly, to unravel the thick bandage. At first there was a bit of a buzz in the classroom, as they didn't know exactly what to expect, but obviously feared the worst, then gradually the room fell completely silent the more bandage was unravelled and the more wrist exposed. I could see their eyes getting bigger and bigger, as they awaited, with horrified anticipation, the grisly sight of an arm mangled by a big lobster!

My great difficulty was in keeping my face straight until, with a final flourish, I pulled off the remaining bandage, only to reveal, no torn and bloodstained flesh, but a smooth, unmarked arm.

There was a great shout of laughter as they realised that I had played a trick on them.

Naturally I took the opportunity of pointing out the dangers of spreading unfounded rumours, and how they should always wait for evidence and proof before letting their imagination run away with them.

As well as lobsters Archie would supply other marine creatures requested by the locals.

Shortly after the BBC visit a friend of mine asked me to get some langoustines from him as she was having a special dinner party and wanted to impress her guests with her culinary skills. At that time of year they were difficult to get but Archie made a special effort and managed to deliver a freshly caught live batch to her house. She was effusive in her thanks, and carefully tipped out the tiny creatures on to the draining board beside the kitchen sink that evening, before leaving, switching off the light and going away to set her dining-room table.

Some time later she returned to the kitchen, switched on the light and was immediately confronted by what she touchingly described as a row of little langoustine faces looking at her, piteously, she imagined, from the draining board.

"How could I kill these poor little things, all sitting there, looking up at me with their sad little eyes, and me an animal lover?" she said to me.

Utterly conscience-stricken, she decided they would have to go back to the sea --- without Archie ever finding out, of course. My help was enlisted and, much later that evening, after the guests had gone home and darkness had fallen, we gathered the langoustines gently together, placed them in a plastic box, and drove to the most hidden part of the shore near the caves of Keil. We kept well away from the big beaches where Archie or John might possibly see us and wonder what on earth we were up to on the shore at that time of night.

Like a couple of smugglers looking out for the excise-man we peered all around, out of the car windows, to see if the coast was clear then, one holding the opened box and the other a torch, we tripped and splashed our way down the beach towards the water's edge --- anything but silently. As I clambered over a seaweed-covered rock I slipped and, waving my arms about in an unsuccessful attempt to keep my balance, lost my grip on the box, which flew out of my hands and disappeared into the darkness, followed by a loud splash. Then, finally, I completely overbalanced and fell, presumably into the same rock pool as the langoustines.

I was now so wet it didn't seem to matter how much wetter I became, so I spent the next few minutes floundering about in the water, trying to locate the missing items, without success. It was too dark by this time to have a hope of ever finding either box or contents, but we knew the tide was on the make, and soon the rock pool and its newly arrived inhabitants would be safely covered by the sea, so I squelched out of the pool and staggered noisily, dripping sea water, up the shingle beach to the car.

As a pair of gangsters we were a total failure, but we felt an inner glow of self-righteousness as we imagined the little creatures now swimming free in their natural element, and we sneaked off home again without being seen, the great burden of guilt lifted from our shoulders.

But my friend spent the next few days trying to dodge Archie, in case he asked her how she had enjoyed the langoustines.

Tale no. 7: Eachann's Tale

John and I were down on the shore barking a large quantity of new manila rope, line and net in readiness for the forthcoming fishing season, at the same time keeping an eye on young Neil Morrison and Calum MacMillan, lads from our local Coastguard station, who were eager to spend their time "helping" us with the various small tasks that we set them, around the shore.

Barking was essential in order to soak the softly pliable manila in the dark preserving liquid which would protect it from rotting in the sea water and darken it enough for the fish to accept it as some kind of water weed, and not avoid it as an unfamiliar threat.

We duly filled the square, brick-built enclosure with water, lit a fire in the space underneath it, and poured in the barking fluid, which consisted of water and tannin from certain tree barks. Soon the dark brown water heated up enough for us to start dipping ropes and nets into the preserving fluid.

It was a messy job --- one which had to be done before the season began, but which we disliked as it required constant attention to both fire and manila, and smelled very unpleasant. In addition there was the time-consuming business of spreading the saturated ropes and nets out to dry on the grass along the shoreline, after waiting hopefully for a spell of dry weather, then folding and coiling the completely dry material before stowing it away carefully in "the hut", the former fisherman's house which we used for a store.

So absorbed were we in our task that we didn't notice the arrival of a police car on the dunes above the fishing station, nor the two Campbeltown policemen who were now walking down the hill towards us.

The boys had spotted them, however, and came at a run to find out what was going on.

"Look, Mr Cameron. It's the police. What do you think they want?"

We didn't usually merit a visit from the constabulary so we were at a loss to explain this visit.

"It's alright. Just you go back down to the river, boys, and we'll talk to the policemen," said John, in case there was anything sensitive that children should not hear.

As always, they did exactly as they were told, but gradually drifted back up the shore again when the policemen started talking to us.

"Hello, there, Mr Cameron," said the taller one, taking in everything in one comprehensive glance, as policemen always do.

"Are these all your boats?" he asked, pointing to *Sheena, Catriona, Zena* and "the punt", which were all moored, bow to stern, in the calm waters of the Conaglen River.

John indicated that they belonged to himself, myself and Archie, and asked if anything was wrong.

In reply the policeman asked another question.

"Are there any signs that your boats might have been moved, or tampered with in any way?"

"No, I'm sure they are just as we left them last night," said John looking at me in some puzzlement. "Why? Is there anything wrong?" he asked again.

"It's just that there has been a lot of activity along the Irish and Scottish coasts recently, and we need to know if any of the local boats have been involved in any way. I'm sure you know what I mean! We've already had a word with the Coastguards."

We knew only too well. This was the time of the Irish political "Troubles" when gunrunning and other activities were rife. It seems that certain persons or groups were reported to have "borrowed" boats off the Argyll shores for various nefarious activities, thus contributing to the increasing violence which we were only too aware of in these days.

The police told us to keep a close eye out for anything different, and to let them know right away if we suspected that someone had stolen, or used, the boats.

They then asked about other boats in the vicinity, so we directed them over to Dunaverty to speak to Archie about *Rex* and *Ace*. At last they went off, apparently satisfied.

We immediately rushed down to the river and did a thorough search for any unnoticed clues to the unauthorised use of our boats, but all appeared to be well. The only way we could increase our security was to transfer our mooring lines from the usual heavy rope hawser on to the massive chain embedded into the shore. The inboard ends of the lines were then padlocked on to the boats, but we knew full well that anyone really wanting to release the boats could do so, simply by cutting the lines, in spite of our precautions.

It was a very unpleasant thought that anyone of criminal intent could just take our innocent boats at will.

Of course, the boys had got most of the gist of what the police had said to us, and were silent at first as they realised how easily trouble could come out of the blue from outside our community, and affect our way of life.

We explained to them how their dads, the Coastguards, were not only important as protectors of all shipping at sea, but also of our shores, and I mentioned how these west coasts had had more of their fair share of troubles from the sea since time began.

John nodded in agreement.

"You have heard of the Viking invasions," I reminded the boys, and young Neil looked pensive as he remembered that his ancestors, the Morrisons, had been Viking invaders of the west coasts of Scotland in times long gone by.

"When did they come over from Norway, and what did they do?" he questioned me.

"Well," I began, "the ancient Annals of Ulster tell of the first recorded raid, by Danish Vikings, in the year 793AD, on the English island of Lindisfarne, followed in 794 by the first attack, by Danes and Norwegians, on the whole of Britain, including the Irish island of Rathlin and our Scottish island of Skye. This was the beginning of continual burning and pillaging in Ireland, Scotland, the Hebrides (which weren't yet part of Scotland) and the Isle of Man.

For us, here in Argyll, the raiding by Norwegian Vikings became continual and never seemed to end. People were horrified by the first vicious attack on our sacred island of Iona in the year 795 and again in 802, when all that had been looted in the first attack had been replaced --- ready for them to pillage all over again.

The Vikings seemed to be especially spiteful towards the Christian communities, although they themselves were supposed to be Christians by this time, and spared neither man nor beast in their cruelty, as well as stealing everything they could lay their hands on.

They were also keen to capture as many able-bodied folk as they could find, in order to sell as slaves, as this brought them a great deal of wealth, and so they emptied whole west coast communities at a time."

The boys looked horrified, and Neil was particularly affected.

"But why did they do this?" he questioned, almost in tears.

"It all started when, long ago in Norway, the population grew too big for the land to support," said John.

"Remember, it's a very mountainous, cold country, where there isn't much land for cultivation and the climate makes it difficult to grow crops, though trees grow well there. The people were poor and often starving, which could make them fall ill with all sorts of diseases.

It soon became vitally necessary to find more land --- and good productive land --- in order to provide for all these people, and give them better lives than they had in Norway. But they weren't able to do much about it until, after many centuries of trial and error, and the discovery of iron, they learned how to make fine, slender timbers from their forests and use them, along with the iron, for building their famous longships.

Now they had the means to go out into the great Atlantic and search for lands to settle in --- though to begin with all they seemed to want to do was to steal and plunder in other people's lands. The Scottish islands, and north and west coastlands, were nearest to Norway so that is why they first came here and why, eventually, they forcibly took our land which they later settled. That is why your long-ago ancestors decided to stay here, Neil. Nowadays the surnames of many modern Scots show their Norse ancestors, such as Morrison, like you, Neil --- also MacLeod, Langwell, Caldwell, Gunn, MacAskill, MacAulay, MacAuliffe, MacCorquodale, Cotter, MacIver, MacIvor, MacKitrick and others. The "Mac" bit is, of course, the Gaelic for "son", which they attached to their Norse names."

"How do you know where they went to in Scotland?" he asked.

"That's really quite easy to discover," I replied. "They named the places where they settled in their own Norwegian tongue. This is so different from our Gaelic language that we can clearly see the difference, and so we know exactly where they eventually put down their roots, and stayed."

"What are the names of the places?" clamoured the boys.

"There are lots in this district. Just look right over there," I said. "The island of Sanda has a typically Norse name, and means *sand island*. Many of our local farms have pure Norwegian names, or a mix of Norwegian and Gaelic names --- we call these hybrid names.

Pure Norse names are Amod --- *river meeting*, and Borgadale --- *fort dale*.

Pure Gaelic names are Glenamuclach --- *boar glen*, and Breackerie --- *speckled shieling.*

Hybrid names are Brunerican --- *brow, or brae, of Eric* (Norse), with *-an* --- little (Gaelic); and Glenadale --- *glen* (Gaelic), with *adale* (Norse), giving *glen glen*

So we can tell what people lived in these places.

An old poem, written in the 11th century, by Bjorn Cripplehand, Court Poet to King Magnus Bareleg of Norway, praised the king's exploits and boasted about how terrified the people were of the Norsemen:

In Lewis isle with fearful blaze
The house-destroying fire plays;
To hills and rocks the people fly
Fearing all shelter but the sky.
In Uist the king deep crimson made
The lightning of his glancing blade;
The peasant lost his land and life
Who dared to bide the Norseman's strife.

So firm was the Norse grip on the land of Scotland that they were to remain for around 675 years, until the last piece of our country, ie. Shetland, was sold, in 1469, to the Scottish crown for 8,000 florins.

Then, of course, some of the Norsemen remained here and became "more Scots than the Scots", as the saying goes."

There was a long silence as the boys took in all this information, and I wondered if new warfare would break out between Neil, our young Norseman, and Calum, our devoted Scotsman.

"It was all a long time ago, boys," I sighed," and we are now the best of friends --- the Scots and the Norwegians --- but we should always remember the dreadful pain caused by the evils of war and terrorism, and that it's always the weak and helpless who suffer the most."

They just looked at one another, and grinned, to my relief --- just a pair of bright young lads with no unhealthy hang-ups about the dark deeds of the past.

It wasn't long before they wanted a real story from the days of the Norse invasions, so, after all the manila had been well and truly barked, we settled down on top of the piles of dry nets in "the hut", and I, like a true seannachie, told them the tale of Eachann and Mairi, the children from Skye:

I remember the day when our troubles all started, and our way of life was gone for ever. It was a glorious morning in the month of July on the west coast of our beautiful, peaceful island of Skye, in the year 794AD, and my grandfather was organising us as usual while our parents were out on the croft and busy at the hay.

"Eachann, my lad, it's a grand morning. Take you the cows up to the high pasture to graze on the hill today.

You are a big lad now, all of ten years of age, and old enough to look after the cattle on your own. Take your little sister, Mairi, with you, and stay up there till the evening. Mind you don't let the beasts stray into a bog, or damage themselves among the rock outcrops. Your mother and father will be busy all day at the hay and not wanting the pair of you under their feet. Here are bannocks and cheese to keep you going till evening. Off you go now."

We wouldn't have dreamed of arguing with any of the grown-ups in our small township, especially our grandfather, so I replied,

"Yes, a Sheanair --- Grandfather. We'll see you this evening. Come on, a Mhairi, let's get the cows together and take them up to the shieling. Goodbye, a Sheanair!"

And off we went, waving to the old man and slowly driving the beasts up the hill to the summer pasture where the grass was long and lush. They required no urging as they knew the way themselves from long habit, and were as anxious as we were to get up to the sweet grass where a light breeze kept the clegs and horse-flies at bay. After our long climb Mairi and I found a spot from which we could see the bay beside which our scattered township lay, but not the houses themselves. This suited us well for we could play around to our hearts' content and make as much noise as we liked, with no grown-ups to interfere with our games. That's not to say that we didn't keep a close eye on the cows, for they were valuable to our family and we daren't let any harm come to them.

At midday, when the hot sun was overhead we found a nice little corrie, and settled down to eat the bannocks and cheese that Grandfather had given us. We washed them down with cool, fresh water from a little burn that flowed down from the nearby mountains, and almost fell asleep in the warmth of the day. Even the cattle lay down to chew the cud in happy contentment.

When we had had a bit of a snooze Mairi got restless again and started looking about her, always alert even when relaxing, and she called out, waking me out of my sleepy doze.

"How calm the sea is this afternoon, Eachann, and look, there's a lovely ship rounding Rudh Stafnish. She's got a big, striped sail with a large black bird painted on it --- a raven, I think. Oh, the wind has failed now and the men have brought out their oars to row her in. I think she's making for our bay. Let's go down to the shore and see the beautiful ship come in."

But I said, "No, no, a Mhairi, we can't leave the cattle. They would stray and Father would be very angry if any of them got lost. No, we'll just stay up here on the hill, as Seanair told us, and go home at sunset, not before."

Mairi looked annoyed, as usual, when she didn't get her own way, but she certainly couldn't manage the beasts on her own, so she sulked and muttered a bit, and kept giving me black looks from under her brows.

I tried to stop her girning, and said, "Don't worry, you won't miss anything. We'll see the ship and the sailors when we get home."

So we stayed up on the hill all that lovely afternoon and into the evening, when the slanting sun told us it was time to get the cattle down from the hill and safely penned up for the night in the little field beside our house.

"Come on, a Mhairi," I said. "Help me to round up the cows. We'll go down to the township now the sun is beginning to set."

She brightened up right away, full of anticipation of seeing the ship and all the new folk down at the shore, for we hardly saw anybody apart from our neighbours and family, and were always wanting news from the world outside our little community.

So she was quick to help me gather the beasts together and we started on our long, winding way down from the high shieling.

Yes, I'm coming, Eachann. Oh look, there's a lot of smoke rising up from the shore. It looks as if a haystack has caught fire. The grown-ups will be very upset, won't they! I wish we had brought the dog up with us. It would be so much easier to keep the cows from wandering. Maybe they'll send him up the hill to meet us halfway. You know how he likes to herd the cattle down that last bit of the path to the infield. But I can't see him yet. It's strange he isn't barking as he sees us bringing down the cows."

She chattered on, quite bright now that we were finally getting nearer our township and she would soon be joining in all the gossip with the other girls from the crofts.

I finally managed to get a word in edgeways:

"I know what it is! Luath is too taken up with the strangers from the beautiful ship to come up and meet us."

I looked out over the bay just in time to see the stranger ship setting out from our bay and heading in the direction of Rudh Stafnish headland.

"Oh, a Mhairi, I'm sorry. We won't be meeting the sailors after all --- there's the ship leaving the bay before we've even got down to the shore, She's got her sail up now. There must be a bit of a breeze out on the water. They probably wanted to leave whenever there was enough wind to fill that one big sail."

Mairi was annoyed again, and I knew she blamed me for us missing the excitement down on the shore.

"What a shame we've missed it all, Eachann," she said. "I wonder why Luath isn't on the way to meet us by now," and then screwed up her face in disgust as she sniffed the air.

"What a horrible smell of burning! Look, there's an awful lot of smoke down at the township ---" her voice started rising in fear as we got nearer to the houses, --- "and I can see flames, and hear the crackle of burning wood. Oh, Eachann, I think the houses are on fire. I wonder what's happened, and why the strangers have sailed away instead of helping to put out the flames?"

She ran faster down towards our croft, scattering the now alarmed cattle as she went.

"Look out, a Mhairi," I yelled at her. "The cattle are frightened by the smoke and you running so fast. They're stampeding! Oh, where is that dog? Where is Luath when we need him now?"

She paid no attention to my shouts. "Eachann, why are there no folk out in the township, putting out the flames, and why is there no-one shouting for help?" I answered, my voice hoarse with the smoke-laden air, and growing fear.

"There's something wrong. There's Luath lying down there at our door. Why doesn't he come up to us? A Luath, a Luath, trobhad a bhalaich --- come here, lad! He's not moving. I'll run down to him."

My heart was thudding painfully in my chest as, with rising panic, I tore down the hill above our croft, overtaking Mairi on the way.

I shouted to her over my shoulder. "You stay here, until I see what's going on. Don't come any further!"

For once she did exactly as I told her, her face pale with the paralysing anxiety that was flooding her body and mind.

I reached the croft after that agonising run, hardly able to get my breath between terrified anticipation and my hurtling descent of the hill. My heart sank as our beloved dog remained motionless in the doorway, not responding in the slightest to my frantic calls to him.

Right away I could see that our Luath would never again rush ecstatically to greet us, tongue hanging out in a doggy grin and tail waving, for he had been killed by a savage blow to the head and the blood was, even now, congealing on his thick fur.

"Oh, a Luath, a Luath, mo charaid bhig, my little friend, who did this to you?" I sobbed, then realised that Mairi was still standing motionless on the hill, watching me as I gathered the dog up in my arms.

She called out, "Is he alright, Eachann? What's wrong with him?"

I didn't want her to see him like this, and shouted back, "Oh, a Mhairi, the dog is dead. Don't come near!" and with tears sliding unheeded down my face, carried the sad little body to behind a row of haystacks where I buried my face in his shaggy neck in farewell, and laid him gently down.

By now Mairi had come out of her paralysis and came swiftly down to the croft.

She spoke the words which were swirling around in my own mind.

"Eachann, where are Mother and Father? Where is Grandfather? Where is everyone? Look, all the houses are on fire! What has happened while we were away?"

She suddenly stopped the flood of her questions and put her head on one side to listen intently.

"What is that noise coming from inside the house?" and before I could stop her she had darted past me into the now fiercely burning building.

I heard her scream, "Help, Eachann, Seanair is in here, lying on the floor and his head is bleeding. We must get him out before the flames take hold of the entire house."

I dashed inside and found Mairi, her eyes streaming and her breath coming in short, ragged bursts, as she bent over the apparently lifeless form slumped on the floor of our burning house.

Between us we dragged the helpless body of our old Grandfather outside, out of the choking, smoke-filled air, and over to the safety of the infield with the burn running through it. Away from the smoke we coughed the over-heated air out of our burning lungs and dragged in great gasps of clear, fresh air.

Seanair was groaning as we washed the blood away from his face with the cool, reviving water, but we could see the awful gash in his forehead which constantly oozed blood even while we tried to staunch the flow with Mairi's kerchief.

He gradually recovered consciousness as I spoke to him.

"A sheanair, a sheanair --- it's Eachann!" I whispered urgently to him. "What has happened? Who did this to you? Was it the men from the ship? Where is everyone, and where are Mother and Father?"

He had difficulty in speaking to us, and we propped him up between us while Mairi rubbed his hands and stroked his white hair in a vain attempt to soothe him, and I dabbed at the blood which dripped steadily down his face. His eyes seemed to sink deeper into his head as he struggled to tell us of the awful deeds that had been perpetrated on our community that day. We leaned closer to him in order to catch his faltering words.

"A chlann, children, it was in the morning, after you two had taken the cows up to the shieling that the fine ship arrived. We all went down to the shore to welcome her crew. We invited them to come ashore and give us their news and share our midday food, never thinking that all the time they were laughing at us behind their hands, for they had no intention of sharing anything with us, but planned to steal everything we had.

We were attacked by these strangers from the sea --- the Lochlannach, the men of Norway --- out of the blue --- without reason, without warning. We welcomed them in their beautiful ship --- but she was an evil ship, a ship of death!"

Grandfather's voice was fading to a barely heard whisper as he continued, "They surprised our peaceful folk and, oh, a chlann, these devils have killed your father and all the men. They have stolen away your mother and the other women for slaves and some of the children as well. The other children, and the babies, too young to be slaves, they have killed. They left me for dead, and set the township ablaze after stealing everything they could carry away with them, before they got back into their cursed ship and sailed her away.

His voice faded away entirely and he seemed to become unaware of our presence. We could see that he was gradually sinking into unconsciousness again, both from shock and his grievous wound then, suddenly, his eyes opened wide and, with a great surge of energy, he raised himself out of our supporting arms, and shaking his fists in rage, shouted,

"I call down a curse on each and every one of them: their kith and kin, man, woman and child; their houses, byres and stables and their accursed ships. Black be the name of their evil tribe, black be their fall, black be their destiny from this time forward and for ever and ever!"

And our poor, stricken Seanair fell back, lifeless, into our outstretched arms.

Tale no. 8: The Blizzard, the BBC and MacBrayne's Big Bus

I awoke that February morning, aware of the cold, soulless white light seeping into my room. It was obvious that there had been a snowfall during the night and I groaned as I contemplated a difficult drive into work in Campbeltown.

Having got myself ready to go out to the garage to get the car I opened the back door, and discovered an unknown and unfamiliar landscape that had sprung silently into being during the dark hours of the night.

I realised I couldn't walk through the yard to the garage as it was buried in a snowfield about two feet deep, so I turned back into the house, looking for some kind of implement to make a path through the white wilderness. The only thing to hand was the coal shovel, so I sallied forth, digging my way towards the yard entrance in order to investigate the situation on the road. It immediately became apparent that I was going nowhere by car that day, as the road had completely disappeared under the snowfall and there were drifts, from about two to at least six feet deep along the stretch of road in both directions. A blizzard of fine snow was still falling, being blown around haphazardly in the strong north wind, and making vision almost impossible.

I'd have to go into the house and phone the school to let them know I couldn't make it in to work that day. Peering around from various manse windows I could see no sign of movement anywhere in the surrounding countryside --- even the outline of the church, our nearest neighbour, was distorted under its white mantle, and Machrimore Mill Farm had almost disappeared from view, being down a little slope from the main road.

I wondered about possibly getting on to the school bus --- if it had managed to get down from Campbeltown --- and if so, how would it get back to town after collecting its usual quota of pupils for the Grammar School. Then, of course, I worried about whether we would all get back to Southend after school, and if we couldn't, where would we all stay in the town? All this speculation was whirling about in my mind as I reached for the phone. I needn't have wondered what to do as it was obvious that the phone was completely dead, and I couldn't inform anyone about anything.

To make sure I had tried all possibilities I struggled out through the yard to the road again and peered out through the blurred haze of still falling snow to see if the telephone lines were okay. I should have noticed the first time round that the lines lay in tangled disarray around the collapsed poles which straddled the road right outside the yard entrance.

Wondering what to do next I went back into the house and tried the electrics --- nothing, of course. How thankful we all were that morning that, like all the farmhouses in the district, we had the comfort of coal or wood-burning stoves in our kitchens --- ours was the trusty Wellstood. At least we could keep warm in one room, and had heat enough to prepare hot food and have hot water from the system.

It was, however, very disconcerting to discover how cut off we had become from the rest of the parish in a few short hours, and a reminder of how things used to be not so long ago when farms had to be more or less self-sufficient in every eventuality. It was, after all, only about ten years since mains electricity had been installed in Southend district, so many farms still had their Tilley lamps and generators from former days. How useful these proved to be in this kind of situation, though it didn't solve the problem of the milking. No electricity meant going back to milking by hand --- a slow process compared with the speed and efficiency of machine milking.

Unfortunately we, in the manse, had no lamps or a generator, so struggled miserably with candles, torches and coal fires for the duration of the snow.

My mother and I checked the food situation in the larder and reckoned we were alright for supplies, for a day or two. We hoped the road would be opened again before too long and we would be able to reach Alf and Morag Grumoli's shop and cafe at Muneroy, right in the centre of the village --- Southend's only shop.

As for milk, Ronald and I decided to try to make it over to the farm by crossing the fields, the more direct route, instead of trying to go round by the road. We were relieved to find May and Douglas Galbraith coping well with the situation at Machrimore Mill Farm, though they were naturally concerned about how to get the milk away to Campbeltown Creamery.

Fortunately the cows were inside for the winter anyway, so they were safe in their stalls in the byre, and we managed to get fresh milk after an adventurous struggle through the drifts. These were unexpectedly deep in places and we had the undignified experience of falling flat on our faces several times on the way over. Of course, we followed our own footsteps on the way back, so managed not to spill any of the milk.

We did notice, however, that many of the sheep had become trapped in the drifts and some were completely covered by the snow, so we decided to come back out from the warm kitchen and rescue our woolly friends by digging them out and ushering them into snow-free areas.

Some of them were nervous of our attempts to pull them free and struggled against our well-meaning efforts. How many times did we exhaust ourselves digging and pulling an unwilling animal out of a drift only to see it dive, panic-stricken, straight back in again into the same drift! This took the best part of the short daylight hours, and we eventually gave up and made for the house but, while out in the fields, we had seen and heard farm tractors out and about nearby, digging out the snow-filled lanes and the road in the vicinity. We hoped this would mean we could get to the village the next day.

What a long evening it was --- no electricity, so no lights, no television and, to my father's dismay, no quick cups of tea from the electric kettle. We lit candles in the study and rediscovered the joys of playing cards and conversation by candlelight and firelight. Looking round the old room I imagined that this must have been a common event in this house (though perhaps not the playing cards!) as the manse was very old, having been built in Georgian times.

The blizzard lasted for another night and it was evident that the road to Campbeltown must now be blocked, but we sallied forth bravely the next morning, with an extensive shopping list, to try to reach the village via the higher ground. We finally made it, but Southend was almost unrecognisable, having caught the full force of the wind, and the fronts of all the houses were buried in snow up to roof level. Doors and windows had disappeared. The only way to get out of the houses was to attempt an exit via the back doors or windows, if they were not too smothered in snow.

Alf and Morag had worked like navvies to clear the way into their shop and cafe, and were now busy attending to those customers who had managed to reach them. It was all very cheery as everyone tried to outdo one another with tales of the storm, though no one lingered for long after being served. It was tempting fate to risk getting stranded away from home as Alf and Morag had only limited accommodation in their flat behind the shop.

"We'll soon be out of bread and flour," said Morag. "I hope we can get more supplies from the town, but when will that be? We can't even phone through to the suppliers."

Fortunately, that very thought had occurred to the same suppliers and, it seems, they were making arrangements to get food supplies out to all the cut-off villages in Kintyre. We plodded off home with our heavy bags of groceries, planning to go down to the village again in the afternoon. These were the days before mobile phones, so we could only get news via the shop, which it turned out, was in touch with the Coastguards and their radio telephone.

So, that same afternoon, it was on again with the Wellington boots, the heavy oilskins and sou'wester, and another exhausting wallow over the higher ground then down to the shop where a cheerful Alf announced that a fishing boat would come on Friday to bring us food and mail, and that the lifeboat would also be coming on Friday to collect a young expectant mother from Glen Breackerie, and take her into Craigard Maternity Hospital in Campbeltown, just to be on the safe side.

We then plodded down to the shore to tell John Cameron the news though, in fact, he already knew. He and Archie were ready, of course, to take out any of our boats to act as tenders to the larger vessels which might find difficulty in coming alongside the slip at Dunaverty, especially at low tide, and have to sit at anchor out in the middle of the bay.

Friday brought the expected fishing boat, and lots of bread, meat and other necessities, so the shop was now fully restocked, and more people were managing to get in to it, all of them by tractor and trailer, or on foot. A procession of tractors brought the farmers who lived nearest the shore, with their full milk cans for the fishing boat to take into Campbeltown, but the inland farmers had the unpleasant task of having to pour good, fresh milk away down the drains because they couldn't reach the shore, even with tractors. We had a busy time getting the heavy cans off the trailers and rolling them along the almost lethally slippery jetty to the tender, then out to the fishing boat where they had to be hoisted aboard and carefully wedged upright in the well of the boat.

I saw Angus MacVicar walking rather too quickly, I felt, out along the jetty, and I called for him to wait for me and my torch before travelling any further. At that speed, with his casual attitude to his own safety, I felt that he was likely to disappear into the bay with a loud splash, especially as it was now the darkening. As an author he was very interested in all that was going on, and I imagined that no doubt he would incorporate all these snow adventures into his next book.

"Let the sailors get to their work," declared the cheery Angus, thinking I was making for the tender at the end of the slipway, and standing back to let me pass.

"No, no," I said, "I just want to make sure you can see where you're going."

To my surprise he added, "We'll try to have a drama practice tomorrow night, at the cafe, as usual, for everyone who can make it down to the village."

Trust Angus not to be fazed by a little thing like a blizzard!

It was getting dark on Friday afternoon when the brightly lit lifeboat appeared. We were glad to see that the expectant mother had managed to get out of her snow-blocked glen, and was making her careful way along the dunes towards the jetty, but surprised to see that her idea of suitable footwear under these circumstances was a pair of high-heeled court shoes! Somehow we got her safely along the slippery surface of the jetty, and into the tender, from which she was assisted a few minutes later, into the lifeboat.

We were also surprised to find that a passenger had come off the lifeboat on the tender's return journey, in the shape of a policeman from Campbeltown. We never did find out exactly why he had been sent --- maybe the powers-that-be thought that Southend might erupt into bread riots! At any rate he took up his quarters at Muneroy with Alf and Morag and had the time of his life for a week, enjoying the corporate life and an impromtu visit to the drama practice in the cosy cafe on Friday night.

"I never realised that Southend was such a great place," he enthused, having been made Assistant to the Assistant Stage Manager for the evening. He was really quite sad to leave when the week was up and he had to go back to his humdrum duties in the town.

While we were on our Saturday visit to the shop Morag informed us that the road to Campbeltown was now open --- but only to tractors! And still there was no telephone communication .

My father had the doubtful pleasure of preaching to a diminutive congregation in St Columba's Church in the village that Sunday morning, but at least the boiler was working so nobody was cold, and there was the additional bonus of a fairly short sermon as everyone was concerned with getting home safely before any more snow fell.

I was relieved that the next day was the official Spring Holiday from school, so it didn't matter that the bus didn't come down the now partially opened road from town. The next day, Tuesday, saw a welcome return to normality when the school bus, after a week's absence, reached Southend at last, and all the adults climbed on in cheerful mood, though the pupils weren't so pleased to be dragged away from their unofficial snow holiday.

It turned out that the Campbeltown teachers had managed to get into their various schools all during the snowy week, and were envious of those of us living outside the town who had been marooned at home.

Angus was anxious to make up for lost time at "the drama", and held rehearsals on that first week back, on Monday, Wednesday and Friday with a final rehearsal of our play, "Tullycairn", on the following Sunday, at 8pm. The reason for all these extra practices was the opening of the annual Scottish Community Drama Association's Festival of one-act plays in the old Rex Picture House in Campbeltown, which doubled as a theatre at this time of year. We were informed that some of the plays were to be filmed by the BBC that year.

As Angus had close links with the BBC, and had been a presenter of Songs of Praise, he had arranged for their Outside Broadcasting Unit to come on to Southend after the Campbeltown broadcast.

The cameras duly appeared first at the shore and John Cameron, the local salmon fisherman, was interviewed at "the hut", the old fishermen's stone cottage where we stored all the fishing gear. He declared himself to have been utterly tongue-tied during the interview, but as he was an unassuming, handsome big man, we knew that he would be bound to appear as a strong, silent hero in the film.

Next to be filmed was "the drama", and we discovered the hard way just how patient actors have to be when a particular scene has to be filmed over and over again before the director is satisfied with the end result.

My part in the play required me to drink a cup of tea at the very front of the stage while the action went on around me. The proximity of the cameras made me very nervous and I couldn't control my shaking hands. The cup began to rattle in its saucer and when I tried to drink the tea it clattered against my teeth. I had to hold the cup and saucer firmly in both hands in order to avoid dropping them and, to make things worse, the audience in the two rows nearest the stage found my predicament extremely amusing and started to laugh. As this scene had to be repeated several times before the director was satisfied I was utterly mortified and threatened to never again take part in any of Angus's ambitious schemes with the BBC.

My parents were not let off either, and they had to endure the attentions of the film crew inside the manse itself. My father, in particular, took acute stage fright and kept forgetting the instructions patiently repeated to him as he stood on the elegant staircase of the house, which was the best place for acoustics, according to the Sound man. He kept on saying, "Hm, hm," when in indecisive mid-sentence and decided there and then that he was not coming back in the next incarnation as a film actor.

The crew then decided to visit St Blaan's Church and film the choir at rehearsal in the Session House as well as during the main service that morning. The whole place was in a flutter and folk, who hadn't darkened a church door in their lifetime, suddenly appeared in church, determined to "be on the telly" --- singing noticeably loudly, with pious expressions on their faces. Fortunately the choir, which had some really good singers, and the organ, in the expert hands of Florrie, our regular organist, all behaved according to plan and gave a good account of themselves.

Angus later told us that the crew had been sorry to go back to Glasgow for they had never enjoyed so many impromptu ceilidhs (and so much single malt whisky), in their entire careers.

That spring would be long remembered in Southend for all the excitement of the violence of the elements, followed by the glamorous presence of the BBC in our midst.

The following week "the drama" gave several performances of "Tullycairn" in Campbeltown and Southend, followed, inevitably, by a lively ceilidh in the Argyll Arms, the village hotel. Then Dunaverty Players went into rest mode until the following autumn when the darkening nights attracted us to "the drama" for another season.

Meanwhile there were the boats to be prepared, and nets and gear to be checked before the salmon fishing season opened in May.

Campbeltown Sailing Club started its racing programme, and all the choirs were getting into gear for the various music festivals and local mods taking place all over Argyll and beyond.

I was delighted to crew for friends during some of the Sailing Club races in Campbeltown Loch and, on one occasion, was particularly pleased to be asked to help aboard a friend's beautiful ketch, currently anchored in the loch. I arrived at the club jetty and climbed into the minuscule dinghy which was to take me out to the ketch. We made unsteady progress towards the elegant boat and soon the oarsman threw our bow line up to be caught dexterously by the crew waiting on deck. I made ready to follow the rope, but a wave caught the cockleshell dinghy just as I was reaching for the yacht's handrail, and it veered away immediately from the boat's side.

"Splash!"

The inevitable happened --- my hands were clutching the yacht's rail but my feet were still in the dinghy, and I hung, suspended insecurely over the patch of sea between the two boats for a few seconds, before toppling noisily into the loch. A great deal of spluttering and gasping went on before I was hauled unceremoniously up into the ketch and it was decided that I should go home and dry off.

This meant, alas, that I would have to drive home saturated with sea water and dripping all over my car's interior so, having been landed back at the jetty, much to the amusement of the sailing club members, I collected my car keys at the clubhouse and slithered over to my car. It was at this point that I remembered that the car was too low on petrol to get me back home, so I'd have to face the ordeal of the filling station.

There was no way of avoiding the next embarrassing scene when I arrived at Neil Paterson's garage at the head of Longrow. This was where I always had my car serviced and repaired so the mechanics all knew me. I drew up at the pump and wound down the window to ask Alec for petrol. I saw the grin spreading over his face as he took in my bedraggled appearance while I mopped at the water still running out of my hair and down my face.

"Left standing out in the rain again all night, were we?" he chortled as he filled the car up. I then had to get out of the car to go to the office to pay, so the entire garage staff observed their usually tidily dressed customer splashing across the forecourt, clothes clapped wetly into sides, water spilling out of shoes, and hair plastered over forehead. Of course the wretches all came out to look at this vision, choking with laughter, uttering ribald comments and threatening to run home for a camera.

"Alright, so I fell in," I spluttered. This sent them off again in fits of laughter. I never lived this down, and had to endure endless digs whenever I went into the garage.

I suppose I should have been thankful that I went to Campbeltown by car that day, as I certainly wouldn't have enjoyed going home on the service bus and trying to explain to the driver exactly why I was dripping sea water all over his upholstery. But the drivers were men of exemplary understanding and kindness, and I suppose that a sodden passenger would have been accepted with their usual tolerance and unquestioning acceptance of the situation.

I remember my mother and I setting off at an ungodly hour one black February morning on a planned shopping trip to Glasgow. This was usually a six-hour journey --- as long as it takes to fly across the Atlantic to America. We were driving along the west coast road out of Kintyre when I felt the unmistakeable pull of the steering wheel that signified a punctured tyre. Groaning, I climbed out of the car and right away found the offending flat tyre. I certainly knew theoretically how to change a tyre as my father always insisted on my learning how to do this whenever we acquired a new car, but the thought of the muddy road, the icily cold tools, the heavy wheels, the lack of daylight, the strength required to jack up the car and remove the wheel nuts, etcetera, all filled me with horror.

There we were, alone on this empty, desolate stretch of coast road, on a freezingly cold, dark morning and miles from both home and our destination. I was distracted with anxiety. My mother was very concerned for my safety and was persuaded, only with difficulty, to remain in the relative shelter of the car.

"She kept calling out, "Are you alright?" and I didn't like to call back, "No, I'm not!" in case she tried to get out and "help" me.

The situation looked bad, but nevertheless I started out bravely to get the jack under the car in order to release the offending wheel. I was always worried about this stage of the operation, even in broad daylight, as I was afraid I wouldn't get the jack in the right position and the car might fall off it, with damaging results to both car and driver. There I was with scratched and frozen hands, mud all over my clothes and watery eyes nipping in the cold, northerly wind blasting into my face. Life could hold no further misery.

Then, unmistakably, I heard the welcome sound of a vehicle engine and, peering with streaming eyes into the mirk back the way we had come, saw the lights of a large vehicle approaching from the south. Soon I could make it out. It was the early bus on its way to Tarbert. Before long it had picked us up in its headlights and, to my incredible relief, drew up on the grassy verge just behind us. I could see the sleepy passengers staring out from the warm bus to see what was going on.

My mother and I were about to abandon the car and take the bus to Tarbert when out jumped the driver who immediately sized up the situation, uttered the magic words, "Right, stand aside, lassie", and proceeded swiftly and efficiently, to change the tyre, remove the jack, get us back to rights again and advise us to go no further as the road ahead was very slippery. Then he jumped back into the cab and drove off, his passengers dropping comfortably back to sleep again. Excitement over!

How could you ever hope to find such gallant courtesy nowadays, and all done so nonchalantly?

On another occasion we were aboard the bus from Tarbert to Campbeltown and had got well down the peninsula at a steady pace when Norman, the conductor, exclaimed, "There's something in the middle of the road!" and Duncan, the driver, slowly drew the bus up. Norman got out, walked a few yards forward of the bus, bent to pick up a round object which he then carried back aboard and showed to the passengers. It was a medium-sized tortoise. Exclamations all round!

Tortoise on the run

"Does anyone know whose tortoise this is?" questioned Duncan. No-one knew. Then Norman piped up, "I think it's wee Jimmy Black's tortoise. It must have got away!" as if the creature had made a swift bid for freedom down the main road.

"We'll just stop at the road-end and see if it's his right enough," announced Duncan, and so the bus trundled on for a short distance to the end of a lane leading to a small cottage. Norman and tortoise jumped out, went up the lane to the door, knocked and waited politely until the door was opened by a small boy whose tear-stained face lit up with joy as he saw the lost animal in Norman's hands. Ecstatic thanks were uttered and tortoise and boy were joyfully reunited before the door shut again, a smiling Norman climbed back aboard the bus and we proceeded on our uneventful way down the road to Campbeltown. Just another unremarkable daily happening in the life of the bus crew.

The West Coast buses still run on many of the routes in Kintyre, though MacBrayne's have disappeared, but alas, the characters have gone, though I think the drivers still throw the rolled up daily newspapers into the usually water-filled hole at the entrance to the Manse of St Blaan at Southend. The Glasgow Herald can be read only when it has been spread out above the Wellstood until it has dried out. Very little changes in some respects

But one noticeable change is the complete disappearance of the "travelling people's" camps around the Kintyre coastlands. We had our usual quota, and they were an integral part of the community. Among the local family were many characters. One in particular remains in my memory for he often travelled on the local bus from Campbeltown of an evening, after a day spent in the town. This patriarch was known as Dan Tuisleach, as, unfortunately, he was extremely unsteady on his feet.

One evening Tuisleach, seated near the back, hadn't rung the bell for warning the driver to stop, and took ages staggering down the central passage of the bus towards the door. He hadn't been noticed by the driver until he reached the front seat and was now well past his stop. He started to berate Paddy in his Gaelic-Scots patois for not stopping in time and an altercation was well on its way when Paddy impatiently threw on the brakes, stopped the bus and opened the door, but Tuisleach had not finished his strop and refused to get off. Paddy then decided that Tuisleach was not, after all, going to leave the bus and started up again, in decidedly frosty mood. But the door was not properly closed. Tuisleach lost his balance and fell headlong through the gap out on to the verge, but with his feet still on the moving bus.

Chaos ensued as the bus moved forward nearly dragging him with it. Passengers started up, rushing to the rescue while shouting to Paddy, who had turned quite pale, to stop immediately, and Tuisleach was hoisted by ankles and arms back on to the vehicle.

What the current "Health and Safety" would make of this is anybody's guess!

Fortunately, kind hands picked Tuisleach up, brushed him down after ascertaining that he was not injured, and sat him on the front seat, while equally concerned passengers calmed the extremely shaken driver and urged him to continue the journey.

Paddy then announced to all and sundry that he couldn't be expected to know when to stop the bus if folk didn't bother to ring the warning bell. This was like a red rag to a bull and Tuisleach started up again blisteringly in his native lingo which, fortunately, no one could understand. The situation was only resolved when the incandescent passenger got off the bus at the encampment on the shore and was last seen, waving his arms about, dancing with rage and shouting at the top of his voice as the bus drew away towards its destination at Keil gates. Paddy had to be revived with strong, sweet tea from the lady at the lodge.

It was never a dull moment on the Southend run!

But Tuisleach had regained his equanimity by the next day and appeared at the manse door where my mother found him just about to open it and walk in.

"What is it, Tuisleach?" she asked.

He put on his most ingratiating expression and mildly inquired, "Any auld claes o'the meenister's, Missus?"

Quick as a wink she replied, "Sorry Tuisleach, he's still wearing them, but just have a cup of tea anyway."

Tale no. 9: Of Duchesses and Dukes

"Make sure you keep a nice fly cemetery for the Captain," said Rose, the stewardess. "He always has a fly cemetery with his morning tea."

This particular delicacy was not some grisly eccentricity of the Captain's, but a well-known, pastry-covered currant confection much beloved by men, on the whole.

The pastry had to be thin, flaky and well baked while the fruit element had to be richly moist, almost juicy and flavoured with cinnamon or some other desirable spice.

My father would have walked a mile to have this cake daily with his morning tea, and our Captain on the turbine steamer, *Duchess of Montrose*, was of a like mind. The expressive name of "fly cemetery" was applied because of the look of the currants as they burst forth from the delicious pastry and in no way put addicts off complete enjoyment of the confection.

We were standing in the after-end of the ship where the cafe was situated, getting ready for the busy morning rush that would start when the ship got under way from her overnight berth at Gourock pier.

Today was Monday so we would be sailing back and forth, zig-zagging from pier to pier, all the way down the extensive Firth of Clyde, as far as Campbeltown in Kintyre, where we would stop for a while in order to let the cruise passengers go ashore and wander round the town. Then there would be the long sail back up the firth to our berth at Gourock.

We sailed this route on Mondays, Wednesdays and Fridays, with the shorter route through the Kyles of Bute to Inveraray on Tuesdays and Thursdays. The latter was a fairly short sail, so we got home early --- about 8pm, on these evenings.

Saturdays usually saw us on the long cruise right out into the Irish Sea, in order to circumnavigate the famous Ailsa Craig, a gigantic, rounded, rocky island where many seabirds roosted, and from whence came the heavy granite stones used in curling. This cruise was not much liked by the crew as we sometimes hit bad weather, even in summer, then the passengers got seasick, and we didn't go off duty till the ship tied up at about 11 at night.

If the sea had been rough during the cruise I found it very difficult to walk in a straight line up the street when I came ashore, and was still bracing myself against the imaginary rolling motion of the ship some hours later. I always feared that any observer would put it about that I had been seen disgracefully drunk and weaving about in the public street.

Other shorter cruises took place, if requested, to the nearby sea lochs of Loch Long and Gareloch, Ayr and the isle of Arran. They were much enjoyed, at least by the crew, as they were of fairly short duration and we came off duty at a reasonable hour of the night.

"Duchess of Montrose" off Arran

The *Duchess* was a beautiful turbine steamer and sister ship to the later *Duchess of Hamilton*, both extremely elegant vessels of around 800 gross tonnes and built for passenger work and cruising. The *Montrose* was built by Denny of Dumbarton for the Caledonian Steam Packet Company, and had a speed of over 20 knots on her trials. She was the first one-class vessel in their fleet with saloon-class passengers throughout --- no objectionable barrier between first class and steerage, as in other passenger ships of that era. It offered extensive accommodation in the form of a bar, a small kiosk, a cafe and a dining-room which could seat one hundred passengers at a sitting. In addition there was a comfortable observation saloon with basket chairs and big windows to allow the best possible view of the spectacular Clyde scenery.

Altogether this was a ship to be proud of, even if you were only a temporary student member of the crew, as I was, and passing the long university summer vacation by working on this prestigious vessel.

Several students were allowed to work in the cafe, but only one as Assistant Purser on the main deck, under the constant supervision of the Head Purser, while the dining-room staff were professional waiters and chefs, and the lady in the kiosk worked on the ship all season round.

The rest of the permanent crew were, naturally, the Captain and deck officers, the Chief Engineer and his gang, the Head Steward and his catering staff, and the deck hands, most of them men from the Western Isles, so there was a great deal of Gaelic spoken on the ship.

The ship's company was a little world in miniature, with a decided pecking order. We in the cafe were most definitely at the bottom of the heap, and got all the dirty jobs to do, like cleaning the toilets at the end of the day, scrubbing some of the internal decks, emptying the slop buckets and even scrubbing the ceiling of the cafe which was, of course, the floor of the deck above.

Cleanliness was noticeably close to Godliness in that ship!

The king of the whole show was, of course, our Captain, whose every word was law, and who had to be appeased by the regular arrival of his cup of tea and fly cemetery on the bridge at exactly the same time every morning. Rose, as senior stewardess, had the privilege of entering the holy of holies, the bridge, bearing the fragrant offerings, while the rest of us saw the Captain only when he made his regular inspection of the ship each week, trailed by a tail of lesser mortals like the Chief Officer, the Head Steward and sometimes the Chief Engineer. We all stood in respectful silence while this majestic progress took place, and woe betide anyone who stood in the wrong place, or uttered a word at the wrong time.

I experienced the Captain's displeasure during my very first inspection, by not standing still as he approached. He said nothing, just glared at me for some time, leaving me practically gibbering with fright, then swooped past, frowning in annoyance, followed by the underlings. I was hissed at by various members of the crew, and told never, on any account, to invoke the Captain's displeasure again.

I found it difficult to accept the rigid hierarchy of the ship's pecking order, especially when I discovered, during lifeboat drill, that the crew member, who would be in charge of my lifeboat, was a particularly fat and oafish cook, who didn't know one end of a boat from the other. He got the job simply because he was on the permanent staff of the ship. I decided that if the *Duchess* sank and we had to take to the lifeboats, I was going to take charge of our lifeboat, not him.

During lifeboat drill it was scarcely reassuring to be told, on having struggled into an ancient cork lifejacket, that I should never --- even if the ship was sinking --- jump into the water wearing this offending article, as it would undoubtedly bounce up under my chin on impact with the sea, and break my neck!

"You throw the lifejacket into the water first, then you jump in, grab it, and hang on like mad. You never actually wear it!" advised Rose.

"Health and Safety", where were you?

But such was our confidence in our Captain and crew that the thought of taking to the lifeboats remained as a fantasy theory in our minds, and we sailed in all weathers without undue worry --- until that unforgettable Saturday when we set out on our usual Ailsa Craig cruise.

The *Duchess* set out from Gourock as usual, well filled with enthusiasts on our long cruise, though the shipping forecast had warned us to expect dull skies and a fairly choppy sea. However, they were not deterred by the prospect of a few waves, and the cafe soon filled up with the sausage roll and cup of tea brigade.

The photographers among them snapped away happily as we wended our way among the channels and islands of the firth, while the band of ex-servicemen, ensconced in their corner on the main deck, played popular songs and more or less whatever the passengers requested, while regularly dodging behind the funnels in an effort to keep out of the snell wind blowing down their necks.

It was when we had passed the Heads of Ayr, and were well down into the open firth, approaching the vast expanse of the Irish Sea, that the sea became noticeably rougher, the wind got up, and even the most enthusiastic passengers took to below decks and huddled in the saloon and cafe. Things were really serious when the lady in the kiosk on the main deck shut up shop and came down to us for a comforting warm-up and a cup of hot coffee.

As always, we were not worried about the safety of the ship, and tried to console those persons who began to look a bit green about the gills, and wished they had not consumed so many sticky buns, sausage rolls, cream cookies, etcetera. Before long there was a steady progression of unhappy souls making for the toilets, or the sides of the ship, and we, lowest of the low among the crew, sighed as we thought of the cleaning up we would have to do when the ship had returned to her berth at Gourock that evening.

We kept reassuring folk that the ship was in no danger as the Captain, completely undeterred by wind and weather, had accepted his tea and fly cemetery with his usual equanimity, and had happily consumed them, as far as we knew. All must be well with the world.

By now the *Duchess* was in the area where the North Channel meets the Irish Sea and the Firth of Clyde. This was where the state of the sea frequently changed, unless in very calm conditions. Today we immediately felt the impact of larger waves and stronger gusts of wind as we approached the great bulk of Ailsa Craig, and many passengers looked longingly at the little town of Girvan, to be seen on our port side. Dry land now seemed infinitely desirable especially to our seasick customers.

Then, as we began to round the spectacular, rocky island, the ship staggered under the onslaught of some very high waves which slammed into her with the force of a monstrous sledge hammer.

Someone started screaming among the crowd in our cafe and had to be reassured, with difficulty, by Rose.

"I hope we don't get any more of this screaming," she said. "You know how quickly panic spreads among scared passengers."

We soon found out that one of the saloon windows had been cracked and that the crew had had to guide the frightened folk out of the saloon altogether, and herd them into other parts of the ship, including the cafe, which was now bursting at the seams.

By this time we ourselves were beginning to feel a bit apprehensive as the ship rolled and pitched violently while rounding the island at the beginning of the return journey. Being on a ship in a rough sea really does sort out the men from the boys, and we had a job to keep calm in front of our frightened customers and not show our own growing fear.

A small child shouted, "Mummy I want to get off!" which caused a few timid smiles and lightened the mood a little, and a kindly deckhand came and chatted to the little one in an attempt to distract his attention from the big waves, and calm his fears.

As we finally turned back into the entrance to the firth the sea gradually quietened and the *Duchess* resumed her serene progress, but the excitement remained among the passengers and they chattered away like budgies about how they, personally, had not been the slightest bit frightened, while everyone around them had been terrified!--- a natural reaction during the gradual release of tension.

We all relaxed as the ship made her stately way up the firth, and by the time Gourock was in sight everyone had more or less calmed down.

As they clambered up the gangways on to the comforting bulk of the pier there were many complimentary comments about the skill of the Captain and the engineers, the kindness of the crew, how strongly the shipyard had built the ship and so on, and we listened wryly as we in the cafe gang got down to work in the shambles of the toilets, the passageways and so on, until the ship had been restored to the state of cleanliness and hygiene demanded by our Head Steward.

At last we were released and staggered off homewards, hoping that the next Ailsa Craig cruise would be calmer than this one.

The next morning one of our number was sent to a store-room down low in the ship's hull to fetch some necessary supplies. We heard him yell as, almost immediately, he pelted back up to our deck, shouting at the top of his voice, "The ship's full of water!" causing an almighty commotion from stem to stern. The *Duchess*'s alarm sounded and we all made for our emergency stations, but instead of taking to the lifeboats, we were directed to leave by the gangways and wait on the pier for further instructions.

So the scenario which we had fondly imagined could never possibly happen did actually happen, but fortunately not while we were at sea. I still shudder to think what might have been the outcome.

It turned out that the slamming of the big waves into the hull had sprung one of her plates and, unknown to us all, she must have been taking on water all the long way from Ailsa Craig to Gourock, and even more water as she lay at her berth overnight, ever so gradually sinking against the side of the pier.

We were temporarily transferred to the *Duchess of Hamilton* which was tied up at the Broomielaw in the upper Clyde, while our poor ship was towed up to Greenock dry dock, pumped out and repairs made to her battered hull.

Not many such exciting events had occurred on the *Duchess* over the years, though she had had a lucky escape many years before while sailing through the upper firth in a thick fog. She ran aground at Kirn, but very gently, so much so that the passengers were completely unaware of what had happened. Three steamers were summoned to the rescue --- the *King Edward*, the *Duchess of Hamilton* and the paddle steamer *Marchioness of Lorne*, but even their combined efforts could not pull her clear, and she had to wait for tugs. Happily, no one was hurt, or even very concerned, except, presumably, the one who was paying the bill!

It was while we were tied up at Inveraray, on Loch Fyne, that I sometimes met my friend, the late Honourable Mrs Marguerite Weir of Dunderave Castle, a spirited redhead with a great sense of humour.

She usually came down the loch by motorboat, from her historic home, and tied up at Inveraray pier near the *Duchess* in order to do her weekly grocery shop. She explained that she hated coming by car as the tourist traffic clogged up the road, particularly through the summer months, and there had been many accidents on a particularly bad bend at Strone, just to the north of Inveraray.

The Castle of Dunderave was open to the public during the tourist months and Marguerite spent many long, tiring hours showing people round the ancient building --- the seat of Clan MacNaughton. Naturally they were fascinated by its turbulent history and she was happy to present it to them, but on one occasion she was extremely irritated by a large, loud American woman who had stuck to her like glue all afternoon and plagued her with endless, often idiotic questions.

"What do you think?" she said. "I spent an age telling the visitors what all the inscriptions in Gaelic and Latin on the castle walls actually meant, but this silly American stood below the family crest above the main door --- which I had just already translated to everyone, including herself --- and asked all over again, "Say,

Ma'am, what did you say that interestin'- lookin' inscription up there meant?"

"Well, my feet were sore, my throat was sore replying to all the endless questions and my back was sore climbing up and down the spiral stone stairs, so to finally shut her up I'm afraid I translated our family motto to her as, *Do not spit upon the floor*, and that finally got through to her, She retreated, muttering, and fortunately the bus arrived to take them all away to plague somebody else."

It was an acknowledged fact that Marguerite had been known, on occasion, to run away and hide in the castle garden when she saw unknown visitors approaching up the drive towards her front door.

There was, of course, a down side to all this open-day activity. All sorts of strangers could legitimately wander around the castle, taking in the layout of rooms, corridors and staircases. In particular, there was a secret stair, leading from the ground floor to the Great Hall which no one, apart from herself and the caretakers, James and Mary MacDonald, was supposed to know about.

Marguerite, as a young widow, had no one continually with her in the castle, apart from James and Mary, who obviously had to have days off and regular holidays.

Often she would be alone at night in the big, rambling building with only her two Alsatians for company and security. The trouble was that the dogs were possibly the most timid of their breed in the entire country, and certainly didn't live up to the usual image of the fearsome Alsatian guard dog.

One dark night when she was alone in the castle, Marguerite heard footsteps on the supposedly secret stair. She knew that James and Mary were in Inveraray at a film show, and became very frightened indeed. Calling the two dogs to her side she waited, breathless and almost fainting with terror, as two men, completely unknown to her, burst open the secret staircase door and crashed into the Great Hall.

It was obvious that they were up to no good and she shakily took the initiative by shouting, "You'd better get out of here right now, or I'll set the dogs on you!"

They paid no attention and moved forward threateningly across the hall.

Marguerite grabbed the dogs by their collars and shouted again, "I'm going to set the dogs on you!" while hanging on like grim death to her canine companions who were barking with excitement and struggling to get away from her. She knew very well that they were trying to make a dash for safety under the huge table that sat in the middle of the hall, and were not at all concerned about protecting their terrified mistress.

Fortunately, as she struggled to hold them back from ignominious escape, the two men, looking at the wide open jaws containing very large, sharp teeth, apparently thought the dogs were about to attack them, and yelled, "Stop yer dogs, missus. We're out o' here!" and dashed back into the darkness of the stairway, from where Marguerite could hear the rapidly diminishing sounds of their footsteps down to the ground floor then out into the castle grounds.

Mary and James, returning only a few minutes later, were shocked to find their collapsed employer sitting on the floor of the hall, crying into the shaggy necks of her two big dogs while they sat there, panting happily and wagging their tails as if they had bravely chased off the intruders.

"Yes, I know what you're going to say, James," sobbed Marguerite. "They are pretty useless at guarding me or the castle, but I love them all the same. If they hadn't been here tonight I might have been murdered in my own home."

Fortunately she soon got over her appalling fright. The Inveraray police came, looked over the whole place and made many useful suggestions regarding the security of the building and its inhabitants, human and canine.

Blessedly, Marguerite's mischievous nature was unquenchable, and James and Mary never knew what she was about to do next.

She recounted to me, with glee how, one summer evening she had been generally tidying up in the castle garden and heard a car draw up on the main road. Shortly afterwards she saw some people peering over the wall at her. It was Ian Argyll (the Duke), with a party of friends who were staying with him and the Duchess at Inveraray Castle.

The Duke called out, "Hello, Marguerite, any chance of a bite to eat?"

"Of course," she said. "Come on in. I think I might find a crust somewhere."

And the party trooped into the Great Hall of the castle where the imposing dining-table sat amidst the painted splendour of the spacious apartment.

Marguerite had, in the meantime, made a quick sortie to the kitchen and had a word with Mary MacDonald, who doubled as cook when necessary.

The guests, although already impressed with the magical beauty of Inveraray castle, were suitably charmed with this smaller version, and said all the right things to its chatelaine, who gave them an extensive guided tour before announcing that dinner was ready and getting everyone comfortably seated.

She herself, poised graciously at the head of the table, gave them the full treatment --- beautiful silverware and crystal adorned the white covered board; crisp white table napkins lay beside each place; there were flowers everywhere; anticipation was in every heart, no doubt. All that was needed was the actual food.

She rang the small handbell on the table beside her, and the door opened. In stepped James in dignified mode. He had been temporarily pressed into service as butler, and carefully carried an enormous silver platter with a domed cover. He paced solemnly round the table to where the hostess sat and ceremoniously set down the platter in front of her, bowing as he withdrew.

She chatted amiably to her guests while reaching for the handle on top of the cover. She slowly picked up the carving knife. Anticipation was on every happy face as Marguerite lifted the cover to reveal to each incredulous gaze --- a long, dried up, crumbly crust of bread!

She then started to count aloud the guests at table and carefully carved the crust into the relevant number of small pieces. As the plates were handed round to each stupefied guest the hostess chatted politely all the while, an absolutely deadpan expression on her face.

The Duke had cottoned on by this time, and played along nicely with his friend's little game. He poured wine into everyone's glasses, seemingly unaware of the stunned silence all around him, and blandly described the state of the salmon fishing on the River Aray that season.

He and Marguerite soon found themselves the only people uttering a word around the table as the distracted guests looked at each other in dismay, wondering whether to pick up their cutlery and start on their minute piece of crust or just drink the wine and pretend nothing had happened.

This state of affairs lasted for several long minutes more, and then the hostess and the Duke, unable to remain straight-faced any longer, bust out laughing until the tears ran down their faces.

Relieved that they had not entered a madhouse, the guests joined in and thankfully handed back their unappetising first course.

A few minutes later a delightful dinner of roast venison, followed by the castle's own raspberries and cream, was produced from the kitchen and brought in by a decidedly twinkling James.

It was a mystery to me how that couple managed to keep their cool while in Marguerite's employ.

The Duke and Duchess, fortunately people with a similar sense of humour, remained her friends for many years.

"You know," said Marguerite to me one day, "You'd really like Ian Argyll."

In fact she was a frequent visitor to Inveraray Castle and its grounds and was often invited to fish on the Duke's beat of the River Aray beside the castle.

On one occasion she had been invited to try for a salmon on a particularly good stretch of the river, along with some other guests of the Duke's, including a renowned army colonel.

Having been allocated her solitary place, just out of sight round a bend in the river from the colonel, she settled down to try her luck for a fish, but spent several fruitless hours in the quest. Disheartened, she considered giving up and leaving the river when, oh joy, she got into a salmon at last!

It soon became apparent that the fish on the end of her line was no small fry, but a big, powerful creature which wasn't going to give itself up without a fight to the finish.

So began a marathon, as Marguerite was absolutely determined not to leave the river without the magnificent trophy she had been seeking all afternoon, and set about the monumental task of landing her formidable quarry. This was more easily said than done as the salmon fiercely resisted all attempts to be drawn in and netted.

Marguerite and the salmon fought each other for over an hour and both parties were becoming fatigued when alas, the poor lady lost her footing on the slippery riverbed and fell headlong into the water, her waders filling immediately and hampering every movement. However, she still kept a vice-like grip on her rod and line, with the desperate and angry fish on the end of it.

What to do?

She was anchored to the riverbed by her waterlogged waders and couldn't get up on her feet again without letting go of the rod, which was unthinkable.

It was impasse.

There was only one solution.

With difficulty she gathered her encumbered feet under her and, getting her waders firmly planked on the pebbles of the riverbed, she swiftly dropped rod and line, hurled herself bodily on to the slippery, threshing fish, and grabbed it round the middle. Both parties now became totally submerged in the River Aray.

A titanic battle then ensued with Marguerite and the salmon locked together in a deadly embrace. All the while the fish threatened to escape as she struggled to keep her grasp on its streamlined body.

Help was urgently required.

Marguerite raised her voice to shout for the colonel, but found this a difficult feat while she and the salmon hurtled back and forth across the river, more often under the water than above it. All that came out of her mouth was a watery splutter. She hastily spat out a mouthful of the River Aray, and tried again.

The result was a bubbling squeak rather than a shout, but had the desired effect.The gallant colonel came galloping to the rescue, took one comprehensive look at the battle taking place in the river before him, was informed, with difficulty, by the lady, that she would not be separated from her catch at any price, and dashed off to find a ghille.

He quickly returned with a very perturbed ghille in tow.

Marguerite, still embattled with her fish, breathlessly reminded them that she wasn't going to let go of her prize after all she had been through, and would they please get her out of the river without making her drop the salmon.

After a swift consultation the men decided that she couldn't be lifted out by the arms so, plunging knee deep into the water, one on each side of her, they grabbed her by the shoulders of her jacket and began to hoist the protagonists bodily from the scene of battle.

The Duke and Duchess, coming to see what had happened to their long lost guest, were astounded to find a party of four, including the salmon, emerging from the Aray in soaked disarray, with an ecstatically smiling Marguerite in the midst of it all, squelching along with a trail of river water spilling from her waders and drenched clothes, and a halo of waterweed plastered over her face, but still happily clutching her salmon.

The ghille was not amused and was later overheard to comment disapprovingly, "Whit a way tae catch a salmon!"

Tale no. 10: Tales of the Unexpected

Christopher slid gently and in slow motion, down the grazing pony's neck and landed on his back on the grass, where he lay, unmoving and speechless, with wide open eyes full of complete bewilderment.

As he was only five years old his mother, Mr Mitchell and I all jumped off our horses in alarm and made a run for the small body lying so still on the ground. We had taken my colleague, Bill's three sons for our usual horse trek along the gorgeous golden sands and through the extensive pine forests of Rhunahaorine in north Kintyre, and the boys were so used to the quiet horses that we were completely caught out by Christopher's mishap.

Christopher on *"Trigger"*

Fortunately he was unhurt and simply bemused by the unexpected happening, so we picked him up, dusted him down and, after we had questioned him about whether he wanted to go on with the trek or not, he decided that he would like to get back on to his pony after all and go on through the forest.

Mr Mitchell, owner of the trekking horses, was more upset by the incident than Christopher, and kept apologising to us, though indeed the pony had done nothing more than snatch a few mouthfuls of grass during a short rest in the forest, and naturally put its head down to get the juicy morsels, thus providing an unexpected slide for a little boy to fall down.

"The Bevs" at Point House

We often went to the Point stables after collecting the boys from school. The two older boys were accomplished riders and, when Mr Mitchell wasn't looking, loved to pretend they were in the Wild West. Malcolm, usually on the brown mare Wendy, would stand up in the stirrups, waving us forward and shouting,"Yo-o", in the fashion of a captain of the United States Cavalry leading the charge against a band of Apaches.This, strangely enough, did not upset the horse and she usually obediently started cantering along the narrow forest paths with Malcolm still leading the cavalry charge.

Kathleen on *"Jean"* at Rhunahaorine

Naturally Mr Mitchell frowned upon such liberties as, on one occasion, Jean, my big half-Clydesdale mare, had been spooked into a full, and wholly unexpected gallop, which I was totally unable to control, no matter how much I leaned back, hauling on the reins and shouting, "Whoa, Jean!"

We were hurtling towards a high stone wall in the distance and I thought my last hour had come. No way would Jean stop or even slow down, and I doubted if I could even turn her. I was sure she was going to attempt to jump the wall in her panic, and for a minute contemplated throwing myself off. Better she should jump without my weight on her back, I thought, though I doubted if it would be better for me to fall off a horse at full gallop!

Before either of us was put to the test she herself decided to stop --- maybe the sight of the high wall in front of her was enough to make her pull up, blowing hard through her nostrils and tossing her head, and both she and I shakily joined the others where poor Mr Mitchell was berating the mischievous Malcolm for potentially causing an accident.

He was very subdued for a while, but it didn't last and he and his brother Johnny, were soon at their tricks again. Johnny's favourite was to get Malcolm to throw him up into the saddle, always when there was an audience around, then overshoot and slide down the other side of the horse, much to the consternation of the onlookers who inevitably rushed forward to the rescue. This made the horse swing around, whinnying, while the wicked Johnny popped up, grinning over its back at the alarmed spectators.

Riding along the sands at the Point on a sunny day was one of the unforgettable experiences of Kintyre. The horses looked like animals in a fairy story while splashing through the waves, manes and tails flying. The islands of Gigha, Jura and Islay lying offshore, their outlines frequently softened by faint sea mist and blue distance, blended into an enchanted seascape, as Keats's poem says, *of faery lands forlorn*. The colours of indigo sea and golden sands were enhanced by the lush greenness of the grassy fields and the brilliance of clumps of pink thrift growing along the verges of the shore and in crevices in the rocks.

As for the well tended cattle and sheep grazing contentedly in the fields ---

What a blessedly beautiful land!

No wonder Magnus Bareleg, the eleventh century king of Norway, cast acquisitive eyes over this land --- *the best island in the Hebrides, excepting Man* --- he is reported to have said. (Kintyre was classed as an island until the beginning of the 17th century).

Argyll was always a place where unexpected things might happen, and still is.

I remember driving down Loch Fyneside towards Tarbert one hot summer day. I was tired, thirsty and had driven many miles since morning, so decided to stop at the next car park and look for a cafe where I could get a cup of tea and something to eat.

Ardrishaig was the next village large enough to have a fairly capacious shore car park and I happily approached the entrance but found considerable difficulty in driving in.

The reason was not barriers or cars or even people, but horses --- about fifteen of them --- hitched on to the seaside railings. I have never before or since been unable to get into a car park because it was half full of horses. Apparently, on this hot day, the considerably sized trekking group had decided to look for a quiet, safe, off-road space in order to have their lunch, and rest and water their horses in the noonday heat.

Ardrishaig car park filled the bill nicely, so in they trooped. The fact that horses are not cars didn't seem to bother them at all. In fact they considerately moved all the horses up to one end and made room for me and other motorists to get our cars into the empty spaces.

Trekking ponies in Ardrishaig car park

As might be expected, most of the car owners were completely intrigued and soon got into conversation with the riders, while patting the beautiful animals so patiently standing at the railings. After some time the place was buzzing with car drivers, horses, riders and happy chat, and I thought that, if it wouldn't have disturbed the horses, a really good ceilidh could easily have been started up in that car park!

After all, this was Argyll --- the land where anything might happen.

Ardrishaig was the place where the annual Ardrishaig Drama Festival was held every spring --- in the tiny village hall which was always beautifully decorated for the occasion, with the daffodils which grew in such profusion all round the village. The local ladies' committee, which one finds in every small community had, over the years, made a feature of the daffodil decorations, so the entire hall was filled with the blooms and fragrance of these prolific flowers and its unimpressive interior was transformed into a magical, golden grotto for the festival.

This was one of the main events of the entire social season in Ardrishaig, as the Duke and Duchess of Argyll came south from their castle to preside over the competition.

On most occasions a very self-important little festival official bustled about in the centre of the group clustered around the couple, chivvying a certain chosen few to be presented to the ducal pair, while he bowed obsequiously.

"Your Grace, may I present so and so," he would flutter, and the person being presented either looked gratified at the perceived honour, or else rather surprised and perhaps somewhat embarrassed by all this medieval-style adulation.

One evening Dunaverty Players, our local Southend drama club, were becoming impatient at being kept penned up backstage during the interminable presentation and wanted to get on with the main business of the evening, the plays. We were raring to go but were then held back by our producer, local Kintyre author Angus MacVicar.

He was about to warn us about the hall's tiny stage which was quite noticeably raked towards the front.

"Whatever you do, don't run or even walk fast towards the front of the stage," he said, "or you'll land, not even in the front stalls on the Duke's lap, but you'll fly right over his head into the second row of the stalls." And it was true --- the stage sloped so decidedly towards the audience that it almost caused a major incident for the actors in the next play who hadn't been warned about this hazard.

Another snag was the fact that there was no room in the hall for the players to change in, so we all had to get dressed and made up in the church hall across the road, then sally forth, in whatever costumes we were wearing, to the edge of the pavement where we waited for a gap in the traffic, braving wind, weather and the comments of the populace, then make a discreet rush across to the hall. Obviously this caused a minor sensation among motorists driving through the village who must have thought they had entered a time warp and had slipped back to ancient times, Brigadoon-style.

The last time Dunaverty Players were at the festival the current Duchess, Mathilda, caused a sensation by appearing on stage at the end in order to make a speech and present prizes, dressed in a beautiful Paris gown of Campbell tartan silk. All the ladies in the place were agog as it was then virtually impossible to buy silk tartan at an affordable price, never mind having it styled by a French couturier. Nowadays silk tartan is fairly easily sourced, but still very expensive.

Some years later Dunaverty Players were intrigued to hear the story of another group of players --- the BBC cast of the film *Doom Castle*, based on the gripping story by the famous Inveraray writer, Neil Munro (who also wrote the *Para Handy* series under the pseudonym of Hugh Fowlis).

The story is set in clan times at Dunderave Castle, the stronghold of the MacNaughton clan, to the north of Inveraray on Loch Fyne.

The cast had put in a morning's hard graft in wet, cold weather out on the castle green, and were thankfully swept up, just as they were, at lunchtime and taken by minibus to the George Hotel in Main Street, Inveraray, a historic 18th century hotel, built in 1776 and much frequented by foreign visitors who loved the quaint atmosphere of the place.

The actors, all Gaelic speakers, were deposited at the front door of the building and, shivering with cold, hurried, still dressed in the costume of poor, barefoot clansfolk, into the front room where a good fire had been lit. They milled around trying to get their circulation going again and chatting away in Gaelic when a wandering American tourist accidentally entered their sanctuary, took one astounded glance at the unusual scene and rushed away to find his tour friends in the bar.

"Gee, they sure are behind the times in these parts," he was heard to utter in goggle-eyed astonishment.

"They ain't got no shoes, their clothes are as ragged as our folks during the Civil War, and they are all talking Gaylic."

He gasped out his news to anyone who crossed his path, fully convinced that he had just witnessed a scene of dreadful deprivation in modern Scotland.

The cast, now warmed up and very hungry, wandered through the hotel to the dining-room where a welcome lunch had been set for them, oblivious of the shock that their appearance was causing among the hotel guests. No doubt the latter would rejoin their tour group and return to the US appalled by the insensitivity of a government which would allow some of its Scottish citizens to suffer such terrible destitution!

Like others who had witnessed the unusual presence of the film cast in the George Hotel that morning, I was amused by the effect it had had on the unsuspecting American visitors, but remembered that the historic little town of Inveraray had indeed been the scene of much poverty and real distress at times during its colourful history.

The famous and talented Neil Munro, himself a native of Inveraray, told a heart-rending tale concerning the tragedy which befell Jean, a poverty-stricken clanswoman and her small child when Rob, the man of the house, along with all other able-bodied Campbell clansmen, was ordered by the Duke of Argyll to take up arms and march northwards towards Inverness, where the Hanoverian forces of King George waited to do battle with the Jacobite army of Prince Charles Edward Stewart on the Moor of Culloden.

The feckless Rob had accepted twenty pounds and a borrowed sword from a kinsman who didn't want to fight and was willing to pay someone else to do his fighting for him --- a fairly common occurrence in those days. He announced that he would take this money with him and buy a few head of cattle to bring back from his adventures in the north as the Duke no longer allowed his folk to "lift", ie. steal, cattle from the clan lands through which they travelled.

The loyal Jean would have died rather than ask her husband for a little of the money when he was going off into the unknown to risk his life among strangers, and fight for King George. So Rob took all the money from the house and, leaving his wife and very fragile little daughter to fend for themselves for only a week, as he imagined, marched off with his fellow clansmen, promising to bring back a White Cockade, the badge of the Jacobite soldiers, for the little one.

Jean was in despair, for there was only a small amount of meal in the cupboard, and a small barrel of salt fish, and she was left without a penny to buy more provisions. The limited food stock was soon almost used up but Jean went out and about the town with stiff-necked Highland pride, pretending that her husband had left her well provided for. All she and her child had to eat was the dwindling supply of meal with shellfish gathered from the shore in the hours of darkness when none of the townsfolk could see her, and a little milk from Mallie, the cow, which was drying up for calving. She gathered wild leeks and nettles with which to make a thin broth, but this was not sustaining for the sick child.

She could have sought help from her cousin, a generous and rich merchant in Inveraray, but was too stupidly proud to do so, and her many friends would have happily shared what they had with her and the little girl who had become noticeably weaker over the bitterly cold winter.

The cold, bleak early spring days dragged slowly past, with no sign of the Campbell army returning.

Gradually the woman and her child began to starve as the cow had gone dry, there wasn't a fish to be had from the loch and the shellfish began to sicken them. The child dwindled away to skin and bone and sat listless by the fire all day long, until the awful day when she could no longer be roused by the sight of the birds hopping about outside the door, or the pretty seashells that her mother brought home for her.

As a last result Jean took a sharp knife and opened the tail vein of Mallie, the cow, to draw blood as starving Highlanders had done in days gone by. But this drastic action came too late. She was mixing this with the last of the meal to make a kind of blood pudding, when the little child gasped and collapsed, calling out for her mother. Jean rushed to catch her and held her fast as the poor little one breathed her last in her mother's arms.

Jean broke out into agonised tears just as the sound of bagpipes was heard out on the road leading into Inveraray.

At last the triumphant, long-awaited Campbell force came marching into town, hailed as heroes by Duke Archie himself, who invited them all to come up to the castle and enjoy a meal fit for warriors, after they had first been home to greet wives and families again. Among them marched Rob, full of pride in himself and his comrades.

He dropped out of the troop as it passed near his door, thinking to himself, "Some home-coming this, with neither wife nor child to welcome me!" and pushed open the door.

"Ho there, Jean," he shouted. "Here I am safely back with you again, with no money or cattle, but look, I've brought the White Cockade that I promised the wee one!"

I was still thinking about all these events as I finally left the horses in the car park and made my way south through Ardrishaig, over the swing bridge across the entrance to the Crinan Canal and down the long road towards Tarbert at the north end of the Kintyre peninsula.

Tarbert is situated around the head of East Loch Tarbert and exists mainly for fishing, sailing and tourism, and supplies the huge refrigerated container lorries from France and Spain which line up along the quays while being loaded with the products of the Scottish seas, mainly shellfish, crabs and lobsters.

On one occasion my friend Fiona had arrived off the MacBrayne's steamer at Tarbert pier which is round the corner from the village and a fair distance from the quays. She had arranged to meet her fiancé, Alan, who was going to take her over on his sailing yacht *Marianna*, from the quays to her destination on the island of Arran, so she set out to walk into Tarbert as fast as she could for she knew that he would want to get going while tide and wind were in his favour.

On arrival at the relevant quay Fiona was concerned to find container lorries blocking the path of a considerable number of local people waiting on the quay to catch the ferry across Loch Fyne. But, as the tide was fairly low this meant that they couldn't embark from the quay anyway so everyone was shepherded down a slippery flight of stone stairs on to a narrow wooden pontoon moored against the quay. Soon the pontoon was jammed with people, including Fiona, waiting patiently for the arrival of their transport, but standing, as the British do, in an orderly queue on the pontoon.

After a long wait, when everyone was beginning to grumble about the delay, Fiona, who was in the middle of the queue, was relieved to catch sight of Alan's boat, *Marianna*, obviously under engine power, rapidly approaching, and she prepared to climb aboard as soon as it tied up.

The onlookers on the pontoon watched disinterestedly as *Marianna* approached them at a rate of knots, and didn't appear to be slowing down in any way.

"Hello," shouted Fiona, waving enthusiastically, "I'm over here, Alan!"

Her loving fiancé, momentarily distracted by her sudden appearance, allowed the yacht to veer slightly off course. Instead of drawing carefully alongside, the boat, still under considerable engine power, came at the pontoon and hit it like an attacking shark. Down went the orderly queue, one after the other, like a set of dominoes, and for a while chaos ensued as the folk gradually picked themselves up and sorted themselves out, while Alan hastily hitched forward and aft lines around a couple of handy bollards.

"Get aboard, Fiona, and let's get out of here!" yelled Alan, in alarm. The situation threatened to become nasty.

Fiona immediately rushed over to the *Marianna* but was hampered by her heavy luggage which she couldn't manage to lift over into the boat, and floundered about between pontoon and gunwale until Alan, in a fever to get away from the restive natives, impatiently reached over, grabbed her bodily and dumped her aboard before turning away hastily to unhitch the stern rope.

"Hurry up, Fiona, and come and give me a hand with this line," he shouted. As there was no response he turned round, only to find his unhappy fiancé hanging helplessly by her jacket collar --- her feet at least ten inches clear of the deck --- from a cleat on the mast which had caught her on her rapid descent on to the *Marianna*'s deck.

"Fiona, stop messing about. Get down off the mast and let's get out of here, pronto!" yelled the unsympathetic Alan.

"I can't get down, you idiot," shouted back the irate Fiona. "It was you who put me here and I'm stuck on this cleat until you get me off it!"

By this time the onlookers were offering a great deal of colourful and unwanted advice and, to make the situation even more urgent, the ferry was approaching the pontoon. The situation was becoming critical. Desperate measures were called for, so Alan whipped out a knife and cut through the collar of her jacket which was holding her to the mast.

Fiona descended at last on to the deck with a resounding crash.

"This is the last time I go out in the boat with you," declared Fiona, picking herself up off the deck. "I'd rather go round to Skipness and get the ferry from there. At least I wouldn't be thrown about like a sack of potatoes."

"And this is gratitude!" growled her fiancé, but hurriedly steered the yacht safely out of the East Loch and into a rising swell from the south west into the more open waters of Loch Fyne. Fiona was sent forward to put up mainsail and jib, while Alan switched off the engine as the sails began to draw well and *Marianna* picked up speed, heeling over under a stiff breeze.

She sailed southwards, with Port Leathan, Ascog Bay, Kilbride Bay and Ardlamont Point on the port side and Inchmarnock Island showing in the distance just off the port bow. On the starboard side they sailed past Fionn Phort, Rudha Lagganroaig and Camus na Ceardaich.

At this point the wider firth of the Sound of Bute, leading into the more enclosed waters of Kilbrannan Sound, appeared on the yacht's bow, and soon Fiona was able to have a good look at the great stone bulk of Skipness ("Ship Point") Castle, originally a 13th century building of Norse origin. This lies at the north end of the Kintyre peninsula and was probably built by the Norseman Suibhne (Sween) the Red, progenitor of the Clan MacSween, or his son, Dougall.

Although the castle was large by the then current standards it was not as imposing as the main MacSween fortress of Castle Sween on Loch Sween. But the Norse tenure of Skipness was fairly short lived as, in 1263, after the long series of skirmishes which eventually became dignified by the name of the Battle of Largs, the Norwegian King Hakon was finally forced out of the Clyde and Hebridean waters and returned, fatally fatigued, to Orkney, where he died.

Marianna now changed tack and sailed diagonally across Kilbrannan Sound towards another Norse fortress, the Castle of Lochranza which sits on the open *oitir* or spit, in its strategically important position on the north-west coast of the island of Arran.

This was built as a hall-house probably by the already mentioned Dougall MacSween. So, between them, Skipness and Lochranza Castles controlled the waters of Kilbrannan Sound when Norse and Scot vied for control of Kintyre, the Clyde estuary and the entire western islands of Scotland.

By this time it was now a lovely, sun-drenched summer evening and the high mountains of Arran glowed yellow, orange and red in the soft light. The wind had died away, so *Marianna*'s sails were lowered and she entered the glassy waters of Loch Ranza under engine again, but this time, there was no pontoon to negotiate, no crowd of threatening, angry onlookers, just a couple of little boys plowtering about in the shallows near the pier. They were delighted to grab the line thrown to them by Alan, and importantly helped to ease the yacht into a berth in the quiet harbour, where a small amount of money changed hands, and ice-creams were enjoyed shortly afterwards.

By this time Fiona had decided that she had actually enjoyed the sail from Tarbert, and she and Alan had re-established peaceful relations again, although secretly she began to wonder if Alan couldn't be persuaded to sell his beloved yacht --- after they were married, of course!

When I belatedly arrived home in Southend Ronald was already in the house and full of another story, and a very recent one.

On the farm where he was temporarily working the farm lads had got up to mischief on the grand scale.

Farmhouse doors were rarely, if ever, locked at night, and the night before, when all was dark, the family had gone to bed as usual and were, presumably, sleeping the sleep of the just, before arising, refreshed and renewed, to their many accustomed tasks early the next morning.

At some hour during the darkness of the night the lads crept into the farmyard and carefully dismantled the large, wooden cart used for transporting feed out to the fields for grazing cows and sheep. They silently carried the various pieces through the back door of the farmhouse and re-assembled it, complete with wheels, in the kitchen then, to add the final touch, filled it to the brim with the turnips destined to become breakfast for the cattle. Thereupon they slipped quietly away to their own homes in the village.

The next morning in the farmhouse Mary, coming sleepily down to her kitchen, thought she must be in the middle of a nightmare and struggled to believe the evidence of her own eyes, only to find that the sight in front of her was no dream but the farm's very own cart, full of the farm's very own turnips, sitting in the midst of her very own kitchen.

What happened then can only be imagined --- yells of anguish from Mary, the rush of feet on the stairs as the rest of the family descended at high speed to see what on earth was going on, and a mixture of gasps of disbelief from the elders, spluttered threats of extreme violence from an incandescent Mary and hoots of unstifled glee from the younger members of the family.

By this time the farm lads, no longer so bold in the cold light of day, wondered what kind of reception they would get when Mary got hold of them, and slid apologetically into the kitchen the next morning to await their fate.

She threatened all kinds of horrible deaths if they didn't remove cart and turnips immediately from the house, clean up every speck of mud from her kitchen floor and take the cart and its contents out to the field for the cows before she would even begin to consider allowing them to live until the end of the day.

They jumped to obey, recognising the threatening voice of justifiable retribution, but as the story went round the district --- no doubt gaining in implausibility as it went --- the lads found themselves quite the heroes of the hour, and were feted among their friends for days and weeks to come.

It turned out that they got the idea from another of Neil Munro's *Para Handy* stories describing a similar incident in a wynd off Longrow in Campbeltown.

Nowadays I travel regularly across the breadth of Argyll and drive through the arches at Inveraray before going up the long length of lovely Glen Aray. When approaching the summit of the pass I always look up to the left at the high stone monument erected in memory of Neil Munro and, if I am alone in the car, I give a wave and a word of thanks to a man who has brought such pleasure to the Scots, and many other folk, with his wonderful short stories and so many thrilling, but historically accurate adventure novels.

Dear Neil, I salute you!

Tale no. 11: Dog and Boss Dog

Boss Dog's Tale:-

My dog and I had many adventures when out of the office in Inverness, especially when we went out to the islands. His name was Roddy Bàn Mòr --- Big, Fair Roddy, and he accompanied me around my extensive area while on education business.

I was the Primary Education Adviser for Inverness-shire, the largest of the Scottish counties, as it included the mainland county of Inverness, along with the Inner and Outer Hebrides, excepting the island of Lewis, which belonged to Ross-shire.

There were 134 schools on my patch and, when we went out to the islands, I had to stay out for two or three weeks at a time in order to justify the expensive car-ferry fare.

Birthday card for Roddy from loving friend

One early spring day we were making for North Uist, South Uist and Benbecula schools and had driven out to Kyle of Lochalsh where we were about to cross, as you did in these days, on the little ferry to

Kyleakin on Skye. The crew were always very nosy about who we were and where we were going, and we always had to go through a most polite, but thorough question and answer in order to satisfy their endless speculation about County officials.

I drove aboard and wound down the window to pay our fare. A big, brawny seaman leaned in, smiling at us, and obviously dying to know all about us. He patted Roddy's head by way of introduction.

"Aye," he said. "It's a fine day that's in it, and where would you be making for, then?"

"Oh, the north, and then the Lochmaddy ferry," I said, deliberately vaguely.

"Oh, aye," said the deckhand. "Would you be having a bit holiday then, seeing the weather's so good?"

"Well no, I'm working," I replied, determined not to make it too easy for him.

"Hm," he tried again. "You'll be from the School Dinners, then?"

Any female travelling alone to the islands outside the normal school holiday time was categorised as being "something to do with School Dinners". But by this time we were drawing into the ramp at Kyleakin.

"No, not exactly that," I said, playing the game to the end. "See you on the way back. Tiori." (Gaelic version of Cheerio) and drove the car off the ferry leaving a very frustrated deckhand staring after us.

"What a nosy parker," I said to the dog. He just wagged his tail.

We drove straight through Skye, without calling in, as we usually did, at all the schools between Kyleakin and Portree, up past the strange rock formations of the Old Man of Storr and the Kilt Rock to Staffin, Digg and Kilmuir, where generations of my family are buried near the grave of the famous Flora MacDonald in the ancient graveyard. On we went around the top of Skye then down to Uig where we were to get the North Uist ferry to Lochmaddy.

I let Roddy out of the car and we scrambled up on to the top deck where there seemed to be a lot of little girls running about. It turned out that they were a party of Brownies from Lochmaddy who had been on a spring jaunt to the big island of Skye, and were now returning home. Roddy liked children, and was always happy to be in among them. Immediately he went over to them, wagging his tail like mad, as Labradors always naturally do --- and an onlooker said,

"He really is a humorous dog, isn't he?

Not for nothing had a class of pupils once inquired of me, "Did Roddy teach the Andrex puppy how to unroll the toilet roll in the TV advert?"

Soon the children and the dog were playing around the deck and all I could see of him was his white tail waving continuously above a sea of Brownie uniforms. Eventually I had to rescue him from being loved to death by the children.

It was getting dark by the time the ferry reached Lochmaddy and it took ages to unload the cars by the old hoist and turntable method of these days.

We were last off, right behind an RAF jeep which was making for the rocket station on South Uist. It was now 11-30 at night.

Our destination was the Creagorry Hotel on Benbecula where we would be living during our three week stay on the islands. To get to our schools we had to go first through Lochmaddy village, drive south through the island of North Uist to the causeway leading to the middle island of Benbecula, and then over the big bridge to get to the southernmost islands of South Uist and Eriskay. The roads were A-classed but were still single-tracked at that time and there were hardly any signposts.

By the time we had left Lochmaddy behind there was only the northern twilight to show us our way. Soon we were out on the twisting little single-track roads with the gleam of sinister bogs and lochans on either side of us and the pale gleam of a new moon to light our way. It seemed as if we were the only living beings on the planet --- no houses, no cars and even the RAF jeep had disappeared. It was a bit sinister and I was getting worried as we didn't seem to be getting any closer to Creagorry. I was afraid Mrs MacAulay at the hotel would have given up on us long ago, and gone to bed after closing up the place for the night.

At last the headlights picked up a signpost ahead of us --- Sollas! To my horror I found that I had been driving north-west instead of south all this time, and was still miles from Creagorry. I drove on looking for a public phone to let Mrs MacAulay know where we were. Round a bend we went --- and nearly torpedoed the RAF jeep which had stopped in the middle of the road, and whose driver was out, holding his map in front of the headlights, trying to make out where he was. I think he was very glad to see us --- another pair of souls lost in this lunar landscape.

"'Ere," said a Cockney voice. "D'you know where we are? I don't know where we are. I ain't never been in this bloomin' place in all me loife. Ain't 'arf creepy, init? An 'ere's me supposed to deliver this 'ere jeep to the Rocket Station. Where is the bloomin' Rocket Station anyway? Noice dog you got there!"

Naturally, Roddy wagged his tail.

I managed to stem the flow of his rapid-fire talk by reassuring him that we were indeed driving south towards the middle island of Benbecula, from where he could get on to South Uist and the Rocket Station.

We decided to try to keep together on the road as the light from the two sets of headlights would be an advantage. However, the RAF corporal must have been expecting his own personal rocket for being so late, for he soon disappeared from sight, leaving us alone in our dark world.

By this time it was 1am, and I was relieved to find a phone box at last, from which to phone the hotel. As has already been mentioned the road was single-tracked and flanked on both sides by evil-looking black bogs. In order to get enough room to install the phone box a small platform had been built out into the bog for the box to sit on. Fortunately the door was missing so, in almost pitch darkness, I had to make a leap off the road, hoping like mad that I would land in the phone box and not in the bog. How I would have got inside if the door had still been there is anyone's guess. As expected, there was no light in the box, so I couldn't see the phone dial. Fortunately I had a box of matches in my handbag and managed to strike a match while struggling to find enough coins to make a call. Of course I scorched my hand when the match burned out, and dropped the coins on to the darkened floor.

Roddy jumped out of the open car door and tried to go to his distressed owner. Alas, for once in his life, he misjudged his jump. He didn't land in the box. He landed in the bog.

I had a nightmare vision of my beloved dog disappearing under the glutinous mud, and, in my fright, dropped handbag, matches and loose coins before leaping back to the safety of the road from where I hauled him, covered in thick, black, viscous slime, up beside me. He then shook himself violently to get rid of the mud and accidentally splattered me, from head to foot, in foul-smelling mud.

So I threw him into the clear water of a nearby burn, and shouted, "And don't come out of there until you're clean!"

This time he didn't wag his tail.

Back I jumped into the phone box and scrabbled about on the floor until I found bag, matches and coins, and started all over again.

Many minutes and many matches later I was delighted to hear the calm, kind voice of Mrs MacAulay at the hotel, saying not to worry about being so late, that we were nearly at Creagorry, and that no, she didn't mind in the least being kept up till the wee small hours awaiting her lost guest. Visitors coming off the last ferry always arrived in the middle of the night.

Soon I saw the welcoming lights of the hotel. In a few minutes we had squelched into the front porch, still dripping dirty water and peat mud, but Mrs MacAulay was not at all put out.

"Och, you should just see the state of some of my guests when they come in from the shooting. Oh, what a lovely dog! He'll be a Boxer."

I was surprised, but realised that Mrs MacAulay's contact with dogs was mainly confined to the collie variety, which are prevalent in the islands, and in any case she had been so kind that I couldn't think of contradicting her.

Roddy just wagged his tail.

The next morning I met the other guests, including a young banker from Dingwall who advised me to look slippy and get over to the local shop if I wanted a newspaper. I thanked him and took his advice.

In fact there were very few newspapers available as they were brought in only when the ferries arrived, and I was about to pay for mine when I noticed it was two days old. When I pointed this out to the shopkeeper he looked surprised and said,"Och, but this is only today!"

In the face of this undeniable fact I could only pay the man and retreat with the stale news.

Then it was on round the schools.

At the first school, Mrs Chisholm, the Sole Teacher, a charming lady about to retire, told me stories of when she was a girl, and how people learned to live off the land. Her father had taught her how to catch lobsters with her bare hands, from under a big rock at the edge of the sea, right at the bottom of her garden. The people of the place lived well off the seaware, as they called it, though it was looked upon as rather poor fare, compared with meat. How ironic that nowadays lobsters, oysters and other seafoods are regarded as luxuries.

As we drove into the playground at our next school I could hear the sound of singing and went inside to find eight little Hebridean faces and one little Pakistani face earnestly practising their song, Little Red Hen, in Gaelic, of course.

The little Pakistani boy was called Nasim. His family had recently arrived in the islands, his father being a packman --- common enough in the Hebrides in these days. Mrs MacDonald, the Sole Teacher, explained what was going on.

"We are taking part in the local Mòd," she explained, "Mairi is Little Red Hen, and Donald, Nasim and Sorley are her chickens."

The children then gave us a rousing rendition of their song, and I thought they were wonderful, especially Sorley, who sang with a wide grin and a slight whistle through the gap where his two front teeth should have been.

"Nasim has picked up Gaelic very well in the short time he has been here," said Mrs MacDonald proudly, "and his mother is hoping to learn English from him, though how this will happen I really don't know because, at present, he speaks only Pakistani and Gaelic."

I was kindly invited to stay for lunch and found myself sitting at the table next to Nasim. Lunch that day was pork sausages swimming in rich gravy, accompanied by mashed potatoes and carrots. The dinner lady dished up lovely savoury platefuls which made our mouths water as we said the Grace. At last it was time to start.

I watched as Nasim, happy anticipation on his little face, picked up his fork, speared a plump sausage, and was about to sink what remained of his front teeth into it, when, like a hawk, Mrs MacDonald swooped down on him, snatched the fragrant morsel from his eager hand, gasped, "Oh, my goodness, what will his mother say?" and swept the entire plate from his grasp.

Shortly afterwards the plate was returned to Nasim, minus the offending pork sausages, and a rather disappointed little boy had to content himself with mashed potatoes and carrots while everyone else was tucking into a savoury delight.

On the day before I had left the office in Ardross Street, Inverness, a memo had arrived on my desk, reminding me to increase the fodder allowance for three ponies at a South Uist school, so I was now on my way there to see what was what.

Previously, consultations had been made with the Depute Director of Education who dealt with such abstruse matters.

It appeared that the request had been made by incomers who were living on a remote croft far from the main road. The children could have quite easily come in by car, like the other pupils, but their parents felt that horses were more stable and reliable than any motor vehicle, on the rough moorland paths, and insisted that they travel, as did many long ago, on horseback.

Inverness-shire Education Department was obliged, like any other county, to pay the costs of travel to and from schools. The fact that the mode of travel was pony made no difference, and an allowance was made to cover the costs of feed and grazing on the croft beside the school during school hours. The children were amazingly good horsemen, especially as they rode without saddles.

Then over the bridge between Benbecula and South Uist we went and I told Roddy to be a good dog and not even think of playing with the ponies, and scattering them all over the countryside, as he had done during our last visit.

He just wagged his tail.

Soon we were in sight of the school and there, attached by halters to a stout hitching rail in the playground, were the three ponies, patiently waiting to be turned out into the neighbouring field which a considerate crofter had made available to them during school hours.

After school, while the other children clambered into warm, comfortable cars, the three young horsemen mounted up, homework in saddlebags, and took to the narrow tracks across the moors, no matter what the weather.

I wondered if these folk would still be as enthusiastic when their children arrived home, soaked and frozen, on a dark December night, during the frequent, long-lasting winter gales.

But perhaps the "pony express" was marginally less exciting than the journey by Landrover driven by one of the more eccentric parents.

The teacher said to me, "Watch what happens when Seumas's father drives out of the playground and up the road." So I watched in puzzlement as, every few yards, Seumas's dad appeared to bob up and down in the driving seat like a demented jack-in-the-box. The

Landrover's progress was marked by a series of spine-shaking jerks, accompanied by loud screeches from the engine.

"What on earth is going on?" I asked.

"Well," said the teacher,"you're not going to believe this, but he seems to think --- and no-one can convince him otherwise --- that he has to stand up every time he changes gear! You should see how many Landrovers he has gone through. The thing is, nobody in the islands will buy them after he has done with them, so they're all away to the mainland to be sold!"

The Dog's Tale:-

We had one other school to visit on South Uist and I was very annoyed when Boss Dog unexpectedly said that she would go in alone and I had to stay in the car.

"No, Roddy, you can't come into the school today," she said. "They are expecting a visit from the Clerk of Works. He will want to inspect the building and see that it is in a good state of repair before sending in his annual report on the state of the island schools, to the Education Office in Inverness, so just you stay here in the car. I'll put the window down so you can have plenty of fresh air, and then I'll take you for a nice, long walk afterwards.

I was not too pleased about this as I always liked going in to see the children, but I lay down, reluctantly, across the car seat while Boss Dog disappeared into the school. After an hour she had not come back and I was getting very restless. I sat up in my seat and stretched myself, then noticed that she had, as promised, opened the window a good way for me to get enough fresh air in the car.

I looked at the open space for a short while and then the great idea came to me --- I would see if I could squeeze through the gap and get out of that boring car. It took only a minute for me to get my front paws, followed by my body and hind legs, out through the window, and suddenly, there I was, out of the car and standing on the pathway up to the school.

This promised to be an interesting adventure so I wandered up the path and in at the big front door which was lying open in the gusty, spring sunshine. From the hallway I could hear the noise of talk coming from the classroom, so I turned to my left and went through another open doorway into what turned out to be the school dining-room. There was nobody there and the place was empty apart from a couple of tables and a few wooden chairs. It was a bit disappointing and I sniffed about for a while but got a bit of a shock when both of the doors suddenly slammed shut in a gust of wind. Now I was stuck in the dining-room and couldn't get out. I didn't dare start barking as Boss Dog would be annoyed with me for coming into the school at all.

I sat down and looked at the door and the window. No use. I couldn't see any way to get out. I would just have to wait until somebody found me. What a bore --- again!

This school visit was turning out to be a big disappointment.

I sat down, then lay down, then scratched my ear, then stood up and got very, very bored. To pass the time I thought I would just have a little chew at an interesting patch on the floor beside me. I quite enjoyed this so I kept on chewing until, unexpectedly, the floorboard gave way and I was staring down into the space under the floor. I thought I'd better not chew any more.

"Chew the floor no more!"

After a long time I heard the school bell ringing and the children running out through the front door. Surely it was now alright for me to give a bark or two and get Boss Dog to rescue me from this horrible room. So I started barking and at last the door opened and in came a surprised Boss Dog along with Miss Smith, the teacher.

"How on earth did you get in here, Roddy?" gasped Boss Dog, then she caught sight of the newly chewed hole in the wooden floor. She and the teacher looked at each other, then at me, then at the floor again, and both of them were quite speechless for a minute or two. Then they both came out of their trance and started to scold me in very loud, angry voices for damaging school property. I hung my head in shame and wondered if Boss Dog would now disown me and leave for the mainland without me.

Boss Dog Again:-

At that moment we heard a car drawing up at the school door.

"Good Heavens, it's the Clerk of Works," uttered Miss Smith faintly. "What on earth will I say to him?", and she hurried away to greet the visitor, a jovial big man, who spoke most affably to the two ladies before firstly going in to inspect the classroom.

The teacher and I looked at one another with something approaching panic. Then I hissed out of the side of my mouth, "I'll just have to come clean and admit that Roddy chewed the hole in the floor. All I can do is apologise and offer to pay for the damage."

"Yes, I think that's best," agreed the teacher.

The three of us stood in a row, apprehensively awaiting the arrival of the Clerk, and I gulped nervously as he came into the dining-room, looked around and then caught sight of the hole in the floor.

I took a deep breath and was just about to make a full confession, but the Clerk got in first, looked seriously at the floor, shook his head then said, decisively, "Ah, I see you've got rats, Miss Smith. Don't worry, I'll soon get rid of them!" and before I could utter a word off he swooped to inspect the outside of the building.

Both of us were shocked into relieved silence, then, like a couple of conspirators, we giggled a lot before deciding that, after all, we would just keep silent about the real culprit and let the mythical rats take the blame.

"And it'll serve you right, Roddy," I said as I quickly bundled him into the car, "if you're sick all night after chewing all that filthy wood.!"

Travelling on to visit the other twenty-four schools from North Uist to Barra, I ran the courses, distributed the books and equipment I had brought from Inverness, and happily renewed old acquaintanceship with the teachers and their families.

All too soon the three weeks passed and it was now time to return to the office so, on a Tuesday night, we set out on the long, tiring journey from Lochmaddy on the overnight ferry, over the stormy Minch, to Uig on Skye, arriving at 6am on the Wednesday. From there it was the long haul by road to arrive back at base by 9am.

Inverness County Council didn't believe in being soft with its employees so, although I had been travelling continually since 4pm on Tuesday I had to work all through Wednesday as usual.

As we left the office that night I yawned and said, "Well, Roddy, I'm really tired, and I have to go to Lochaber schools for the rest of the week. You'll come with me again, won't you? But absolutely no chewing, mind!"

As usual, he just wagged his tail.

So, off we went the next day to Lochaber and points west.

At first there was the usual scrimmage down the long length of Lochs Ness, Oich and Lochy with cars, caravans and commercials all trying to make good time on the narrow, winding road --- with little success.

May, my colleague, had once arrived three hours late for a conference in Fort William, having suffered an absolutely infuriating fifty-eight mile journey from Inverness down Loch Ness-side, while trapped in a slow-moving caravan rally.

I had left inverness with the intention of going straight to Fort William without stopping, then turning westwards along Locheilside to Glenfinnan with its wonderful monument commemorating the 1745 raising of the Jacobite standard in the presence of Prince Charles Edward Stewart, and the unforgettable railway viaduct which featured so spectacularly in the Harry Potter films.

Unfortunately I got into a convoy of cars moving at a snail's pace while their drivers gazed happily at the scenery around them. I was becoming agitated as I wanted to get to the two Arisaig schools before they closed for the day.

There was a car with French number plates immediately ahead of us and it became obvious that its driver, too, was impatient to get up speed on the cluttered road. He tried to pass the little Honda in front of him several times, without success and, winding down his window, stuck his head out hoping to see a suitable place in which to overtake this annoyingly slow vehicle.

He started weaving from the one side of the road to the other, looking for a gap through which to overtake --- dangerously so, and I muttered dire warnings about what was likely to happen if he tried to pass on the wrong side. I actually considered taking his registration number in case there was an accident when I might be obliged to give evidence. It was all becoming very tense.

We could see the Frenchman now waving his arms about in growing frustration while the totally unconcerned Honda in front of him sailed on majestically at under 30 miles per hour, the driver apparently in a coma. The Frenchman then leaned on his horn and then subsequent, sudden, blaring racket brought the startled Honda driver back to life with a jolt, at last realising what was going on.

He pulled his car as far over to the verge as he could, leaving the smallest of spaces for the irate Frenchman to pass. The latter swept through, missing the Honda's wing mirror by a millimetre, and, as he passed, shouted the most appalling of French insults from one male driver to another:

"Et ta soeur, elle tricot aussi?"

I burst out laughing and the dog looked at me questioningly.

"It's okay Roddy," I giggled. "Nobody is going to commit murder."

The Frenchman has just yelled at the Honda driver:

"And your sister --- she also knits?"

Vive la France!

Tale no. 12: How Worthy of Respect is the Ocean

Dr Bill Stewart stood up to the thighs in the sea while steadying his fast sailing dinghy by the gunwale as she sat, bows facing seawards, ready to sail out of Dunaverty Bay.

John Cameron stood holding the opposite gunwale, protected from the sea by his long waders, and shaking his head at the bold doctor who was just about to leap aboard and set sail for the open water of the North Channel.

His plan was to go sailing around the Sanda archipelago, a wonderful sanctuary for breeding seabirds, past Sanda itself and the smaller islands of Sheep island, the Scarts, Glunimore and Paterson's Rock then possibly, if conditions were right, venture further out into the Irish Sea towards the northern Irish coast.

Dunaverty and Sanda on a good day

This was in the days before the arrival of the mobile phone so, once out of sight of the land, a small-boat sailor could not communicate with the shore at all.

144

John was not at all happy with this arrangement as, although the sun currently shone benevolently out of an azure sky, the weather forecast was for rising wind and choppy seas in the Malin area --- our sea area --- during the course of the late afternoon and evening.

"You know, Bill, that area around Sanda is full of wrecks, and no wonder. The currents and tides can be fierce over there, and the forecast is definitely against you today. It looks fine and calm right now but it can change very quickly and catch the unwary without warning. I wish you would take someone with you --- and, better still, wouldn't go at all!" said John. "There are thirteen big ships lying wrecked on the rocks around these islands and I don't know how many smaller ones. I don't want you to become yet another casualty."

But the intrepid Bill was determined to go in spite of warnings from John and his brother Archie, both of them highly experienced seamen and professional fishermen.

"Oh, it'll be okay --- anyway I've told the Coastguards," replied Bill casually, then he jumped aboard, hauled up the mainsail and jib, and shot away quickly from the shore leaving a worried John staring after him.

It seemed that morning as if nothing could disturb the calm waters of the sunny bay, and I had taken *Catriona*'s sails and mast down, raised the drop-keel and attached an outboard engine on to her flat stern. I was going to take my mother out for a little wander about Brunerican and Dunaverty Bays, and also --- never passing up a good opportunity --- have a quick look at the stake net for possible salmon as we went past.

My mother duly arrived at the shore, as expected, but I was amused to see that she had come complete with gloves, handbag and flowery hat, and fully expected to go out in the boat thus attired.

"Mum, you can't go out in the boat dressed like that. This isn't the Women's Guild outing," I chortled.

"Well, you never know who might see me and I am the minister's wife, after all," she replied. "You have to be prepared for all eventualities."

I sighed and gave in to the inevitable.

I took the boat out on the engine until I reached the head of the net right out in Brunerican Bay, then cut the engine and gently pulled her along the length of the net and the leader while gazing steadily down through the crystal clear water of the bay.

There were several salmon swimming around inside, also one or two caught by the gills in the skirts of the net and one trapped in the leader.

Naturally I had come prepared for a possible catch, so was able to lean over the gunwale, haul the relevant sections of net over *Catriona's* broad stern, carefully avoiding the outboard engine, and start to get the fish out of the sea and into the fish boxes lying on the bottom-boards.

To my astonishment my mother decided to give me a hand, fortunately first discarding gloves and handbag, but I was sure she could be clearly seen from the shore, still wearing the flowery hat while helping me to extract the very slippery salmon from the net and place them in the boxes.

Soon we had finished the job --- wiped any fish scales from the gunwales and thwarts and restored the net to the sea --- then she carefully rinsed her hands in the water before sitting back, satisfied that she had been of great use to me at the fishing and no doubt planning to boast about it to her husband, who was busy writing his sermon, when she got back to the house.

After some time we decided to turn around and go back to Dunaverty. The water was still glassy calm and the hot sunshine beat down on our backs. It was blissfully peaceful and the sea was at slack tide.

Past the Conaglen River mouth we sailed, then the gaping cavern of the Roaring Cave --- not roaring today --- and on towards the huge bulk of Dunaverty Rock with the rocks and reefs strewn around its base.

Usually there was a bit of a swell around the Bow Reef, a big, rocky projection, lying mostly under water right at the front of the Rock, but today there was hardly a movement of the sea, and the tide had completely covered the reef so that, unless you knew the place, you wouldn't know there was a hidden menace there at all. But, to the uninitiated, under even moderate sea conditions, this was a place to be wary of, for there was frequently a big surge of disturbed water as the tide flowed back and forth around the Rock.

John, Archie and I watched the tides very carefully at all times and especially when rounding the Rock on entering or leaving Dunaverty Bay, and judged our high tides on the tidal constant of Belfast plus one (hour), and obviously Belfast plus two during British Summertime.

Unfortunately there always were people who played around in small craft in the bay in good weather and were lulled into a false sense of security by the calm waters of summertime into wandering out lazily on rafts, canoes and even lilos.

I spotted one such wanderer as we started to turn to starboard around the base of Dunaverty Rock in towards the bay. It was a girl sitting casually with her feet and legs over the side of a very small inflatable raft and, to my consternation, holding a tiny baby on her lap. There was no way she could steer or control the raft while both hands were holding the baby only inches above the sea. The raft was now floating towards the top of the invisible Bow Reef.

What turned my blood cold was the fact that a large container ship was rapidly approaching the Sound of Sanda, between Dunaverty and the island of Sanda. I knew that when the ship had swept past a large wave would surge inshore in its wake and, meeting the underwater obstruction of the reef, would cause a violent upsurge and disturbance of the water which no small raft could possibly withstand.

"Look, Mum, that girl and that baby are in awful danger," I shouted. "They are sitting right over the Bow Reef and that big ship's wake will swamp them in a minute or two."

So the pair of us started shouting and waving at the raft, but the girl just waved back, oblivious to the danger and completely unaware of the approach of the ship.

I gunned the outboard engine and we shot round the Rock and came alongside the raft.

"Quick, you must get inshore," I urged her. "You see that big ship back there, well, when it passes there will be a big wave which will knock you over. You must get out of here at once."

"Why? The sea's calm," she objected.

"Yes, I know, but you are sitting right above a big reef, and the wave will cause an underwater disturbance when it hits the reef. For goodness sake get back right inside the raft, put the baby down safely on the bottom boards and catch this rope that I'm just about to throw to you. We'll tow you back to the beach."

I had decided not to attempt to persuade the girl to pass the baby over to us, then clamber over herself, into *Catriona,* being not at all confident that either of them would make it across to us in safety. I thought it better that they should stay put and let us tow them inshore.

By this time the girl had looked back towards the Mull and at last saw the approaching container ship. She still looked sceptical at my warning about the ship's wake, and reluctantly caught the line I threw her but I think it was my mother's flowery hat that finally convinced her that we were honest folk and not trying to hijack her little craft.

Thankfully I attached the line firmly to *Catriona's* stern and put the engine into gear.

Immediately we went off rapidly shorewards and soon tied up both craft at Dunaverty jetty. The girl watched in horrified fascination at the big wave rolling in when the container ship passed, and in disbelief when she saw the upsurge and boiling of the sea right in the place where, a very short time ago, she and the baby had been sitting in their flimsy raft.

There was no need to tell her what might have happened to them --- she could imagine for herself without me spelling it out, and she declared that never again would she venture forth so casually, without any experience of boats, in such a cockleshell of a craft, without lifejackets or any other safety equipment, and without any adult companion, especially with a little baby on board.

I was glad she took this attitude, for so often people were resentful if we tried, in even the smallest way, to interfere with their venturing out into deep water, well meaning though we were. Even HM Coastguard had been known to be physically beaten off if they tried to rescue a boat which they considered was in danger but whose crew were enjoying a bit of risk-taking on the water.

Alas, the beaches of Kintyre were all too often crowded with completely inexperienced holidaymakers wandering happily offshore in what were really just inflated pieces of plastic or rubber, sometimes with tragic results. People just didn't realise the unpredictable power of the sea and didn't treat it with the respect which it undoubtedly deserves.

No wonder the Coastguards were nearly always on full alert during the months of summer in particular.

My mother was appalled at the complete lack of preparedness, not to mention imagination, of the girl we had rescued, and shared her emotions with my father when we got home.

At the same time I have to congratulate my long-suffering parents for never, at any time, trying to discourage me from spending most of my time, when not teaching in a Campbeltown classroom, out at sea in various small boats. I realise now how difficult it must have been for them to keep quiet when I went out, especially at night, either fishing with Archie or John, helping on the Sanda run, or sailing *Catriona* around the dangerous waters of the south coast of Kintyre.

I am sad now when I look back and think how I may have caused them needless anxiety, which they never showed outwardly, but I also feel pride at their confidence in my ability to act competently around our six-boat fleet.

Of course, I was practically brought up in boats, and was well instructed in boat handling by great teachers --- John Sands, a master yacht builder who was involved in the construction of the 12 metre America's Cup yacht *Sceptre*, and who taught me to sail the yachts which he himself had built, as well as the professional boatmen, his brother Archie and his father Bob, who taught me and my friends how to row, and to handle their motorboats (and how to shell mussels).

Also, my parents had unlimited confidence in the seamanship, commonsense and efficiency of Archie and John Cameron of Dunaverty and Bayview, two wonderful, kindly men and very special friends of our family.

Alas, even the best can make mistakes, and John and I were very abashed on the day when we were almost late for the evening bus which usually transported our freshly caught salmon into Campbeltown for transfer on to the evening Glasgow bus. On arrival in the city the salmon would be loaded aboard the midnight train to London, thus arriving, still in excellent condition, at Billingsgate market at 6am the next day.

So we emptied the net hurriedly and John rowed the exotically named *Silvery Dawn*, our little maid-of-all-work clinker boat, otherwise known as "the punt", at high speed back to the Conaglen mooring where we leaped out, fastened the boat hastily to the big hawser, and dashed up the shore with our catch. Never were salmon so quickly packed in their layers of grass in Hailstones and Unkles' wooden boxes, and stowed in the boot of John's car, after which we roared away across the machair and just managed to catch the bus as it was slowly drawing away from Keil gates.

"That was a bit too close," said John as we drove more sedately back across to Dunaverty.

"We'll just tidy up the nets and the boats and then we can get home."

"Right," I said, quite glad to be finishing early at the shore, as I should have been busy up at the house helping my mother to prune her 150 rose bushes, a daunting task which required more than one person to carry out on a regular basis in summertime.

We pulled up outside Archie's house of Dunaverty and, in leisurely mood, got out of the car, stretched ourselves a bit and wandered down the slope to the shore where "the punt" waited to be washed down and tidied up.

Only, "the punt" wasn't there!

We both did a double-take, firstly at the hawser, then at one another, without any clue as to what had happened, after all, we definitely had come ashore in the usual place and had been away for only a few minutes.

"The punt" was not anywhere in the river mouth, nor had she beached herself on the shore. Never before had we actually mislaid a boat!

We separated and went off in opposite directions to search the surrounding land and scan the shoreline in a desperate attempt to find the elusive little boat, both of us really embarrassed at such a ridiculous situation.

Then John let out a shout from the top of the bank from where he could see past the high rocks at the river mouth and well out into Brunerican Bay.

"There she is," he yelled. "She's gone to sea on her own. We'll need to take your *Catriona* and go and get her before the Coastguards see her wandering about out there. They'll think we've fallen overboard at the net."

So we dragged my boat down into the river, jumped in and John rowed like a demon well out into the Sound of Sanda where we took the little boat in tow then made for the shore as hurriedly as possible, hoping that no one had seen our shameful mishap.

By this time we reckoned that in our hurry to take the salmon ashore we hadn't properly checked that the little boat's mooring line was properly attached to the big hawser with the usual rolling hitch. But which one of us was the guilty party? I was sure it was me, but John said that, no, it must have been himself. We were both each still trying to take the blame when Kenneth, the Glasgow dentist who regularly holidayed in Southend, appeared at the top of the slope.

"What are you doing, taking out two boats to look the net?" he questioned. John and I must have looked as guilty as we felt, and we both mumbled some vague reply which Kenneth obviously didn't believe.

"The pair of you are getting as bad as the Otter," he said.

We both bristled at this as Bob the Otter was an annual holiday visitor from Sutherland. In fact he had just the one boat, and was the only other person, apart from ourselves, to have a boat on the Southend shore. He was such a bad seaman that he should never have left the sanctuary of the beach in his poorly maintained craft.

We remembered, with a certain amount of uncharitable glee, that he had once set out to sail to the northern Irish coast armed only with a road map, lost his way in the North Channel and was reported to have called in at a nearby lighthouse to ask the way home!

The Otter's idea of an anchor was an ancient item of household technology in the form of a "mangle", a large iron contraption built to squeeze the water out of the weekly wash, not to anchor a boat.

So we were not at all amused to be compared with such a complete lubber. However, we knew Kenneth would keep on at us until he got at the truth and, anyway, we really wanted to know the reason for our apparent inefficiency so we decided to go back to the hawser and see if there was any clue to the mystery. There was nothing obvious but we did notice that the entire mooring line was still attached to "the punt's" bow and a bit of experimenting soon showed us the reason for her unexpected departure.

The Campbeltown chandlers had got in a supply of a new type of rope, called courline, which was really a form of nylon. We used to always favour manila, but we had decided to give the new stuff a try, thinking it would be harder wearing than the soft, pliable manila, and bought some for the mooring lines. But it was difficult to tie a knot in this material as its springy fibre wouldn't fasten tightly and, unless there was quite a bit of tension on it, it would begin to loosen and gradually untie itself. It looked as if "the punt's" rope had untied itself during our quick dash over to Keil with the salmon.

So we tried out our theory and attached the springy nylon line to the hawser with the usual rolling hitch, but with difficulty. Sure enough, within a few moments the knot started to unravel and then fell away from the hawser. "The punt" had gone off to sea because she was no longer attached to her mooring. What a relief to find a reasonable explanation for her departure!

151

Kenneth had, grudgingly, to take back his acid comments.

Later we discovered another flaw in the new rope. Where the courline lay over the concrete jetty at Dunaverty it started to fray when the attached boat moved up and down in the swell. Eventually the line frayed right through and soon there could be another boat floating away from her mooring.

That was the end of the experiment with the new, up-to-date courline rope at both Dunaverty and Conaglen.

While all this was going on we stood about on the shore in the gathering dusk of evening and soon became aware that the sun had gone in, the wind had got up and the sea was getting quite rough to the point where "white horses" were beginning to appear in both bays.

John interrupted our blethering with a look up at the clouds gathering overhead and the "white horses" on the surface of the previous glassy sea.

"I think the weather forecast was correct and we're in for a blow," he said, "I'm getting a bit worried about Bill. There's no sign of him so far. That little boat of his is fast but no use in a big sea. I think we'll give him another half hour and then I'm going to contact the Coastguards. I'll just go up to the hut and get my binoculars."

This altered the mood immediately and both Kenneth and I were concerned enough to go over to Dunaverty and consult with Archie whose launch, *Zena,* had been winched ashore and was now up in the shelter of the old Lifeboat house. It was typical of these men that they didn't waste time criticising anyone who got into difficulties on the sea, but went about their business efficiently and quietly, though both John and Archie must have regretted that people went out so often without taking heed of local knowledge, official weather warnings, not to mention notice of tidal rise and fall and local hazards like reefs, skerries and powerful tidal currents.

So the four of us stood there on the dunes, looking southwards towards the nasty collection of rocks off the south-west of Sanda. If Bill was in any trouble it would possibly be somewhere around there. We each went off to a different vantage point to keep a look out for Bill.

By this time the wind had increased considerably to about Force 5-6 and there was now a big sea running. The sky had darkened ominously and it became difficult to see clearly through the flying spume. Bill's wife appeared over the dunes and her anxious face told clearly how frightened she was.

It was while Archie was telling her what we proposed to do that John, peering through his high-powered glasses, shouted out,

" I think I've got him now. He's off the west Sanda reefs and not making much progress as far as I can see."

We all rushed over to John and peered out into the murk of the gathering dusk. It was difficult to see Bill's little dinghy against the white flecked waves but we all strained our eyes and eventually made out her white hull against the threatening bulk of the savage, reef-strewn west coast of Sanda.

Archie ran over to the house and phoned the Coastguards in their station on the hill just beyond Brunerican Bay. They said they would let Campbeltown lifeboat know, and would come over themselves with rescue gear, knowing that we would keep a sharp look out for Bill's boat until they arrived.

But Archie and John went into a confab together and finally announced that they wouldn't wait, but would relaunch *Zena* and go out themselves towards the stricken boat as she could sink long before the lifeboat appeared.

Kenneth and some other men who had appeared declared that they would go as well, but Archie would allow only Kenneth to go with them as he was used to the *Zena* and could handle her efficiently if need be.

So about six strong men got the launch winched back down the shore into the choppy waters around the jetty and held her steady until her engine fired then, with Archie at the helm, she turned, surging away into the foaming swell of Dunaverty Bay and heading out for the rock-strewn area on the west coast of Sanda.

John later described how they kept the launch heading for the small white streak tossing helplessly among the sharp teeth of the Sanda archipelago, hoping that Bill would be able to keep his boat away from disaster long enough for them to get to him.

As they drew nearer it was obvious that his mainsail was flapping in shreds around the mast and the foresail had completely disappeared. He was evidently sailing under bare poles and had little or no control over the dinghy which would no longer answer her helm.

He was utterly drenched and, although wearing a lifejacket, looked white and tense with the strain of trying to fend the boat off the rocks as she pitched and heaved wildly in the now ferocious waves.

Archie steered the *Zena* infinitely carefully in through the maze of jagged rocks, many of which were submerged at this state of the tide, while trying to keep enough way on her to avoid her being thrown on to the reefs herself. She gradually crept nearer to Bill's boat and John yelled over the racket of the screaming wind that he was going to throw Bill a line. Bill nodded to show he had understood and readied himself to catch the line.

Five times he missed it as the wind caught it in mid air and whipped it down into the surging, boiling sea. By this time the stricken dinghy was being rapidly swept in towards the violently breaking surf around the rocks of the shoreline, but on the sixth throw Bill caught it and managed to hold on long enough to haul it in and make it fast around the mast. John decided that it would be completely impossible to tow the dinghy through these towering waves and shouted to Bill to haul on the line and pull the dinghy closer to the *Zena* as they would have to try to transfer him into the launch and abandon the dinghy altogether.

There was no room for argument, or even discussion, as Bill was now in a life or death situation. He nodded agreement and managed to pull the dinghy in towards the wildly yawing *Zena*, herself now in danger.

But it seemed as if the situation was now manageable and a successful rescue was about to be forthcoming. Bill scrambled to stand up in the boat and was reaching forward toward *Zena's* gunwale when a sudden downdraught off the island's high shoreline slammed the boom hard across the dinghy and it caught Bill full on the back of the neck. He staggered forward, dropped the lifeline, fell across the gunwale and slid slowly into the sea between the two boats, where he hung, face-down, in the commotion of the waves.

Near panic ensued as John and Kenneth struggled to push the two boats apart in case they would crash together and crush Bill between them. With muscles cracking under the terrific strain Kenneth held the boats apart while John, hanging perilously over *Zena's* gunwale, his legs wedged insecurely under a forward thwart, got hold of Bill's hair, yanked his face above the waves, then transferred his grasp to the lifejacket, and heaved like crazy.

Bill was no light weight at the best of times and now, with saturated clothes and lifejacket, he was a dead weight in John's arms. Archie did not dare leave the helm as his whole concentration was on holding *Zena* as steady as possible. Kenneth was left, suspended across the space between the bows of both boats and still holding them apart. Now it was down to John.

Drawing on every ounce of strength and determination, he threw himself backwards into the body of the launch, hanging on grimly to the inert man and dragging him gradually up the outside of the launch's hull. A superhuman heave from John brought Bill up and over the gunwale and both men collapsed in a heap on to the floorboards.

But John's ordeal was not yet over as Kenneth, hanging perilously between the two boats, could not get back into the *Zena* on his own, and had to be hauled bodily away from the now waterlogged dinghy into the relative safety of the launch.

"Okay, let her go, and let's go ourselves," yelled John breathlessly, while turning the unconscious man over on to his back and trying to find a neck pulse.

Kenneth, the dentist, now took over and used his professional skills to judge the situation.

"He's obviously concussed and now beginning to suffer the effects of hypothermia, but I can't find any sign of broken bones," he said. "We need to get him to hospital as soon as possible though."

They watched sadly as the dinghy, released from its lifeline to *Zena,* was finally gripped in the terrific undertow and thrown against the shoreline rocks where it smashed into a thousand pieces and disappeared into the maw of the sea.

Little more was said as the infinitely reliable Archie, by some miracle, got the *Zena* safely out through the maze of currents, reefs and rocks off Sanda's rugged coast, and eventually brought her into the open waters of the Sound of Sanda.

"There's the lifeboat!" he shouted, pointing to the northward where the beautiful, sleek hull of the Campbeltown lifeboat appeared, throwing up a considerable bow wave as she surged down towards us.

"Good, she's seen us," said Kenneth. "I'll bet the Coastguards spotted us and told her exactly where we are."

In a blessedly short space of time the lifeboat was circling the launch and many strong arms transferred the recumbent Bill across into her warm cabin. Kenneth went over with him to advise the crew about what had happened and report on Bill's physical state.

The lifeboat coxswain then inquired about Archie's and John's state of health, and kindly asked if *Zena's* engine was functioning alright and did she require a tow into Dunaverty. Having been reassured that everything was fine, the lifeboat surged off northwards into the darkness towards Campbeltown Loch.

An exhausted John and Archie were now left to bring the launch back to her mooring at the jetty, where a crowd had gathered, including Bill's wife, desperate to know what had happened.

John was left to tell her that her husband was in good hands, while willing volunteers, under Archie's close supervision, brought the heroic *Zena* up out of the water and into the shelter of the old Lifeboat house.

The next evening, after many hours of interviews by police, press and Coastguard John, Archie and I met on the dunes above Dunaverty and stood looking down at a serenely calm sea --- so different from the raging beast of yesterday.

"Aye, it's true," said Archie quietly. "The sea has many moods. She is calm tonight, and she is beautiful, she is wide and she is mysterious, but she is deep and can be wild, and she can be cruel and unforgiving, as she was yesterday."

"Indeed," answered John. "Nach urramach an cuan. How worthy of respect is the ocean!"

Tale no. 13: God Bless America!

I stood in Glasgow Airport waiting, in pleasant anticipation, for the appearance of my American friends, Frank and Eleanor, off the incoming flight from Florida. They had got together a group of fellow countrymen and anticipated a leisurely tour of Scotland, but not the usual city tour, rather a meander around the highways and byways of the west coast.

They were caught up in their American enthusiasm for all things Scottish --- many had "Scots-Irish" (as they put it) ancestors, and they were extremely eager to see where their "folks" had come from, so the next step was for Frank, Eleanor and myself to herd them on to three minibuses and take them on their long-dreamed of trip of a lifetime through Argyll and Inverness-shire, with myself driving one bus while acting as tour guide, and Frank and Eleanor doing the really difficult tasks of driving through what was unfamiliar territory to them, keeping everyone up to date with travel and hotel information and dealing patiently with all complaints.

After the usual scrimmage of the baggage carousel we got our happy band on to the minibuses and set off westwards down the M8 to McInroy's Point and all roads west --- fortunately, in brilliant sunshine. The west coast always looks spectacular in good weather.

My bus load chattered non-stop and were delighted with the beautiful views of Ben Lomond, Dumbarton Rock and the Firth of Clyde which opened before their eyes as we drove down the motorway towards Gourock and beyond.

At the Western Ferries terminal at McInroy's Point we waited in the queue to get on to the red and white vessel *Sound of Scarba,* now approaching the ramp.

"Gee, are we goin' on that li'l boat? It's surely too small to take us," uttered Mildred, the elderly, white-haired lady, apprehensively.

"Why Mildred, Honey," uttered Flloyd, her devoted husband, "You know these li'l ferry boats sure are safe. They've bin sailin' back an' forth across this waterway for years. So come back aboard the minibus right now, why don' you. You'll be jus' fine."

"Yes, that's our ferry, and it can take buses, lorries and lots of cars, no trouble at all," I said reassuringly (I hoped).

But "Mildred, Honey" was not at all happy as she watched the embarking cars bumping over the ramp on their way on to the ship.

"Ah ain't stayin' on this bus on the way over," she declared and, abandoning her husband and friends to a possibly watery grave, she insisted on getting off the bus and standing beside the ramp all the way across the firth, presumably to get a head start swimming for the shore if the ferry sank!

I felt it was time to put in a good word for the ferries which are the lifeblood of the Cowal peninsula, so started to tell my passengers a bit about the fleet.

The astute American businessmen among us were most interested in, and very approving of, the great success story which is Western Ferries, after a precarious and tragic beginning.

I started my tale.

"In the mid 1960s the western islands off the Scottish coast were served only by old-fashioned steam lighters, which we call "puffers" --- you'll see a great one at Inveraray.

They took the ground at low tide on arrival at their island destinations. Horses and carts were then brought into the shallows alongside the boat where loading and unloading of cargo took place while the tide was out. This usually took the best part of a day, then they refloated with the high tide and went on their way. You're going to see a typical example, the *Vital Spark,* tied up permanently at Inveraray pier. This, of course, was a slow and laborious procedure. The only other form of ship transport was the MacBrayne fleet of cargo/passenger ships, which were side-loaders and so needed specialised piers at which to load and unload.

By 1966 as there was a considerable increase in sea traffic three enterprising people set up a service with the aid of an HIDB (Highlands and Islands Development Board) loan for a landing-craft type vessel plying mainly between Tayinloan in Kintyre and the island of Gigha.

Tragically this barge capsized at Gigha, ditching a lorry and drowning its driver. It looked as if this were the end of the service but eventually some Scottish businessmen got together, subscribed £100,000, and set up the highly successful company now known as Western Ferries."

My Americans murmured their approval, and listened patiently while I told them the rest of the story.

"This is still a private company, based in Dunoon, and manned mainly by local people. The Clyde service began on Sunday 3rd June 1973, and has never looked back, now providing a bow and stern-loading, roll on-roll off service which runs from early morning to late at night, seven days a week.

It also provides a wonderful life-saving role, the crew coming out at any time of day or night in order to take emergency cases across the firth to the big hospitals in the central belt of Scotland."

My Americans said just how impressed they were at this revelation.

"But," I continued, "I have my own personal stories of our wonderful Western Ferries --- nothing to do with business efficiency and all to do with human kindness."

My Americans said, "Go right ahead, Ma'am. We sure would be glad to hear what you got to say."

"Well," I began," I was on one of the older ferries one very dark, stormy December morning, where all of us walking passengers were penned up in the gloomy, ill-lit accommodation immediately under the car deck. The only sources of light were the rather dim electric lamps distributed throughout the saloon and, as usual on an early morning, we all sat huddled over our newspapers, grumbling about the draughts, the poor lighting and the uncomfortable seats, and wishing the journey was over.

Suddenly, all the lights went out, and we were left in stygian darkness, as the ferry pitched and rolled her way across the firth. There was, at first, the total silence of complete surprise until, after a few minutes, there were raised and frightened voices. It was obvious that, unless we could see our way to the heavy doors at the top of flights of stairs on each side of the saloon, people would start to panic, and then chaos would undoubtedly ensue with folk rushing and pushing their way up to the car deck. Fear spreads terribly quickly on a ship and a few were already on their feet, stumbling about in the darkness and falling over the still seated passengers. The tension in the air was palpable and it was the perfect scenario for a tragic event.

But just as it seemed that hysteria would get the upper hand, a door in the bulkhead suddenly opened, light from the engine room spilled out into the blackness, a diminutive mechanic clad in a grimy white boiler-suit popped out and, grinning from ear to ear, shouted in the tones of deepest Clydeside, "Ony o' youse yins got a shullin' fur the me'er?"

I had, of course, to translate this for the Americans as, "Have any of you got a shilling for the meter?" They were very amused.

"This simple but brilliant tactic immediately broke the tension, and we all burst out in relieved laughter at this typically Clydeside, down-to-earth reaction to a potentially dangerous situation. The lights came back on again within a few moments and everyone settled down fairly calmly again for the few minutes of the voyage that remained."

The visitors murmured their approval and wanted to hear more, so I continued:

"Some weeks later I left my car in the then parking area at McInroy's Point before boarding the evening ferry *Sound of Sanda*, to Hunter's Quay. I planned to collect the car the next morning and, for security purposes, fastened a crook-lock on to the steering wheel then got out and locked the car door, as usual.

My hands were full of coat, handbag, umbrella, briefcase and other assorted belongings, and, as the ship was about to leave, I ran down the ramp, dropping things as I went, so had to stop and pick them up before she sailed out. But I just made it and collapsed, catching my breath while the ferry made her way across the firth. I hoped I had picked up all my bits and pieces.

The next morning I crossed to McInroy's Point, again on the same *Sound of Sanda* and, unconcerned, walked over to where my car was parked, while struggling to get my keys out of my pocket. I found them, unlocked the driver's door, then started to look for the little crook-lock key without which I couldn't release the steering wheel and drive the car away. However, I couldn't find the key and, with mounting anxiety, looked over and over again through every pocket, the briefcase, my handbag and even the inside of the umbrella. But no key!

It seemed probable that, in my usual morning rush, I had left the tiny key in the house in Hunter's Quay, so I rushed back down the ramp on to the *Sound of Sanda,* which I had just got off, where the astonished deckhand said, "That was a quick journey!" and was forced to admit that I had carelessly left my key in the house, and would have to run back home to get it.

He just laughed, and shook his head. "You'll have to get a move on. Women and keys!" he said.

Normally I would have challenged this patronising comment, but this morning I was in no position to argue!

On arrival at Hunter's Quay I moved like smoke along the road to the house, dashed inside and went straight to where I was absolutely certain I had left the key. Of course, it wasn't there! Frantically I went through the entire house like my Labrador looking for a buried bone. But there was no key --- anywhere. I'd have to go back to the car and try to get it started somehow.

But now would I be in time to reboard the *Sound of Sanda* before she sailed again for McInroy's Point? Completely bewildered I sped back along to where the ferry was just about to leave, slithered down the ramp, and admitted my abysmal failure to the deckie.

I thought that maybe I had dropped the key while rushing down the ramp the previous evening --- I would have to check the ramp again, though the key would probably have fallen into the sea when the ramp was raised. But I'd still have to check because, unless I found it, how on earth was I going to start the car?

I fretted all the seemingly endless way back across the Clyde and at McInroy's Point abstractedly wandered up the ramp, searching it the whole way --- unsuccessfully, of course.

Then I heard a whistle behind me and looked round.

There, following me up the ramp, was the white-boiler-suited engineer, with cutting gear draped over his shoulder, closely attended by a junior acolyte from the engine-room trailing a series of mysterious cables and grinning all the way up to the car.

My deckie friend had obviously reported the situation to the rest of the deck crew and they had decided to come to the rescue of their dozy passenger so, without a word to me, they had got the engineers out of the engine-room, carrying the cutting gear, knowing it would take only a minute to cut through the crook-lock and send me on my way.

Only on wonderful Western Ferries could this have happened!

In fact their good deed was not necessary. The car which had been parked next to mine when I locked it at night, had moved off during my absence. There, in the middle of the space where it had been was the little key. I must have dropped it during my scramble to catch the ferry the previous evening and it had bounced under the next-door car. Untold relief!

I grovelled with abject apologies to my friends the engineers, who graciously returned to the ship without a word of reproach, while I slunk off, full of remorse, blaming myself for always being in such a tearing hurry.

So, God bless our Western Ferries! Though the ships may be small, the goodwill is great," I said, finally.

The Americans expressed their total appreciation of the ferry crews.

"My, they certainly are a very fine body of men," approved Mildred's husband in sincere and sonorous tones, and immediately climbed off the minibus to get Mildred and inform her, in his rumbling bass voice, about how lucky they were to be travelling with such a wonderful ferry company.

Mildred, however, would not listen and refused to get back on to the minibus until it had rolled off the ship at Hunter's Quay.

There I led the minibus procession through the car assembly area and turned to the right, westwards, along the shores of the Holy Loch, past the scene of the late, controversial US Polaris submarine base, all peacefully quiet now with nothing more lethal than the sailing club yachts, and the cargo ships carrying timber from the Argyll forests.

We passed through the village of Sandbank to Sandhaven where the US officers had had their purpose-built houses then swung off to the left at the head of the Holy Loch on to the winding, single-track road through Glen Lean which would lead us, eventually, to our destination that first night at Tighnabruaich on the shores of the picturesque Kyles of Bute.

Between the fatigue of the long air journey from Florida and the warmth of the sunshine striking through the minibus windows my passengers were beginning to doze a little in spite of their acute desire to stay awake and drink in every feature of the beautiful mountainous scenery we were driving through. At last we began the long, slow descent into Tighnabruaich when Harvey, still alert in the back seat, spluttered:

"Say folks! What do you think --- I just do not believe it --- did you see that? If that ain't jus' sumthin' ---!" and more splutters and exclamations.

Everyone shot upright in their seats, wondering what was wrong with him.

"I sure ain't imagin' it, but it seems ---" and he paused for maximum effect, "--- there are wild elephants in this here countryside!"

"Aw, c'mon now Harvey" chorused the rest, "You're jus' tired right now, man."

But Harvey insisted that the road sign we had just passed warned of possible elephants on the road. I was highly dubious about his loud voiced insistence and thought this must be a fatigue-induced illusion, but there was such a clamour among my passengers that, after much discussion, I was forced to turn the minibus, with great difficulty, in the next lay-by and drive back up the road to where Harvey had seen the sign, and there it was --- a beautiful elephant straight out of the pages of Jungle Book.

"Well I'll be doggoned," said one. "Harvey's quite right. That there sign sure is warnin' us about elephants. Nobody told us there was wild elephants roamin' around Scotland when we booked our trip. This is fantastic!" and plans were made to phone the US of A as soon as possible to let the folks back home know just how exciting this trip looked like being.

I was completely puzzled and, after depositing my excited, chattering passengers at the Royal Hotel, went to confer with mine host about the phenomenon. He winked, rolled his eyes humorously and disappeared into the back premises without a word. So back up the road I went to check that our collective eyes had not deceived us.

Sure enough, there was the road sign with a very realistic elephant on its surface. I went nearer, in fact, right up to it and peered closely at the sign.

Then I saw what had happened. Some wit, obviously with a considerable flair for art, must have very carefully sneaked up the quiet road, probably in the dark of night and, with consummate skill, had transformed a very normal, unexciting sheep into a most convincing elephant. It was tremendously well done, and I was really sorry to have discovered the mundane truth, for elephants on the loose at Tighnabruaich was an infinitely more interesting proposition than mere sheep.

I had a strong suspicion that mine host at the hotel was very likely in cahoots with the artist. How many Scottish hoteliers could boast of such a unique wildlife attraction in the vicinity of their establishments? It was all so good for trade!

I wondered about keeping quiet about my discovery as the Americans were so delighted about the unusual turn of events but, after consultation with Frank and Eleanor, decided they should be told the truth, disappointing though it was. When told they gave a collective sigh of resignation.

"Ah jus' noo it was too good to be true," said Mildred, amazingly unfazed at the prospect of encountering wild elephants, while being really afraid of crossing the Firth of Clyde on a nice, stable ferry.

After dinner and many excited phone conversations with family and friends back home they all drifted sleepily off to bed, no doubt to dream happily of ferries and elephants.

The next day we set off via the little ferry from Portavadie across Loch Fyne to Tarbert at the head of the long Kintyre peninsula. By this time Mildred was getting bolder and enjoyed the calm crossing on the very small ferry without a qualm. I didn't let on to her that this was not a wonderful Western Ferry.

On the way across I regaled them with the history of King Magnus Bareleg, the 11th century king of Norway who succeeded in conning Edgar, King of Scotland out of the whole of the Kintyre peninsula in 1098, by calling it an island. In fact successive governments of Scotland designated Kintyre as an island until the beginning of the 17th century.

Magnus really wanted Kintyre which he described as, *the best island in the Hebrides, excepting Man,* so he sailed his fleet down the west coast, round the Mull of Kintyre and northwards into the broad Firth of Clyde. This, in turn, led into the mouth of the great sea loch of Loch Fyne, then Magnus turned westwards into East Loch Tarbert. There he had one of his ships pulled ashore, climbed into it and sat holding the helm while his men portaged the vessel across the peninsula to West Loch Tarbert where it was put back in the water. Having thus "sailed" right round Kintyre he cunningly claimed "the island of Kintyre" as his own."

Harvey commented, "Ain't that jus' like the kind of dirty, low down, land grabbin' trick that happened so often in our own Wild West?" Loud agreement all round.

Turning northwards at the head of East Loch Tarbert we set out on the long drive to Lochgilphead, passing on the roadside a little, ruinous heap of stones which had evidently been a small building in days long gone by.

So, in the best *seannachie* tradition, I told them the true story of what had been a local sensation in the early 18th century:

"Morag, a young teacher, was walking through the forest one snowy winter morning, to get to this building --- the little school where she worked --- and became aware of a lurking presence shadowing her and keeping pace as she hurried along. Becoming extremely frightened she increased her speed, but the faster she walked the faster the shadow kept up with her. She could see nothing clearly through through the haze of falling snow and the thick screen of bushes. Finally she broke into a stumbling run as the welcoming shape of the school building came into view.

As Morag slipped and staggered along, shaking with terror, and by this time sobbing aloud, the awful presence finally emerged from the undergrowth in the shape of a huge wolf which lunged at her, snarling ferociously, and fastened his powerful jaws in the skirt of her coat.

She screamed and struggled to reach the safety of the school but, by this time, the wolf had transferred his grip on to her left arm and was pulling her away in the direction of the forest. Just as she gave a despairing wail, sure that her last hour had come, the school door was jerked open in front of her and the youthful headmaster appeared in the doorway armed with a pitchfork.

He dashed out, yelling at the ravenous beast, and trying to get at the wolf without hurting Morag or losing his footing on the slippery, snow covered ground. Circling the struggling pair he got in a few sharp jabs on the wolf's back, but it still held grimly on to Morag's arm until he managed to stab its hind leg right through. The huge animal yelped in pain and turned on him, thereby letting go of Morag's arm.

The headmaster saw his chance. He hurled the pitchfork with all his strength straight into the now exposed throat of the wolf, which instantly dropped like a stone, twitching, as its lifeblood poured out over the snowy ground, flooding the whole area scarlet.

Having made sure that the wolf was finally dead, the headmaster turned to the shaking and hysterical Morag, wrapped gentle arms around her and led her into the shelter of the school, where he bathed the wounds on her arm and comforted her with soothing words until she had recovered.

This turned out to be the last ever known attack of a wolf in that part of Argyll, and wolves became extinct in Scotland shortly afterwards. (ie 1680 or 1700 or 1743!)

The very best part of the story is that young Morag and the headmaster married soon after and lived happily near Lochgilphead for the rest of their lives."

There was enthusiastic applause for the hero and heroine when I finished my story.

"Say, Scotland sure is full of stories wherever you go," said Flloyd, "jus' like our own Wild West, but mostly considerably older."

The others agreed and thought it was a marvellous true tale. Naturally they started to recount similar stories of danger and extreme hazard in their own country's history. Of course I had no stories to match those of attacks by Apaches, Grizzly bears and rattlesnakes, as they had, though I was later to curdle their blood with tales of our ancient clans.

Our convoy of three minibuses swept on up the road to the mid-Argyll town of Lochgilphead where the story of the wolf attack resides in the Argyll Archive. Then we all decamped to The Stag for morning coffee and my tour group happily pottered around in the warm sunshine buying postcards and small souvenirs to take home.

On the whole they were a most appreciative band of happy wanderers though Eliza was inclined to remind anyone who would listen that her ancestors came from north Argyll in the early 1900s which made her, in her own estimation, an expert on all things Scottish. It seemed to have slipped her mind that everyone else in the group had Scottish ancestors too, that being the main reason why they were in Argyll in the first place. She always went around decked out in Campbell tartan and attempted to overwhelm every conversation with her own, loud "expertise" until I addressed her in Gaelic. That silenced her (temporarily).

Poor Eleanor was the unfortunate usually left to deal with Eliza and keep her away from the others as much as possible. This was fairly easy when not on the bus but, during every journey her fellow passengers couldn't get away from her, so we all ended up talking like mad so as not to let her get a word in edgeways, and we all got sore throats from talking too much.

"Oh dear, there's always one flea who irritates everybody, isn't there?" Eleanor said.

But the party was mostly quite irrepressible, especially the men.

We were travelling northwards, as always, towards historic Kilmartin Glen having passed the iconic Pictish, later Scottish, fort of Dunadd which is the ancient heartland of the country of Scotland. I always get a lump in my throat as I climb to the top of the fort where the symbols of our ancient glory are carved into the bedrock in the form of the Boar, the Footstep, the Basin and the Ogham script.

Dunadd Fort

"This," I explained to my listening group," is where our ancient Scotland began --- the land of the Scots from Ireland actually.

Right here, on this rock, was a large defensive fort, known since Pictish times, comprised of five smaller forts, one above the other, standing high above the surrounding widespread marshland, known as the Moine Mhòr, the Great Moss, and an outstanding landmark from which the approach of any enemy could easily be seen.

The Boar of Dunadd Fort

The Boar was the original symbol of the kings of Scotland --- the Lion came much later --- and the Footstep was where every new king stood to take the oath to protect his people, at the time of his inauguration.

The Basin, it is thought, was where sacred water, or sacrificial blood, was held, and the Ogham script was widely used in ancient times though no one seems to know the origin or meaning, of this particular inscription, as it is in an unknown language. Examples of the later Viking Ogham writing are to be found in various places, but theirs is a different form of Ogham, and has been translated.

Footprint and Ogham script

This place", I went on," is particularly venerable in that our great Saint Columba actually stood where you are standing now while visiting his kinsman, King Connel of the Scots, in the 6th century, for this was the royal palace of the Scots."

For once the group was utterly silent, digesting the grandeur and importance of where they were standing, and it was an almost reverent group who clambered carefully back down to the floor of the glen and the waiting minibuses.

But it didn't take long for their natural, chirpy humour to break through and, as I drove the leading bus through the head of Kilmartin glen, pointing out the impressive prehistoric remains which are thick on the ground there, we turned a corner in the narrow road, and there was the wonderful Kilmartin stone circle, looking like a miniature Stonehenge. I hoped they would continue to be impressed, but forgot about my cheery male passengers.

Harvey, leaning out of the open bus window and pointing over to the stone circle, yelled back to the two following buses:

"Hey folks, just look over there --- a Stone Age barbecue pit!"

Tale no. 14: Dragons and Cattle Raids

We were at Garmony on the north-eastern coast of the beautiful island of Mull on a mild July day, though the sun shone only fitfully on our little group of Director/ Cameraman, Sound man, Presenter, Assistant Producer and me.

We were preparing to film the exploits of the famous Celtic war leader, Somerled, later king of Argyll and progenitor of the Lords of the Isles, and I had been asked to contribute to the forthcoming BBC production in honour of his people, the future Clan Donald --- the MacDonalds.

I had happily discussed the entire material several weeks beforehand with the director and felt fairly relaxed about the whole thing, but now was about to experience actual filming in the open air, at the mercy of the vagaries of Scottish west coast weather, without the aid of an autocue, and far away from the comfortable, dry, controlled environment of a studio.

We should have been filming in the district of Morvern on the northern bank of the Sound of Mull, at Ardtornish Castle, headquarters of the Lords of the Isles but, for various reasons, we were shooting instead from Garmony on Mull, across the Sound towards the castle and so had to walk a considerable distance over the rough, saltburned, grassy moorland from the main road to get to the edge of the sea --- at least a mile, I thought.

We leaped over salt-water inlets and fresh-water streams, avoiding many lichen-covered outcrops and seaweed-covered rocks. Inevitably we became increasingly hot and bothered as we struggled and slipped towards the rugged shoreline.

I had forgotten to bring water for my increasingly dry throat; the Director, Tony, who was carrying the heavy camera on his shoulder, was looking a bit strained; the Sound man, Jake was glowering at me from the midst of his extensive equipment as if it was all my fault; the presenter, Alan, kept telling me to watch where I was going and the Assistant Producer, Molly, was sweetly and patiently trying to keep us from barking at one another.

I led the team into the right place almost directly across the Sound from Ardtornish Castle but thereafter was instructed, like a small child on the first day at school, in the correct procedure for making a film, and found it incredible that we had to repeat the opening sequence thirteen times before the Director declared himself satisfied with the "take".

"You are standing higher than Alan," shouted Tony. "Move to another part of the bank so you are lower than him. Don't get too close to him. Walk slowly towards me and keep looking at Alan while he is asking you a question, then point towards the castle as if you are showing him the headquarters of the Lords of the Isles."

I tried to remember all that and obey instructions but, while gazing steadily at Alan, tripped over an unseen tussock and fell into a patch of squelching bog. Alan kindly extricated me, brushed off some of the mud and asked the question again, smiling calmly all the while.

We continued, walking unsteadily along the uneven banks of the Sound while I pointed to the castle on the opposite bank, as directed.

"That's no good. You are bobbing about all over the place. Go back to the beginning and do it again," shouted Tony. We did.

Then we did it all over again, and again --- twelve more times!

"The sun is shining too much on the left side of your face. Turn to the left, into it a bit," added Tony. I turned.

"She is still holding her glasses," the surly Jake pointed out. I apologised.

"Right, give them to Molly," said Tony. I gave them to Molly.

"There's a drizzle coming on. We'll need to wait until this shower is over as I'm getting rain on the lens," he said. We waited.

My head was beginning to ache with trying to remember all these instructions.

But now Jake had his say:

"Stop saying "he", say "Somerled", he growled. "You have already said "he" fourteen times".

I tried to concentrate on not saying "he" but, alas, in growing panic, went on saying "he" in spite of myself, which made Jake more bad-tempered than ever. I became like the proverbial rabbit in the headlights and got more panic-stricken the longer we continued.

Eventually I got into the awful state when I couldn't remember what Tony was telling me to do, or what Alan had just asked me. I seemed to be having an out-of-body experience and didn't know what I was saying while I was saying it.

"Anyway," I thought to my resentful self, "what right has Jake to tell me what to say? He is only the Sound man, not the Director."

Then my throat began to dry up and my voice descended into an intermittent croak. I had no water. It was a mile away in the car. Next, my lips went dry and I couldn't articulate my words. The only available water, and there was plenty of it, was in the Sound of Mull and no use to me.

How I longed for the ordeal to be over. Never again, I promised myself, would I allow myself to be beguiled into appearing in a film. I salute the acting profession who do this for their daily bread.

The rest of the filming became a hopeless blur as I staggered through all the questions and blindly walked about as Tony instructed me. This was stage fright without the stage.

Never was I so glad when the unflappable Molly reminded us gently that I should be taken to Craignure for the last ferry back to Oban, which left in an hour, and that they had to pick up another poor soul coming off that same ferry for the next day's filming beside Glengorm Castle at the north end of Mull.

Babbling gratefully, I was taken back to Craignure and put on to the last ferry, off which came the lecturer from Edinburgh University who was doing the next day's filming. Tony, Jake, Alan and Molly met him with smiles and welcome, while happily waving me off into the sunset. I was sure they were glad to see the back of me!

I was never so glad to see CalMac's big ship, *Isle of Mull*, and subsided thankfully into the comforting anonymity of the ferry's cafe, wondering if the new man would be as dreadfully ill at ease as I had been.

I thought probably not. I reckoned I must be the world's worst actor.

Eventually I went up on deck to get a breath of air and, hopefully, drive away the unwelcome memories of my encounter with the BBC, and was immediately and happily distracted by the sight of the *Aileach,* a replica of a small Viking ship, sailing past us in the opposite direction. She was obviously making for the Sound of Mull and points west. Her single big square sail was set and drawing nicely, so rowers were not required. The busiest man aboard was the steersman who had the sole, almost unnerving, responsibility of holding this most unusual rig under control, knowing he had no fall-back to an engine if things became difficult.

The uninvolved, relaxed rowers of the *Aileach* waved up at us from her open deck, and the little ship soon disappeared into the distance. My mind began to wander back to the time when other crews had sailed their ships all around these coasts, and Scotland was all too aware of the threatening presence of Viking longships in the waters of the Kingdom of the Isles, as this area was called.

As we were sailing past the district of Morvern, in which Ardtornish Castle lay, I visualised the great war leader, Somerled MacGhillebhride, as a young man of probably thirty, about the year 1130, distraught with rage and frustration as he watched the inexorable progress of Norwegian Vikings towards supremacy over the entire west coast of Scotland, including his family's ancestral lands in Argyll, by means of their beautiful but sinister longships.

I imagined Somerled's conversation with his ailing father, Gillebride, lord of Morvern:

"Father, we must get our lands back. But we have to rely on something other than a pitched battle to get the Norsemen out of Morvern, They're everywhere," said Somerled in great agitation.

"Well, but what?" muttered the self-pitying Gillebride. *"I've tried long enough, Heaven knows, to defeat these grasping, evil pirates but, even with the help of the Fermanagh men, we can't rid the land of this plague. They're now claiming all the islands from the Isle of Man to the Orkneys, and the mainland from Dumbarton to Caithness."*

Somerled shrugged helplessly, acknowledging the fact that his father was now a broken reed and truly incapable of leading the fight against the Norsemen.

Their conversation was interrupted by the sound of running feet and a voice calling urgently for Somerled. He looked round to find several, breathless tribesmen approaching him, their voices rough with anxiety as they called his name.

"Lord Somerled," began Seumas their leader. *"All of us of the Clan MacInnes of Morvern can see that your father, the Lord Gillebride, is unwell and unable to lead us against the Vikings. We think he should take shelter in the caves nearby until this last wave of the enemy has left and then you should get him away to safety in the islands."*

He hesitated before beginning an impassioned plea,

"Oh, Somerled, our own chief has been killed in this last fight. Will you not take over the leadership? We will follow you anywhere if you will lead us against these interlopers, and the Fermanagh men will help, as long as they can see some chance of a victory."

"What are you saying?" rasped Somerled. *"Are you saying my father should be replaced? By me?"*

"Aye, Gillebride of the the Cave," muttered one of them. *"That's all he's good for --- skulking in a cave while we are left to carry on the struggle against these Viking fiends."*

"If you do not take on the leadership we will all be wiped out," said Seumas flatly. *This is the end of the road for all the Celtic folk of the west, and the king in Scotland is too far away to care. In any case he has no ships to match their accursed longships."*

"Leave me to think about this," said Somerled. *"You know that I am young, and inexperienced in leadership."*

Seumas pleaded, *"The elders of our clan, the Clan MacInnes, have allowed us to say that you have shown your mettle in this last battle. How ferociously and fearlessly you retaliated against our attackers! Also, you are young and fit while our ageing leaders have no stomach left for the fight. You are the best, and the only, man fitted for such a post. Oh, please, my Lord. There is no time left!"*

"Very well, my friends," replied Somerled,*" you have made the case for myself as your new chief. But will you follow me loyally and do whatever I ask of you --- and swear on the iron to do that?"*

"Yes indeed, Lord Somerled. We will do your bidding no matter what," said the smiling Seumas, fervently.

The clansmen standing around him shouted their delight.

Somerled was in charge.

"Then let's get down to business," he said, showing immediately the inspiring personality which had attracted the clansmen to him in the first place, in spite of the odds stacked against him --- his father now lost, the Norse apparently immovably entrenched, few fighting men available apart from the men of Fermanagh, and his family name humiliated by the manner of its downfall at the hands of the usurpers.

Now was the time for desperate tactics. The battle must be taken right to the enemy in the form of lightning guerrilla attacks, immediately.

"Do you see that herd of cows grazing in the field? Well, go and kill them, then skin them," ordered Somerled in a whisper to the

band of men hiding with him in woodland near the Viking encampment. *"When you have done that, get up and march openly around the summit of that hill over there.*

Then come back, put the cattle hides around your shoulders in order to disguise yourselves and repeat the action.

After that, reverse the cow hides and go round the hill a third time, in order to look like a strong force of three divisions.

Then we'll attack them before they have time to work out what is going on."

The story goes that Somerled then attacked the Norsemen and drove them back, with significantly reduced numbers, to the River Shiel, which they struggled across before finally escaping to the relative safety of the islands.

This was the beginning of the resurgence of the Celtic forces in western Scotland, instigated and led by Somerled, who went on to become King of the Isles, and progenitor of the later great Clan Donald, the MacDonalds.

He recognised the importance of the longship in taking and holding his possessions in the Kingdom of the Isles.

He probably had a Twenty-Five, a longship very much bigger than the *Aileach,* with twenty-five pairs of oars, large enough to be suitable for a king. Although we would like to think of him as having the biggest design of warship available at that time there is no evidence that he had one of the Dragon Ships, also known as Great Ships, the equivalent of modern-day battleships --- enormous Norwegian vessels which were terribly expensive to build and maintain, and not able to manoeuvre as fast as the standard Twenty-Five longship.

There were only sixteen recorded Dragon Ships built in Norway between 995 and 1263, ending with the *Kristsuden*, built in Bergen for King Hakon Hakonnssonn.

Initially Somerled would have obtained his warships by piracy or as spoils of battle, and later by having them built by his own shipwrights to a recognised Norse design.

I came back to reality as the *Isle of Mull* sailed carefully into the busy harbour of Oban Bay and tied up at the pier there.

I wondered to myself, "Oh, Somerled, just imagine what you could have done if you had owned this big ship, the *Isle of Mull!"*

But the ship which is most commonly associated with Mull is, of course, the famous Tobermory Galleon.

In the Autumn of 1588 the Spanish invasion fleet of King Philip II of Spain was defeated by the English navy, and many of its ships, attempting to get back to Spain, scattered north and westabout around the northern coasts of Scotland and the west of Ireland, rather than risk further confrontation with English ships in the Channel. At that time of year the weather is always very unpredictable and many of the Spanish warships were lost during fierce storms on the dangerous voyage.

One battered vessel appeared in Tobermory Bay where she had run for shelter, and also to replace sails and spars destroyed in the storms, as well as during the naval battle.

Tobermory

Her name was *Santa Maria de Gracia San Juan Bautista,* a galleon of 800 tons, built in Ragusa (Dubrovnik) and commanded by Don Diego Tellez Henriquez.

It looked at first sight as if she had landed lucky in her choice of sanctuary, for the chief of Clan MacLean of Duart promised to help the Spaniards as long as they fought for him against his old enemy, MacDonald of Islay.

The result was a series of successful raids on MacDonald islands in the Hebrides and the mainland of Ardnamurchan when many

MacDonalds were killed by the Spanish sailors, and MacLean was later declared an outlaw.

The galleon then returned to Tobermory Bay where she anchored safely until the November of 1588. Perhaps the Spaniards were unaware of the strength of feeling among the Scottish clans for it seems they were totally unprepared for the violent explosion which suddenly blew their ship apart. There is no doubt that her magazine exploded, the ship caught fire and sank quickly in the middle of the bay, killing most of her crew.

This could possibly have been the result of an accident, but is more likely to have been a revenge attack by the MacDonalds or sabotage by English agents. At any rate the shattered hull disappeared into the thick mud of the bay, and gave rise to the romantic legend of the Tobermory treasure ship.

Over the centuries many people have dived in the bay, searching hopefully for the lost ship and its supposed treasure, including representatives of several Dukes of Argyll, but very little in the way of artefacts has been found, never mind treasure.

It seems unlikely that anything will ever be found as the whole area is now thickly silted with mud, and so many treasure hunters have disturbed the entire site that fragmentation of the remains has probably already taken place.

But it certainly makes a good story!

The next time I journeyed along that same road from Craignure to Tobermory was soon afterwards and in totally different circumstances.

I was taking part, with my Gaelic Choir comrades, in the annual provincial Mòd in Tobermory, the main town of the island of Mull. These smaller events are held throughout the summer months in various parts of the west and, as well as being a pleasant interlude when old friends in the Gaelic world can meet and ceilidh together, are considered a useful practice run for the main competition festival of the choir year --- the National Mòd of An Comunn Gaidhealach, always held in mid October in a range of different venues.

Several of us were to sit our Gaelic test that day as choirs must present a proportion of their members who are proficient in Gaelic in order to gain a desirable Bronze, Silver or Gold card. So there we were, crammed on to the local bus, and not enjoying the journey up to Tobermory one bit, for worrying about the test. I had been asked to take it along with the others although they had had instruction in the language but I had not, my Gaelic having been acquired informally from my Skye grandfather during my childhood.

I just wished they would all be quiet and stop testing themselves against one another as we journeyed along. What should have been a pleasant journey was anything but, as folk kept bemoaning the fact of not knowing the word for this or that, asking generally who knew the correct idiom for such and such, and making mistakes in grammar all over the place. By the time Tobermory appeared in view I was a nervous wreck and wishing I had never come.

After decamping from the bus we were directed to a local church hall where the tests were to be held, and shown into a long, gloomy little room where we had to wait our turn to be tested.

The first of our number was a native Gaelic speaker from the Western Isles. Catriona was obviously going to pass brilliantly and get her Lifelong Gold Card, the highest accolade possible. She was supremely confident. Alright for her, we thought! The rest of us --- one of whom was an Admiral (Engineering) --- twittered with nerves and made unhappy comparisons with the endless exams of our schooldays.

Catriona was called first and went off in fine, relaxed mode to the next room where the testers lurked. She was away, we thought, for ages, and eventually returned, beaming, the happy recipient of a Life-long Gold Card.

"Sorry I took so long. I was just having a great craic (conversation) with the testers," she said. "We know so many folk in common."

Off she went. A steward then appeared in the doorway and told me to get ready to go through next. Nervously, and without waiting to be called, I shot out of the small anteroom, straight into the larger room next door where the examiners sat in stately formality, waiting for the next victim.

I started in at once, thinking that if I could guide the subject for discussion it would be a decided advantage --- and was cut off in midstream by the testers who hadn't quite finished their discussion about Catriona and the folk they all knew in common. I was requested, but quite kindly, to go back out and wait until they called me in.

Covered in confusion I rattled out, "I beg your pardon," in Gaelic, and scuttled out of the room, feeling extremely silly. My partners in the ordeal looked astonished at my sudden reappearance in the anteroom.

"Heavens, did they fail you right away?" asked the Admiral anxiously. "You hardly had time to get into the room!"

"It's okay, they'll call me when they're ready," I uttered bravely, shaking with nerves.

At that I was called again by the steward and entered the test room much more cautiously. I was waved into a chair and this time, waited in silence until the lady tester asked the first question.

Gaelic is a complex language and is spoken on many different islands as well as the mainland. All have their distinctive local accents and many use different idioms, but all are linguistically acceptable. The trick is to get the hang of what the tester is saying, in whatever dialect, before making a suitable answer.

I therefore listened with as much concentration as I could muster and, after asking several questions --- and receiving several apologies from me for wrong answers --- the lady tester asked me to describe the appearance of her male colleague, sitting in the next chair.

I took a deep breath and started in on him. All seemed to be going well until I described his hair.

"You have very nice, thick, brown hair," I said enthusiastically. There was an embarrassing silence. What *faux pas* had I just made, I wondered unhappily.

The gentleman looked rather sour.

"You have just told me I have a very nice, thick, brown wig," he said, without the vestige of a smile on his face.

Yet again I stammered, "I beg your pardon," to the solemn faced testers. Why was I always having to apologise to them, I thought to myself? At the same time I knew it wasn't really a good idea to insult the examiner if you want to pass the exam.

However, he turned out to be quite magnanimous and, smiling at last, admitted that Gaelic does have this unnerving habit of using the same word for several different meanings.

After a conversation in extremely quick-fire Gaelic the testers generously informed me that I had passed my card. I thanked them profusely and fairly skipped out of the room to where my friends waited in trepidation for the next call into the test room

Blessedly, we all passed, and one of our number, who had secreted a half bottle of whisky in her handbag, made us all go out to the railings by the shore to have a quick, celebratory dram. We needed little persuasion and were quite a merry band when we finally joined the rest of the choir slogging away at a final rehearsal before going on stage in the Aros Hall.

Congratulations were offered all round.

The competitions went on slowly throughout the afternoon and, after what we considered to be a reasonable performance, we waited in hopeful anticipation for the Gaelic and Music adjudicators to give their judgment.

This time we had done remarkably well, and everyone was in buoyant mood when we got back to Craignure for the five o'clock ferry.

Naturally, as we were still so "high", we started out to sing the entire Mòd programme again with many extra songs thrown in for good measure. This was nothing new --- we always did. Sometimes irate ferry passengers would leave the saloon/bar, muttering darkly, because we were making so much noise and they wanted to enjoy a peaceful voyage, but most folk enjoyed the impromptu performance, sung with gusto and glad relaxation, as the songs always should be.

This time we had an appreciative audience of Americans aboard. They loved the songs, they loved our tartans, they cheered, they clapped, they whistled, they stamped their feet where appropriate, they took many photographs, they told us our performance was the highlight of their trip and they almost wept over us when the ferry docked and we had all, reluctantly, to get off the ship, and go on our various ways.

The power of music to unite!

Tale no. 16: Roddy, Ace Footballer

"Do you know what he did yesterday?" I said to Chris in great agitation.

"No, what did he do?" giggled Chris in gleeful anticipation of the latest of Roddy the Labrador's dreadful deeds.

Roddy sitting on his cushion

"I can't go back to that school ever again, or we might get tarred and feathered and run out of town," I groaned.

"What on earth did he do? Tell me, tell me!" she urged.

"Well, as it was a warm, sunny day very near the end of term I offered to take the senior class down on to the shore, for a bit of hunting for crabs, sea anemones, starfish, shellfish and so on, in the rock pools. The Head Teacher said that would be fine and she could get on with writing her final reports before the kids went on to the secondary school.

Off we went with a delighted Roddy, happy to be in the midst of the children who, straight-faced, had once told the rest of the school that he had taught the Andrex puppy all his tricks!

We got down to the beach and everyone started searching the pools for interesting sea life. After a while we had a rest, looked at all the creatures the kids had found, then someone produced an old football that he had found jammed behind some rocks.

Naturally they all started to play football on the sands when Roddy, who had been let off the lead while on the shore, joined in uninvited, grabbed the ball and raced away with it, obviously thoroughly enjoying being chased along the beach by the yelling mob of children. He finally gave it up after stern commands from me and the game continued.

This time one of the girls accidentally kicked the ball into the sea and it floated out some way. Roddy plunged in to the rescue, surging forward like the paddle steamer *Waverley* rounding Ardlamont Point, while the kids cheered him on from the shore.

Eventually he caught up with the ball, grabbed it in his jaws and paddled back to the shore where he emerged, shaking himself violently and showering his shrieking fan club with sea water. He dropped the ball in front of me but, when I bent down to pick it up he grabbed it again and dodged about, refusing to give it up to me or anyone else. I'll swear that dog was laughing at us in pure mischief. You should have seen his face --- if a dog can be said to grin, he was grinning and, as usual, wagging his tail.

The next minute off he went again, straight into the sea and, still holding the ball, started swimming out towards where a local fisherman had laid his nets.

As always, the tops of the nets were festooned with plastic floats to mark their position and keep them afloat. Roddy immediately lost all interest in the battered old football and swiftly abandoned it to its fate.

He became far more interested in the bobbing floats, which were roughly the same size and shape as the football. To my horror he swam in among them, grabbing them whenever he could get a grip and happily towing them all over the place. Naturally where the floats went, the nets followed and soon there was the most almighty tangle of fishing nets and floats that you can imagine. He paid absolutely no attention when I yelled at him to drop the floats and come ashore at once.

Some of the boys offered to go in after him and bring him ashore but, of course, I couldn't allow that in case they got into difficulties. *Health and Safety* and all that.

So we all had to watch helplessly while the wretched dog played havoc with the fishing nets. Moby Dick himself couldn't have made a bigger commotion.

At that point the worst happened."

Chris was agog with curiosity by this time. "For Heaven's sake, what happened?" she demanded.

"Didn't the fisherman himself appear on the beach!" I uttered, shuddering, reliving in my mind the whole awful scene.

"I thought he was going to have a stroke when he saw the state of his nets, and he started shouting and swearing at the top of his voice at the dog, at me, at the children ---. It all became extremely fraught and all I could think of was getting the kids away before the man resorted to actual physical violence.

We were all very scared and I quickly rounded everyone up, gave a last despairing scream at Roddy to come ashore immediately, and started scrambling hurriedly up the sandy beach, trying to herd the kids together and usher them up on to the road like a distracted mother hen shooing her chicks out of reach of a ravening fox. It's not that easy to run quickly through soft sand and it seemed as if we would never get off the shore before the ogre caught us and possibly killed us all."

Chris was saucer-eyed by this time and quite obviously unsure as to whether to laugh or commiserate. "Go on, go on," she urged.

"Well, Roddy finally realised in his doggy mind that his friends were in some kind of trouble, forgot the entrancing floats, paddled ashore at high speed, dodged the irate fisherman and raced after us while the man threw every missile he could lay hands on at us and threatened us with all kinds of litigation for ruining his nets.

I gave up gasping out breathless apologies over my shoulder as we all struggled off the beach and finally fled up the road to the sanctuary of the school building. Never were children more eager to enter their school than these children yesterday afternoon!

I dreaded having to explain the situation to the Head Teacher who had appeared at the school door to greet one distraught Primary

Adviser, one very wet Labrador and a class of highly excited, extremely voluble children all talking at her at once.

Blessedly she was a personal friend of the fisherman and his wife and, having calmed everyone down, declared that she would make it alright with him, and seriously discourage him from sending the local policeman up to the school.

I'm telling you, Chris, I'm absolutely affronted, and I can't go near that school again for a very long time, if ever!"

"What a bad dog!" said Chris, grinning all over her face. "I expect he just wagged his tail and offered everyone a paw."

I groaned.

That summer term was unusually dry and sunny on the west coast of Scotland and soon after the fishing net episode my dog and I were travelling out through the wonderful scenery of what used to be called *The Rough Bounds* of Lochaber in order to visit the local primary schools. We were making for the little coastal village of Morar, and looking forward to many walks along the unbelievably gorgeous, white sands of that shoreline, and to enjoy the fantastic views of the islands of Rum, Eigg, Muck, Canna and Skye dotted about throughout the western ocean.

We climbed out of the car at the hotel and went inside to be greeted by our host, and old friend for, when travelling about on education business you get to meet, and become acquainted with, a lot of local people in every district.

Sorley MacPherson was one of these and he greeted me warmly and patted Roddy as he showed us up to our room.

"You'll be going to the football match on Sunday afternoon," he announced.

"Will I?" I asked in surprise, for I had never even discussed football with him before, never mind expressed an interest in watching a match.

"Oh yes," said Sorley. "The weather is just right for it, the ground is completely dry for once, and all the locals will be there. It's a charity match, you know, between the Ladies and the Men of Morar and we want a nice, big crowd to cheer the players on. So, you'll come?"

"Sure," I said, planning to show willing and turn up for the match since it was for "A Good Cause".

"That's fine then," he said. "You'll be playing for the Ladies, of course."

"What?" I spluttered. "Now look here, Sorley, I never said a word about taking part. I'll just be a supportive spectator.

"Oh, go on," he said in his best wheedling tone. "We've got plenty of boys for the match, but we're short of young, fit ladies."

"Flattery will get you nowhere," I retorted. "In any case what would my Director say if he found out?"

But Sorley kept on and on at me until I, with very bad grace, relented. I wasn't surprised there was a shortage of lady players available. I had seen the young men of Morar --- a crowd of large, burly, athletic fishermen with the turn of speed of international rugby players. What on earth had I got myself into? We were likely to be annihilated.

I didn't let on to anyone in my four local schools --- the two at Arisaig, one at Mallaig and one at Morar. I didn't think my Director of Education in Inverness would be very impressed by his Primary Adviser cavorting about on a public football pitch --- and on a Sunday, too! --- no matter what "The Good Cause". Talk about making a public spectacle of yourself! I could just hear him --- "So undignified for Education Personnel, you know."

But alas, I had committed myself.

So, on a blazing Sunday afternoon, a very bashful Primary Adviser, accompanied by the entire complement of the hotel and her faithful hound --- who howled the place down if left alone in the hotel --- sidled timorously over to the football pitch which was, I was horrified to see, crammed with eager spectators, from what looked like the whole of Lochaber. The place was buzzing with anticipation, and bets were being taken as to which side would win.

Strangely enough, many folk bet on the Ladies to win, as they had cunningly used feminine wiles, hoping to distract the men, in the guise of the Belles of St. Trinian's.

I shudder to think what kind of spectacle I presented, dressed in an ancient, tattered and faded gymslip, disastrously laddered black tights and wearing an enormous, floppy tartan bow in my hair. In addition we were all plastered with pancake make-up and every other kind of cosmetics we could lay hands on.

"You're enough to scare the horses!" shouted one uncomplimentary spectator.

"Oh, you just shut up! Anyway, there are no horses," snapped our Lady Captain. "You'll be singing a different tune when you see us win."

I admired her confidence, but privately was sure we were about to be wiped out.

However, I handed Roddy over into the tender care of Sorley who promised not to let him go during the match --- I knew exactly what havoc that dog could cause if there was a ball in his vicinity.

The whistle blew and the match began.

We all ran miles around the football pitch during that long, hot afternoon but, in spite of much cheering and whistling on behalf of the Ladies, it soon became evident that the Men were by far the better team. Time and again they attacked our goal, and were building up a considerable number of points while we had absolutely none. Half-time came round, with much confusing advice being offered from Sorley and all the other spectators, some of whom were beginning to drift off in boredom. This was hardly Rangers v. Celtic.

Matters were becoming desperate. It was high time for serious measures to be taken.

It was at this point that my beloved hound was pressed into service. Before I could stop him Sorley had unleashed the over-excited Roddy and urged him into the Ladies' goal just as a blinding shot came rocketing towards our beleaguered goal-keeper. Before she could get hand or foot to the ball Roddy leaped joyously into the air, intercepted the ball in mid flight, streaked away down the pitch with it in his jaws and raced into the Men's goal where he dropped it in front of the astonished goal-keeper.

A huge cheer went up from the Ladies' supporters. "Hurray! Great goal!" they yelled.

"Nobody warned me you were carrying hidden weapons," shouted the goalkeeper to the Ladies' team, unable to stop laughing as he shooed Roddy out of the goal where the wicked Sorley was waiting to grab him and escort him sedately, on his lead, back to the Ladies' end again.

"Sorley," I shouted, "Don't let him off the lead again." Once more I was affronted at the unruly behaviour of my dog, but the place was exploding with cheers for Ladies and dog. Those who had been leaving the ground turned around and streamed hurriedly back in again, determined not to miss anything, and the umpire blew his whistle to continue the match.

Of course, the same thing happened again. Sorley let the dog off the lead the next time the Men's centre forward came near the Ladies' goal.

Roddy shot in like a space rocket, whisked the ball away from right under the astonished player's feet just as he was about to kick it, and pelted away up the pitch to the accompaniment of loud cheers and shrieks of laughter from the spectators, while I ran helplessly up the pitch after him, in acute embarrassment, shouting to him to stop, and quite sure we would be banned for ever from yet another Highland village.

But, no. It seemed that the spectators were delighted with the outcome.

"Leave the dog alone, lassie," advised a white haired old gentleman. "This is the best football match we've ever had in Morar. And he is the best player we have ever had."

The chaotic match eventually ended with a three-all draw. The Ladies hugged and kissed Roddy ecstatically. He just modestly wagged his tail, enjoying all the fuss that was being made of him.

We were immediately inundated by happy spectators all trying to pat the dog at the same time, and totally ignoring me altogether. I was just the person who had brought the hero of the hour to the game. I suppose I was worth my temporary invitation on to the Morar Ladies' Football Team for that reason alone. It certainly wasn't for my football ability.

Never were so many complimentary toasts offered to a Labrador dog as were in the hotel that night and Roddy went down in the history of Morar as the best footballer the village has ever seen.

A fortnight later it was off to Sabhal Mòr Ostaig, the Gaelic college at Sleat in south Skye. I wanted to get my childhood Gaelic updated before including the subject in the schools' curriculum when the new term began.

I had to take Roddy with me as my mother declared herself to be totally unable to look after such a powerful, big dog if he was left with her for three weeks. This was understandable as he had, in fact, caused her to fall headlong into a large rhododendron bush during a recent evening stroll, and an irate mother eventually appeared at the back door with her face covered in black smears from the dusty bush. And recently, while being walked along the pavement, he had pulled out of her grasp and run into the middle of the road after an inoffensive cat, causing frantic braking and swerving of the car ferry traffic streaming in both directions.

He ignored my mother's shouts to him to came back at once. The motorists were rightly incensed and threatened all kinds of vengeance from their car windows. My mother, mortified and realising that she couldn't get him to come back, gave up the struggle, pretended he wasn't with her and walked away along the pavement, gazing innocently into the far distance and hoping no one would associate her with the current chaos on the road. That no car actually collided with him was a miracle.

In his own time the wilful Roddy forgot the cat, wandered casually off the road and attached himself to her again looking, as always, as if butter wouldn't melt in his mouth. For some time she kept up the pretence of not being with him until the last of the irate drivers had disappeared into the distance, before clipping on the lead again and berating the totally unconcerned dog for his disobedience. As always, he just wagged his tail.

"I have died a thousand deaths over that dog," she complained, "so don't leave him with me. For goodness sake take him with you to Skye and let him scare the life out of the Sgiathanaich (Skye folk) for a change."

So off we went, driving out westwards towards the island of Skye and the now famous college of Sabhal Mòr Ostaig, part of the University of the Highlands, where all instruction is given in Gaelic. I knew many of the staff there through education connections and was looking forward to meeting up with them again.

Iain MacKerracher was the tutor for my group, which comprised several Canadians and Americans of originally Scottish origin, from whose forebears had evolved many strange idioms and unusual accents when speaking Gaelic. Iain had constantly to stop the flow of whoever was speaking and tactfully correct their pronunciation, not to mention their basic grammar and vocabulary.

He admitted to me that he often found it infuriating, frustrating and, on many occasions, actually boring, having to listen to the regular massacre of such a beautiful language. I commiserated with him, having been surprised, myself, at the outlandish forms of "Gaelic" being aired in the class.

The college was in its very early years at that time, being originally an abandoned farmstead on the estate of Sir Iain Noble, a merchant banker and big landowner in the island. He had generously donated the farm buildings to the fledgling college with the aim of encouraging, and indeed, saving Gaelic language and culture throughout the islands and the entire Gaeltachd.

Roddy was confined to the car while classes were going on, but allowed out at lunchtime when he and I wandered into the "dining-room" which was really a crumbling, wood-lined, high ceilinged old room in the ancient steading. When it rained the water fell straight into your soup through the gaps in the roof, and the wooden lining hung haphazardly from the ceiling, so nobody lingered there for long. I found it quite difficult to hold a full plate of soup with one hand and a boisterous dog in the other. Inevitably most of my soup ended up on the floor or on Roddy as I tried to negotiate my unsteady way from kitchen door to lunch table. So lunchtimes became a nightmare at Sabhal Mòr and I spent as little time as possible indoors, finding it more relaxing to take my dog for a long walk away from the steading.

The entire centre of the quadrangle of farm buildings was filled with rubble and building materials as the college gradually took shape, and the one side which would later become the assembly hall was completely derelict at that time. The library, where many classes were held, could be used only during daylight hours as the electricians had not yet finished their work and electric cables sprouted, unconnected, out of the walls, ready to catch the unwary walking past. Truly it was a potential death trap. *Health and Safety* hadn't been thought of as yet.

In the fulness of time the building would emerge from its dusty chrysalis and become the heart of the brand new college, with a later, beautiful extension down on the shore, whose dramatic views across the Sound of Sleat towards the uninhabited, unspoiled district of Knoydart with its incredible high mountains made it, surely, one of the most beautifully situated university buildings in Britain, if not the world.

It was while I was in the dining-room and about to get back to my classroom for the afternoon session that another class came bursting in, full of glee at the hilarious mistake made by one of the Canadians.

"It's true," I heard one of them say. "He actually translated *maor sìthe* as *a big fairy*."

And everyone fell about in fits of laughter. *Maor sìthe* in fact means *peace official* and would normally refer to *a policeman*. I had an instant inner vision of a burly policeman going about his duties dressed in big boots, a tutu, wearing fairy wings and carrying a magic wand.

I headed for the car park with a reluctant Roddy in tow. It was time for me to get back to class again and for him to climb back into the car for a while.

I met Iain on the way.

"Oh, just bring him into the class," he said. "He'll be no trouble." So I hesitantly agreed and the bold Roddy expressed his pleasure in the usual way --- greeting every student as if a long lost friend, with doggy grin and wagging tail.

We settled down to some abstruse points of grammar which seemed to go on for ever, and the class was becoming a bit restless.

So, unfortunately, was the dog. He wriggled and uttered small squeaking noises in his throat. I knew these would soon evolve into a fully fledged whine, and told him, rather sharply, to be quiet. He subsided briefly, but then began to try to get the attention of the American sitting next to me. The lad had a waterproof jacket folded over his knees and Roddy started to paw at it, his claws scraping noisily over the stiff, shiny surface. The noise seemed to fill the entire room, and I hauled him off unceremoniously and hissed "Shut up!" at him. This was not the time for niceties.

It was no use. He started to whine quite loudly and many of the class were staring at us with obvious annoyance. It was definitely time to leave.

"Please excuse us," I muttered and stood up, almost bowing apologetically towards Iain as I dragged the offender out of the room while he howled at the top of his voice.

"Roddy, you wretch. Here I am embarrassed at your dreadful behaviour yet again!" I shouted. "You're going straight back into the car and I don't want to hear another squeak out of you."

I returned to the classroom and entered like a mouse, desperate not to antagonise my fellow students any further. They paid absolutely no attention to me and I could almost feel their displeasure, though I think this was partly because they were fed up with the boring grammar lesson and wanted to display their annoyance somehow. Roddy was barred from all classrooms and remained in the car during all lessons, from that time forwards.

Anyway, the course continued, as planned, with humorous bits, difficult bits and boring bits, and Roddy was eventually forgiven.

We finally reached the end of the course and all joined in the inevitable end-of-term party. Songs were sung by the traditional singing group; clarsachs, accordions and fiddles were played by the instrumentalists; stories were told by the bardic groups; there was piping from the piping students; dancing from both Highland and Country dancers; speeches were made by the Principal and by a delighted Iain Noble, founder of the college.

At the very end of the programme the Principal stood up and announced an unusual extra presentation which he was quite sure was unique in the then short annals of the college. To my astonishment he called out, "Roddy, come and receive your certificate."

We both climbed up on to the stage with me slightly apprehensive, not knowing what to expect.

A large sheet of parchment was handed over, its gold lettering declaring that this award was presented to Roddy the Labrador, being the only known Dog ever to have regularly attended classes at Sabhal Mòr Ostaig!

Tale no. 17: Alarms and Excursions

Janet and I were sitting in the dining room of a well known hotel situated on the loch side of an equally well known Hebridean town on a bitter, blustery 1st November, waiting patiently for our lunch to materialise. The hotel was not busy and there was no one else in the room, but we had already waited for some considerable time and the food had not yet appeared.

We were getting quite impatient and thinking of moving to another hostelry when the small side door, which opened directly on to the street, suddenly burst open and a freezingly cold blast of air, straight off the loch, funnelled destructively throughout the entire room.

Every napkin, every menu, every piece of paper and every lightweight object was swept away from all the tables and from behind the bar, and deposited randomly all over the floor and on every flat surface, by the icy whirlwind. Then the door slammed shut again, apparently of its own accord.

As one, we leaped to our feet and scrambled about picking up the detritus and replacing everything in approximately its correct position. It took some time to bring order to the dining room and, laughing at the unexpectedness of the event, we then impatiently continued our wait, rather surprised that none of the hotel staff had appeared. Surely they had heard the commotion.

We shivered in the suddenly reduced temperature and, losing patience, eventually began to gather our belongings together before departing, in annoyance, to a better organised hotel when, without warning, the side door burst open again, with the same outcome --- a cyclone of paper and assorted objects, whirling about the now cold room like confetti.

For some unknown reason we again sprang into action. Once more we spent a considerable time restoring order from the surrounding chaos, and once again none of the hotel staff appeared in the dining room. Why did we bother? We tried to analyse our repeated good deeds, without success.

"It must be the Girl Guides in us," suggested Janet.

"I certainly wouldn't like the hotel staff blaming us for vandalising their dining room when they weren't looking," I answered. "However, it's their own fault for not paying attention to their business. I think we should go, don't you?"

And for the second time we started to get up from our table, but were stopped in our tracks.

This time it was the main door leading from the front hall that burst suddenly open, accompanied by the usual cold draught of air, and we suddenly sat down again, in expectation of our long awaited soup.

But no --- in staggered a vision in ancient, filthy dungarees, bowed under the considerable load of a hundredweight of coal in a grimy sack which lay across his back, pressing heavily on the back of his neck. It seemed that he was intending to carry this unsavoury burden right through the middle of the dining room.

While he staggered slowly past us we noticed that a corner of the sack had fallen open and, as he swayed, almost unbalancing, among the tables and across the open floor, a thin, black streak of coal dust trickled down his back, following him across the carpeted floor like a long, sooty serpent.

We gazed, in open-mouthed fascination, at the apparition who was heading, unsteadily, for a small door which we hadn't noticed earlier, on the far side of the fireplace.

"'Morning," grunted the vision.

"'Morning," we chorused back, unable, in our dumbfounded state, to think of any other reply.

"It isn't still Hallowe'en, is it?" whispered Janet.

"Don't think so," I muttered.

He finally reached the door but couldn't free a hand to open it, so kicked it open and lurched heavily through into the space beyond. On the way a large lump of coal detached itself from the sack and fell with a muted clunk on to the crimson carpet, causing a small avalanche of coal dust to spill out in its wake.

By this time we were giggling helplessly, but not at all confident about the hygiene arrangements in the hotel kitchen. What on earth might we expect to find in our long awaited soup? We decided to make our escape before anyone could stop us.

As we sneaked across the front hall and emerged out into the lochside gale the heavy glass-fronted door was whipped out of Janet's hand and slammed shut so heavily that the glass cracked from side to side.

Paralysed, we gazed at one another for a horror-stricken minute, then decided to run for it.

We hared desperately to the shore lay-by where we had left the car, leaped aboard and drove off in a panic, declaring that we could never dare to enter that hotel again --- and we never have!

All this happened in the days before the Scottish Tourist Board exerted its almighty authority over all hospitality in Scotland.

But not all hotels were so badly managed.

As the Primary Adviser I used to love my winter visits to the Coolin Hills Hotel in Portree on the island of Skye and would happily ask the switchboard in my office in Inverness to get me Portree 3, the hotel's unforgettable phone number, and exchange complimentary greetings with the hotel's telephone operator.

Because there were almost no tourist visitors to the island in January and February, Inverness-shire Education Department officials were given very advantageous rates for Bed and Breakfast and Evening Meal, and were delighted to take advantage of this generous offer, particularly when the weather was bad. We certainly appreciated the warmth and comfort of the lovely old hotel after braving the elements all day while going round the many primary schools of the island in winter weather.

On my first visit I was given an entire corner suite to myself --- oh, the luxury of the spacious apartment with its extensive desk, capacious wardrobe facilities and endless hot water for a thoroughly chilled Primary Adviser to wallow in before descending to the elegant dining room where the waiter offered a delicious choice of fresh island food, like Aberdeen Angus steaks, haunch of venison, local wild salmon, sea trout, lobsters, crabs, oysters and other shellfish, followed by typically melt-in-the-mouth Hebridean desserts such as Cranachan and Carageen, along with locally produced island cheeses --- not all at once, of course!

It was well worth the discomforts of the winter days on the road.

The hotel owners told me to look out of my corner window on to the grassy, tree-dotted slopes of the gardens.

"Do you see the snowdrops out there?" they said. "Look how big they are."

"Yes," I replied, "they are quite lovely."

"They are Crimean snowdrops, and bigger than the native variety," I was told. "They were brought back by Skyemen returning from fighting in the Crimean War in 1856. They planted the bulbs out there in memory of their fallen comrades. The climate must suit the snowdrops for they have been spreading year by year, much to our delight."

I was very touched by this story and always looked for the carpet of delicate, tiny, white flowers with their poignant history whenever back in Portree in January.

But there's always a drawback, however, no matter how good the island hospitality and I found it in the provision of a courtesy car when my own car broke down on the road to Elgol. It had to be towed up to Portree and the garage offered me a substitute in the shape of an ancient Hillman Minx, a car I was not at all acquainted with. But, as beggars can't be choosers, I gratefully accepted it and set off back down the road to Elgol.

I had driven a mile or two along the quiet road out of Broadford towards Loch Slapin, muttering uncomplimentary things about the Hillman's highly suspect suspension and, feeling increasingly stiff, I leaned heavily against the back of my seat in order to relieve my now aching back.

Immediately the back of the seat fell off into the well of the car. I nearly went after it and just managed to keep my balance by hanging on frantically to the steering wheel. Unfortunately my feet were jerked off the pedals, the engine stalled and the uncontrolled car swerved right across the opposite carriageway. Momentum carried it onwards to the edge of a deep ditch where it hovered, see-sawing, before toppling in and settling on its right side.

Fortunately it hadn't overturned but now lay with the driver's door firmly jammed against the banking. I had been thrown hard against my window, and couldn't get out. There was water in the ditch and I could feel it seeping steadily into the car through the broken windscreen. Although used to occasional emergency situations on our fishing boats at home in Southend, I have to admit that I could feel panic beginning to rise in my throat. I was lying helplessly on my right side and couldn't get my feet under me in order to climb up the inside of the car, somehow force open the heavy weight of the passenger door and struggle out. I didn't think shouting for help would be of any use as the road was very isolated. I was trapped here in the steadily rising water of the ditch. There were no mobile phones then, so I couldn't summon help in any way. It was terrifying to feel so utterly helpless.

Eventually, to my inexpressible relief, I heard another car drawing up on the road directly above me and looked up to see a concerned face staring down at me.

"Are you okay?" a tall, dark-haired man questioned me, anxiously.

"No, I'm not. The water's rising inside this wreck and I can't get out. The back of my seat fell off and I lost control of the car," I wailed. "It's not my car. The garage lent me this one while my own is being repaired."

I babbled on, wishing he would do something about getting me out.

"Right, don't worry. I'll soon have you out of there," said the stranger in a calm and soothing voice.

"Hang on." And he yanked open the passenger door, stretched down a large hand and hoisted me bodily up and out of my trap in one energetic pull.

At last we stood side by side on the road, peering down into the back of the car.

"Would you just look at that," he said, pointing to a small spar lying underneath the driver's seat.

"The back of the seat must have been detached from the rest of it, and they have just propped it up with a bit of firewood! What a disgrace! Jump in, and I'll give you a lift back to Portree."

I got into the stranger's car in a state of thankful relief. He introduced himself as Donald MacKay and informed me that he was a banker from Dingwall, and often on business on Skye. I thought he looked vaguely familiar and it turned out that we had already met, in Mrs MacAulay's renowned Creagorry Hotel on the Outer Hebridean island of Benbecula.

It's a small world in the Western Isles!

Very serious words were uttered when I eventually entered the garage in Portree. The garage owner, recognising that I could make things very hot for him at the local police station, fluttered around me, frantically apologising and offering all sorts of inducements not to do so.

I'm afraid I snarled at him like the proverbial Dragon Lady. I wasn't going to let him off easily. And I absolutely insisted that he tow my own car round to another garage to be repaired, at his own expense, in spite of his voluble reluctance. He was well aware that this wasn't going to do his reputation any good in the island, where news travels almost faster than the speed of light.

Modern MOT tests might often be a real nuisance to car owners but they certainly have made a difference when it comes to car safety. Before that it was every man for himself.

Neil, a young veterinary student friend of mine, studying at the Glasgow Vet School, owned a real old banger, in which he, and several friends, drove home to Campbeltown on most Friday nights and back again on Sunday evenings. He kindly offered me a lift any time I might need one, and I sometimes took him up on his invitation.

On my first Friday evening I met Neil's battered car at the corner of Byres Road and Great Western Road in Glasgow, and was taken aback to discover that the back door was held on with binder twine and the car was, as a mariner friend of mine would say, *well down by the stern*. I really didn't want to know what other eccentric alterations had been made to the car and climbed in gingerly, becoming wedged between two large students, Sandy and Brian. The car now sank down on to its back wheels even further. The front passenger seat was occupied by Davy, a huge lad introduced as an international rugby player. No other person shared the front seat with him.

I think every rule in the book was broken by Neil, even for these days. We streaked out of town and along the Boulevard towards the area of Loch Lomond where the road became a narrow, winding menace, full of blind corners, with sheer rock faces on the left and the depths of the loch on the right, although it is one of the main highways to the north.

Round each bend we screeched until the usual nightmare on Loch Lomond hove into view. It was a little Morris Minor, puttering along in the middle of the carriageway at about ten miles per hour. It wouldn't pull over to let is through. Neil drove as close to the little car as he dared and we crawled along for several miles, the Morris's driver either unaware of, or uncaring about, his snail's pace up the lochside. We couldn't get past, being prevented by lorries, buses and other large vehicles coming down the loch towards the city. The corners were a nightmare, with vehicles having to slow right down and edge carefully past one another, there being absolutely no room for manoeuvre.

Neil tried a few blasts on the horn --- no result. He then flashed his headlights at the back of the Morris. Still no result. It carried steadily on its way, right in the middle of the road whenever traffic permitted, and just wouldn't let us through. We trailed miserably behind him for many miles with everyone seething with frustration.

By this time our fellow passengers were stirring angrily, and full of suggestions, most of them highly colourful and some downright criminal. This was war!

"Wait till we get to the junction at Tarbet," snarled Davy. "We'll get the wee toad there. The road's up just now and there are temporary traffic lights. He'll have to stop there."

"Okay, but I'm going to try to pass him before that, so he can't sneak away from us when the light turns green," said Neil.

A touring bus coming towards us provided the situation we were hoping for. The Morris was forced back on to his own side of the road in order to let the big vehicle pass and as soon as it had crawled past him, and before the Morris had time to get back on to the crown of the road, Neil put his foot to the floor, leaned on the horn and we roared triumphantly past in a cloud of black exhaust smoke, narrowly avoiding taking the side off the offender.

We swept past the insufferable pest and Neil held on his way until five minutes' driving brought us up to the traffic lights at Tarbet.

It being fairly early on a Friday night there was no other car waiting there so we were first in the queue at the red light. The Morris crept up behind us, its driver gazing impassively at us as he drew to a halt, apparently not a whit abashed.

"Great," said Neil. "Let's deal with him! He's wasted enough of our time."

I didn't know exactly what the boys had in mind --- and I was a bit apprehensive in case blood would be spilt --- so was not prepared for what followed.

Out stepped our squad from the car, marched two by two, back to the Morris, then Davy and Neil went to its back wheels and Sandy and Brian to its front wheels. To my stupefaction they bent down and, each grasping the underside of the wheel arches, lifted the vehicle bodily into the air and turned it right round, before putting it down again, none too gently, on the road, facing the way it had come.

I could see the alarmed driver opening his mouth to yell as he was turned, helplessly, through 180 degrees.

The lads dusted their hands together, strode back to our car and got in, just as the light turned green. We drove off, leaving an altercation between the Morris and a following car, as its driver wanted to know what on earth he thought he was playing at, facing the wrong way in a queue at a traffic light.

We never did find out exactly what happened after that, but our way was now clear right through to Arrochar and the Rest-and-Be-Thankful.

I'm glad to say that the return journey on Sunday night was entirely without incident.

That was the weekend when I met my new boss for the first time.

I was in the kitchen at Southend on Saturday morning and, as it was a showery day, had thrown the newly washed sheets over the kitchen pulley, where they would soon dry in the heat from the Wellstood, rather than risk them out in the drizzly garden.

The back door was open but I hadn't heard the arrival of a car in the yard outside, or footsteps in the scullery, and was intrigued suddenly to discover, below the level of the sheets, a pair of sturdy bare legs in khaki shorts above a pair of well worn sandshoes.

A cheery voice called out, "Anyone at home?" and Hector MacNeill ducked under the sheets and came forward, smiling broadly and holding out his hand.

"You're my new teacher at Millknowe, aren't you?" he asked. "I'm the head man on the premises. I was just passing and thought I'd drop in and introduce myself."

I was considerably taken aback, having never experienced such jovial informality in my previous post --- a secondary school where the headmaster floated about in his black, academic gown and never permitted a smile to crack his face. New teachers there were treated liken recalcitrant pupils --- endlessly frowned upon and regarded as a nuisance.

My parents heard our voices and came through to the kitchen to meet Hector. Soon we were all seated round the Wellstood, chatting easily, drinking tea and eating my mother's newly baked pancakes. Hector kept cracking jokes and I was so unused to this informality that I was scared to laugh out too loudly in case it was The Wrong Thing To Do!

But I couldn't keep my face straight for long.

This was the beginning of a lifetime's friendship with Hector and his charming wife, Iona, and a real privilege for me.

Myself, and another three young, newly arrived teachers, were invited for dinner soon after our arrival, to their house in Campbeltown. They were so hospitable and took a lot of trouble to make us feel at ease. I was especially impressed by Iona's culinary expertise, and later told my mother about the sizzling hot croutons which were served with the soup. "They kept on sizzling even after dropped into the soup, "I enthused. "I don't know how she kept them so piping hot. They were delicious."

I later taught their young son who, though ostensibly very quiet, was constantly sizing me up and reporting each day, to the delight of his parents, on my exasperated sayings in the classroom. Hector used to relay this to me, with great hilarity:

"Good Grief! Oh, my Sainted Aunt! Give me Strength!" etc. he would recount, uttered when my pupils drove me to distraction.

But I got my own back. It so happened that, when in the music room, I sat at the piano, facing away from the class. The kids were disturbed to find out that, no matter what tricks they got up to, ostensibly behind my back, I always knew what they were doing.

Hector said that the children put it about that I had supernatural powers as how else could I know what they were doing when my back was turned to them? They were sure I had eyes in the back of my head!

I gave away my secret, but swore him to secrecy for I was enjoying my sinister reputation for being all-seeing, all-knowing in the school.

"It hasn't dawned on them that the front of the piano casing is extremely highly polished," I explained. "It's just like a mirror, and I can see into every corner of the room without having to turn around."

Hector was highly amused and promptly told all the adults in the school, but the children were never enlightened.

We were privileged, in Kinloch Primary School --- comprising the two buildings of Millknowe and Dalintober --- to have the presence of three men who had given incomparable wartime service to their country.

Hector was aboard HMS *Hotspur*, one of the warships taking part in the infamous battle of Narvik, and also in the battle of Cape Matapan in March 1941, and suffered the appalling experience of being on the bridge when his ship was attacked by a deadly Stuka dive bomber. He survived, but many of his comrades did not.

Bill Beveridge, who worked with us in the Millknowe building, had been a Royal Marine and had taken part in the North Africa landings, after Field Marshall Rommel's retreat. He and his comrades had run the gauntlet of booby-trapped buildings wherever British troops went.

Mr Cunningham and friends in Millknowe playground

Mr Beveridge, Pr 6/7 and forester on a summer outing

Our janitor, Mr Cunningham, was unfortunate enough to have been a prisoner of the Japanese and had experienced the horrors of the Burma railway. He died as a result of injuries from a local road accident, no doubt exacerbated as a direct result of his dreadful experiences.

Perhaps these three were determined to bring light into the lives of the young children in their care after the darkness of the war years, for you couldn't find kinder and more considerate men towards both the adults and children with whom they came into contact.

At the end of the summer term the mood was lighthearted in anticipation of the long summer break, but the niceties had to be observed, as always.

The girls in Bill's senior class, knowing that they would return, not to Millknowe, but to Campbeltown Grammar School, wanted to impress the entire school with their sadness on leaving their primary school for ever. They had a serious discussion about whether they should cry or not. The majority opinion was that they ought to cry, so they went around all morning, dabbing at suitably reddened eyes, and sniffing dolefully into their hankies.

That lunchtime Bill came into my empty classroom with a decidedly heightened complexion.

"Come over to my classroom," he said, "and look at this. "I followed, not knowing what to expect. He said nothing, but just pointed at the blackboard. There, in huge capital letters, scrawled right across the board, was the brief but telling message --- BEV IS FAB!

He was too overcome to speak, and I felt a tear in the corner of my eye.

What a very well deserved compliment to a lovely man.

Tale no. 18: Midge Attack

My father's colleague, and the family's good friend, the Reverend Tom Titterington (yes, really!) was staying with us in the manse at Southend one summer weekend.

My mother was anxious to do a bit of baking for the forthcoming Women's Guild annual Sale of Work in Southend village hall, so I was detailed to take Tom, who had never been in Kintyre before, down the road to the village and round by Keil and Glen Cattadale, to show him our beautiful district. This was no hardship for he was one of the most interesting people I have ever met.

He had married a Danish lady and had visited the Scandinavian countries on a regular basis, having acquired family connections in all four countries as a result of his marriage.

He was also a skilled linguist and had taught himself Norwegian and a bit of Swedish as well as being fluent in Danish, and could make a stab at Finnish, an extremely difficult language with no apparent connection to the other Indo-European languages.

As if this was not enough he was also a fluent Gaelic speaker, and was thus able to identify the Gaelic and Norse elements in our local place names. I was looking forward to our walk through the Kintyre landscape, with its fascinating farm names, showing their Celtic and Norse origins.

Tom himself was the typical dark type of Celt, with plentiful black, waving hair, deep blue eyes and, at this time of year, a darkish, tanned complexion. Actually, he looked slightly satanic in the evening light!

Looking at him, I could imagine him performing heroic deeds among the ancient clans of Ireland and the west coast of Scotland --- though some of the deeds might be highly questionable. This thought was enhanced when Tom, writing a letter of thanks to my father after his visit, declared his intention to visit "fiends" in Lochgilphead on the way home.

But on this lovely summer day fiends were far from our minds as we strolled along the country road to Southend village. I called out the name of each farm as we passed and Tom, having mulled it over in his mind, would then declare whether it was the original Gaelic, or incoming Norse, or a hybrid of the two.

He started off by mentioning the Anglicisation of the name, Campbeltown, itself a monument to the perceived importance of the Campbell House of Argyll. "Ceann Loch Cille Chiaran, the *Head of Saint Ciaran's Loch*, is so much nicer, don't you think?" he asked. I certainly agreed.

"Yes, Machrimore is definitely Gaelic and means *big field on the machair,* and of course Machribeg is *little field on the machair,*" he said. "Dunglass is Gaelic for *grey fort;* Aucharua is *red field,* referring to the reddish earth hereabouts, and is also Gaelic, but Brunerican is a Gaelic-Norse hybrid, meaning *Eric's brow--,* Norse, with the Gaelic diminutive *-an* ending.

As we passed the road-end to the aforementioned farms we were startled to see the middle of the single-track road obstructed by a large Ayrshire bull which lumbered along, head down, on some private mission of his own. We immediately contemplated leaping the nearest fence and taking to the hills, for these animals can move extremely fast when they want to, and are renowned for their unpredictable tempers.

Tom had had enough experience of farm animals to know that you take no chances when it comes to a bull, or even a cow if she has a calf at foot, so was in complete agreement with me in taking avoiding action.

We louped over the nearest fence and stood, gazing anxiously at the big animal as it plodded purposefully along the road towards us. Then Aucharua car appeared, crawling up cautiously behind him. It pulled into a lay-by and John, the farmer, jumped out, holding the most enormous spanner I have ever seen. This was obviously the first line of defence against bovine attack.

We were riveted to the spot as John plus spanner approached the bull from behind, moved carefully round to its front end, grabbed the ring through its nose and led it, protesting a bit, round in a circle and back up the road to the farm. But it followed John placidly enough and both slowly disappeared into the distance.

We commented on how many people have a too relaxed attitude to farm animals, especially bulls, through just not realising the latent power in their mighty frames.

While Tom and I breathed more easily I told him about a regular holiday-maker, a doctor from Lanarkshire and owner of a beautiful Bentley who, while travelling down the single track road between Polliwilline and Macharioch, came across two Glasgow lasses on holiday from the city, wandering languidly along the single-track road. They were coming down the road behind the car and seemed completely unfazed by the sight of an enormous Hereford bull on the loose, swaying heavily up the road towards them.

The doctor wound down the window and called out to them. "Don't you see that bull down there? He could be very dangerous. You should get back up the road as fast as you can."

"Is that a bull right enough mister?" said one. "Is it no tame? It looks okay tae me." and they wandered on.

The doctor was getting very hot under the collar by now and drove up alongside the girls.

"For Heaven's sake, get into the car," he advised. "Do you not understand? That's a Hereford bull!"

His voice conveyed the seriousness of the situation and they reluctantly climbed into the Bentley.

The car was pulled over as far as it would go into the side of the road --- another inch and it would have been in the ditch. Unfortunately the car was so big, and the road so narrow, that there was no way the doctor could turn the vehicle and retreat back up the road and alas, he didn't seem to think it necessary to reverse.

As the enormous animal came nearer everyone held their breath. The girls were now silent, stunned by the sheer size of the beast.

Nobody moved a muscle and it seemed as if the leviathan would lumber past without incident then, for no apparent reason, he swung his massive head and butted the front wing of the car several times. There was a horrible crunch of metal as the wing crumpled under the onslaught. The women all screamed and the doctor turned pale as his pride and joy was assaulted so comprehensively.

"Hold on," he said,"I'm going to try to drive away from him," and he revved the Bentley's engine --- fortunately still functioning --- and, while receiving more direct hits from the unpredictable animal, managed to extricate the car from the scene of battle and escape away down the road.

The doctor, understandably, was incandescent, blaming the owner of the bull for allowing it to get out, and imagining the cost of the repairs which the farmer would undoubtedly have to pay.

He never returned to Southend again.

Meanwhile, Tom and I climbed back over the fence on to the road again and continued our serene journey past Dunaverty, Keil, Gartvaigh, Carskiey, Lephenstrath, Glen Breakerie, Drumavoulin,

Cattadale, and Dalbhradden before coming back round by Keprigan, Dalmore and Kilblaan to the Manse of St Blaan again, with Tom revelling in being in a landscape whose names told of such an incomparable history.

Manse of St Blaan, interior

When we arrived back at the house we found, to our astonishment, the sitting-room full of an English Boys Brigade company who were currently camping in the fields at Macharioch Farm. My father, a fervent supporter of the Boys Brigade had been told they were there by the farmer, and had gone over to speak to them. Apparently they were thoroughly enjoying their camping holiday but would very much have liked to see an important international cricket match which, they knew, was being televised that very day.

My father, always the soul of hospitality, had invited them all, lock, stock and barrel, over to the house to watch the match, without warning my mother in advance. There were no mobile phones in these days.

She was therefore stunned, on opening the front door in answer to their knock, to be overwhelmed by a mob of young lads, all eager to see the match. Naturally she couldn't refuse them entry so stood back while they piled into the sitting room and settled down in eager anticipation of the important event.

"You should have warned me," she hissed at my father.

"I never thought there would be so many," said he, helplessly deflating in front of our very eyes.

"Men!" she spluttered. "What am I going to give them to eat? How many are there? Thirty-six!" and she returned to the kitchen rolling her eyes in understandable exasperation.

Tom was grabbed by my father who kept him standing strategically between himself and my incensed mother. I followed her into the kitchen. The scones and pancakes she had been baking for the Sale of Work disappeared like snow off a dyke. She and I then started pancake making on the grand scale, while the ever tactful Tom conveyed a steady stream of hot pancakes, straight off the griddle, into endless consumption in the sitting room. The pancakes disappeared as fast as we could make them. Tea was made, it seemed, by the gallon and Tom discovered previously unsuspected talents as a waiter.

At last the demand for hot pancakes diminished then, blessedly, ceased altogether. The excitement of the match overtook all other considerations, and food became irrelevant.

After what seemed an eternity the match stopped, the boys were highly satisfied with the resulting score and eventually trailed happily out of the house and away over the road to Macharioch, having politely thanked my mother and father for inviting them. My mother smiled back at them through gritted teeth, while Dad looked as if he wished the floor would open and swallow him.

My mother and I had to start baking for the Sale of Work all over again and Dad was in the doghouse for ages after that.

Two of our young Coastguard friends arrived at the door that evening, hoping to see the three kittens our Manx cat had recently produced.

Both Neil and Calum were entranced by the antics of the little animals and Calum had been given permission by his parents to choose a kitten for himself. He eventually decided on the beautiful little brindled grey and white tabby and solemnly produced his pocket money while asking me, shyly, "How much does the kitten cost?"

We all burst out laughing.

"Nothing at all to you, Calum. Just promise you'll look after her well, and be very good to her," I said.

"I sure will. Thank you very, very much," he earnestly assured me and the boys, obviously wanting to play with all three kittens for a while, were invited to stay for tea.

They were introduced to Tom and were fascinated to hear that he was a frequent traveller to Scandinavia, where his wife came from. Neil especially, was intrigued by our guest.

"My name is Morrison," he proudly announced," and John Cameron, the fisherman, told me that the Morrisons were originally from Norway --- and were probably Vikings," he added with a flourish.

"Yes," said Tom. "The Morrisons of Lewis are supposed to have been descended from a Norse family who were shipwrecked on the shores of the island long, long ago, and saved themselves by clinging on to a piece of driftwood which floated in to the shore. There the family settled. That is why the clan took the driftwood for their crest. Eventually they became one of the ancient clans of Lewis."

A wide-eyed Neil looked impressed. "So they were really just like immigrants today," he said. "They were in danger and stayed in the Hebrides because they couldn't get back to Norway."

"Something like that," said Tom, "The trouble was that, although they stayed in Lewis for many generations, and became brieves, or law enforcers, the government accused them, in the 16th century, of harbouring rebels. Also they got into serious trouble by getting into feuds with other Lewis clans, the MacLeods and the MacAulays, and eventually lost all their lands. After that about sixty of the families had to flee to the mainland of Sutherland."

Neil looked a bit downcast at this reversal of his clan's fortunes but took all this in very thoughtfully.

"I suppose if you go and settle in someone else's land you shouldn't get into a fight with them," he said.

"Out of the mouths of babes --------," said Tom to my father.

By this time Calum, who was always being put in the shade by his Viking pal, wanted to hear what Tom --- obviously the expert --- had to say about his own clan.

"I am a MacMillan," he said proudly. "And there are far more of us in Kintyre than there are of you Morrisons. See!" This was uttered with a triumphant look at Neil, who was obviously getting a bit above himself with his Viking ancestors, and needed bringing down a peg or two.

"Now, boys, both your families are well known and respected in the Highlands and Islands," said Tom, the peacemanker. "There is room for us all as long as we don't get greedy and try to take more than our fair share."

The protagonists subsided, and Tom was again urged to tell what he knew about Calum's clan.

"Well," said Tom, gathering his story-teller's cloak around him. "as I expect you already know, the name MacMillan is a religious one, meaning *son of the bald, or tonsured man* --- that just means, a monk, in this case."

Neil sniggered, and Calum punched his arm.

Tom continued, paying no attention to them, "As far back as I can tell they were well known around the banks of Loch Arkaig, in Lochaber, and in later years they had lands in Knapdale, on the Argyll coast."

Calum was suitably impressed and stuck his tongue out at Neil.

"And, Calum, you should be very proud, for their chief, Maolmuire, sheltered the great Robert the Bruce while he was on the run from his enemies, then fought for him at Bannockburn in 1314. What a man!"

Calum was almost crowing with delight.

"And," went on Tom," as if that wasn't enough, the clan later fought for Prince Charles Edward Stuart at the battle of Culloden."

Calum was ecstatic, He couldn't wait to get home and tell his Dad about their illustrious ancestors.

"They don't seem to have acted much like monks, do they?" said the envious Neil, dourly.

However, it looked like game, set and match in the ancestry stakes, both sides having memorable forebears, and off went the boys and the kitten, well pleased with their visit, and the wonderful Tom.

The next afternoon Tom accompanied us to the Sale of Work, the major event of the year for the Southend Church Women's Guild, as my mother had a plan to include him in the opening remarks expected from the minister at such functions. Tom could always be relied upon to crack a few mild jokes suitable for the genteel occasion while my father was left to wander happily round the stalls admiring the goods and taking advantage of the gathering to speak to his parishioners from the furthest outreaches of the parish.

Dad always had a hankering after brightly coloured clothing --- for himself that was --- but was always given presents of knitwear in restrained hues suitable for the clergy.

"Even the Clergy tartan is dark blue and green," he sighed while looking longingly at the bright tartan ties in the tartan gift shops.

That afternoon he remarked pensively to Tom, "I never get to wear anything but black or grey. I expect it's the same for you. I would really like a nice Canary yellow or Sky Blue pullover for a change," and then he spotted some brightly coloured knitwear on one of the stalls. He homed in on it like a bee to nectar and was observed by Mrs MacDonald, the President of the Guild (and a rather straight-laced lady) who had her own ideas as to what was suitable for a minister to wear), holding up a multi-coloured Shetland knit with the obvious intention of bargaining for it.

He had actually completed the transaction with the stall holder who dived under the table to look for a nice piece of wrapping paper. While she was out of sight Mrs MacDonald hurried over, plucked the offending article out of his hands and said, reprovingly,

"Oh, no, Minister! That is not at all suitable for you to wear. You want this nice Lovat Green over here, or this lovely Dove Grey. These are the right colours for you." And she absolutely refused to let him have any other colour. The stall-holder, who had emerged from under the table with the wrapping paper, was positively affronted at the cavalier attitude of the President, but poor Dad was persuaded to take yet another dull, grey pullover and wandered off disconsolately, carrying his parcel. Tom, who had observed all this from a safe distance, dared him to sneak back when Mrs Mac wasn't looking, and just get the Shetland knit which had so nearly been within his grasp.

Unfortunately, the same Mrs Mac obviously suspected possible mutiny and kept a strict watch on her minister's movements all that afternoon. He didn't dare arouse her wrath by going back openly to the stall, but the cunning Tom took the parcel from his hands and slipped unobtrusively over to the knitwear table where he and the stall-holder conspired to exchange the dull grey for the bright Shetland pullover. She wrapped the latter in very thick paper, heavily sealed with enough sticky tape to defy even the most suspicious of Guild Presidents.

So Dad wandered round the house all evening, preening himself in his illegal clothing and congratulating his good friend on being so successfully light-fingered.

"I don't think Mrs Mac suspected a thing," said the highly amused Tom. "My word, that woman is a real dragon, isn't she? Thank goodness I don't have any like that in my congregation."

The next day dawned warm but dull and drizzly, and not the best of weather for our annual Highland Games, planned to be held on a grassy sward behind the Argyll Arms Hotel. By midday an elusive sun shone fitfully through the heavy cloud cover and the rain dried up, to our great relief.

Unfortunately, the combination of warmth and dampness brought out that notorious menace, known and dreaded throughout the west coast --- midges! These diminutive tormentors have gained a well-deserved reputation for almost making grown men cry. Their merciless stings cause eyelids to swell up, blisters to appear wherever they strike, and they get into the eyes, noses, ears and hair of chosen victims. They are truly one of the most refined forms of torture devised by the animal kingdom.

It is virtually impossible for the victim to continue with what he or she is doing when a midge strikes. Only, it is never a single midge, but whole battalions of them descending in full cloud formation when the conditions are right.

On this particular evening the local Pipe Band was scheduled to play a selection of marches, strathspeys and reels before the sporting events took place, and they marched smartly, in good order, on to the pitch where they took up their stance in a large circle, facing each other, and started on their programme.

It seemed as if the midge host had been waiting for just this very opportunity for they descended on the pipers with, it seemed, malice aforethought. Soon the unfortunate pipers were unobtrusively hopping on the spot, trying to dislodge all the evil insects from their bare legs, scratching hurriedly at faces and ears whenever a hand could be freed from the chanter, and swiping at the intruders whenever they came near. The trouble is that you can't really see a midge approach, so are unprepared for the onslaught until it is too late and they have got you pinned down.

Our little party of spectators was filled with pity for the pipers who couldn't escape and who were obviously suffering. Fortunately we had come prepared for just such an eventuality. We, at least were able to take such steps as seemed effective in trying to protect ourselves. The ladies whipped their chiffon scarves off their necks, threw them over their heads like bridal veils, and tied the loose ends round their throats, collars were turned up, bicycle clips issued from pockets and were clipped round the ankles over closely folded trouser legs as well as around tightly covered wrists, and hands were buried deeply in pockets. We were as completely covered as we could manage, but still they got us!

Tom and my father produced cigarettes and handed them round the entire company, even to those who didn't normally smoke. Attempts were made at forming a protective smokescreen around our little group, but none of these extreme measures stopped the grim armada one iota.

The spectators stood around as the Games events proceeded, not wishing to desert the competitors on the field, and smiling bravely at one another while heartily wishing to be somewhere else.

It was worse for the Highland dancers, runners and heavy-weight athletes who forced themselves to keep going in spite of the rapacious attacks. Concentration flew out of the window and many, who had been expected to do well in their competitions, struggled desperately to get through them and not flee shrieking from the field.

The beer tent and the tea tent became clogged with unhappy spectators striving to find sanctuary under canvas, but even there the midges found them.

Eventually mothers had to remove their crying children from the scene of battle and only the most hardened spectators remained till the end, then fled to the shelter of the Argyll's bar or into midge-free cars.

I had suffered such an onslaught many a time when spectating, along with my teacher colleagues, at Highland League shinty matches if our school team was playing. I had even experienced this malignant menace when in my boat, well out at sea, and in midwinter!

My brother, Ronald, also had a close encounter with the midge kind when taking part in the BBC series of *Para Handy*, filmed in the district around the Crinan Canal. The situation became so bad, and the actors and extras so distraught and clawing at themselves, that filming had to be postponed and the venue altered.

Afternoons and evenings in the summer months are definitely not good times to take part in outdoor filming on the west coast.

Apparently even the toughest of commandos, reduced to frantic scratching while out on manoeuvres, were forced to look for a solution to this eternal problem and, surprisingly, discovered a beauty preparation for the skin, produced by a well known cosmetics company.

From then onwards they went around the forests, moorlands, mountains and other rough territory, protected from the worst of the bites, with the added bonus of blissfully softened skin, and smelling as sweetly as a garland of flowers, no doubt to the great amusement of their girlfriends and wives!

Tale no. 19: Death at the Doirlinn

It was half-tide and we carried the clean, dry net carefully out of "the hut", the former fisherman's cottage on the shore, which now served as a store for our nets and gear, and stowed it on the wooden hand-barrow in order to carry it down to where the *Sheena,* John's boat, lay moored against the bank of the Conaglen River. We hoisted the heavy net into the stern of the boat then pulled on our yellow oilskin tunics and our long, rubber sea boots. We were almost ready to go out to lay the big stake net in Brunerican Bay where it would stay for the week, unless the weather changed for the worse.

John sitting on net

John started the engine and swung the boat around in the river mouth so that she was facing out to sea. There is a sand bar across the mouth of the river so we had always to watch the state of the tide before entering or leaving the Conaglen, otherwise the boat could strand on the bar or get caught in rough water.

This had happened to me once while coming back into the river in my boat, *Catriona*. The boat, lifted by a big incoming wave, hit the bar, checked a little, then was slammed down --- fortunately on the sandy spit on the port side, and not on the rocks on the starboard side --- where she stuck fast until I managed to push her off into deep water again by using an upturned oar as a lever. The force of the stranding was so great that I was afraid the boat was damaged but, fortunately, the hull was alright, at any rate we didn't sink --- but I got a considerable fright!

This morning I looked back at the low, green hills of Southend and the gently rolling expanse of the fertile farm lands of this lovely district. On the horizon blue skies met blue seas, the islands of Sanda and Sheep Island lay in a slight sea mist ahead of us, and sea birds floated serenely on the surface or cartwheeled slowly about the sky. As I stood in the stern beside John I felt the steady rise and fall of the boat under my feet as her bow met the slight swell of the incoming tide. I felt very content.

The sights, sounds and scents of this pleasant land will remain in my memory always.

John Cameron, whose boat this was, pointed out to where the marker buoy lay bobbing gently in the tide, and gave me the helm while he went forward to the engine and opened up the throttle now we were clear of the rocky river mouth. *Sheena* answered her engine and helm, and soon we were approaching the buoy marking the place where the net would be anchored.

"What do you think, John. Will there be good fishing this week?" I asked.

He sniffed the wind before answering, "Aye, I think so. The wind has been from the north these past few days and that always brings a big swell on to a beach like this. That's why we had so much damage to the net last week. The leader gets ground against the shingle beach and that tears it as much as any seal, so the salmon can't swim in. That courline --- you know, the new nylon rope and yarn that we tried recently --- is very easily worn through when rubbing against anything hard, like this stony shore, so from now on we'll just stick to the old tried and tested manila. Anyway, it's much more flexible than the courline. We'll bind a bit of tarry spunyarn around it where it might rub. That should keep it from fraying for some time." And we stopped talking.

We had arrived at the buoy.

The next half hour was spent in hectic activity as John slowed the engine and put it in neutral while we got the bag of the net out over the stern, and its head roped on to the head-pole with a couple of half hitches. The boat heeled over at an awkward angle while we worked, bracing ourselves against the gunwale with our knees, while the head-pole, along with its attached net, was forced down into the sea bed. The side ropes were attached next, and that was the stake net in place. This wasn't made any easier by the steady rising and falling of the boat in the considerable swell now coming in from the south-west.

We then went back to where the leader net meets the stake net and attached the one to the other, paying out the clean leader behind us until we reached the shore. There the inward end was attached to the land-stick, and a straight line of floats now marked the entire length of the leader from the shore right out to the stake net. The job was done.

When the salmon comes inshore from the ocean on his miraculous journey to the river of his birth, he swims close to the shoreline and follows it towards the river mouth. He then hits the leader and then follows it, right out to the stake net where he swims into the bag of the net.

I must admit I always feel a pang of sadness when I see the beautiful, gleaming silver fish swimming round and round in the net, his fantastic journey across the Atlantic stopped short just as he is about to enter the fresh water of his home river. It seems rather a cruel fate.

Then it was back to the river mouth where the net which had been brought in on Saturday had to be cleaned of all the growth and debris of the previous week. It was spread out over the beach and we started brushing out the seaweed and removing any jellyfish which had accumulated along the cork floats and throughout the meshes. Gloves were definitely advisable as jellyfish stings are really quite painful and we could be stung even if there were no jellyfish actually trapped in the net. Their poison remains on the net for some time after the creature itself has gone, and the painful, stinging effect lasts for ages on the hands.

When the net was looking clean again we spread it out fully along the length of the beach, to be further cleaned by the rain and, or, to dry before being gathered up on to the hand-barrow, carried back up to "the hut" and hung up over the rafters for a final, thorough drying.

Some nets are so badly damaged by sea conditions or the depredations of seals that they have to be slung up on dock poles and mended with manila twine. This can take a long time if there is a lot of damage, but John always insisted on mending the nets himself.

"It's just like your knitting," he would explain."Everyone has his own way of mending, and uses a particular tension so, if someone else tries to mend the net, the tension and the size of the mesh will vary and the meshes will be unequal, distorting the shape of the net."

So I was limited to loading the wide, wooden needles with the brown mending twine which I coiled around the central prong. John usually needed a lot of needles.

"This is a very labour intensive business," I said to my father as I staggered into the house that evening.

"Well, why do you do it?" he asked, logically.

"I suppose a lot of it has to do with being out on the sea in a small boat, when your safety and that of others lies completely in your own hands, in the way you handle the boat and how she responds. It's a fantastic feeling --- the boat responding so quickly to your direction. Then there is the sea itself in all its moods and colours, as well as those of the surrounding land. Even the most familiar sights ashore are quite altered when you are looking at them from the sea. It's a different dimension altogether."

Dad nodded, unable to get a word in edgeways. I was now on a roll and carried away with my own magical memories.

"I'll never forget the translucent depth of the water in Dunaverty Bay last Friday night.We were floating in still, clear water about twenty feet deep, which acted like a glass, magnifying the sea bed so that every crab, starfish and shell could be clearly seen, as well as tiny fish and waving strands of seaweed. Oyster-catchers were running along the beach, calling to one another, and I could hear curlews trilling somewhere up on the machair. It was like a scene from a fairy story.

I feel it is such a privilege to be part of all this, and with such friends and experts as John and Archie," I tried to explain.

Dad just smiled.

"You're lucky. Hold on to these memories. They're what keep you going when things are not so good," he said.

"Of course," I admitted, "it's not always so idyllic, and then the sea shows her teeth and reminds you who's boss, and just how small and vulnerable you really are, like that time when Doctor Bill got into such trouble out on the Sanda reefs."

Dad nodded. He remembered the near tragedy of Bill's encounter with an angry sea.

I didn't like to say too much to my mother and father about the dangers inherent in sea fishing, as I didn't want to make them anxious every time I went out in the boats, and I was acutely aware of how dangerous it can be working, or even just sailing, out on the sea.

To add to the natural hazards, like most fishermen, neither John nor Archie could swim!

I knew we were always at risk, every time we took the boats away from the security and shelter of their moorings in the Conaglen. Even within the river mouth itself a boat heading out to sea could get caught in an incoming big wave and be dashed against the rocks within a few minutes, as I had once nearly been in my boat, *Catriona*.

That was only the beginning of it. While fishing the stake net in a big swell there was always the danger of the boat capsizing, or of the engine stalling if water got into it, and oar power alone could not possibly get the boat out of danger. Under these circumstances she would be completely out of control and might well end up being smashed against outcropping reefs or the rocky shore itself by the force of the breakers.

The final, and most severe hazard was, of course, coming back inshore again, when a momentary loss of concentration at the helm could cause the boat to veer off her course and be swept against the rocks, or on to the sand bar where she would broach to and capsize, at the entrance to the Conaglen River.

On a recent occasion we had had a near miss at this point. As *Sheena* approached the river mouth I saw an enormous, green wall of water rapidly rearing up behind us. I was too scared to watch as the boat was caught up in the huge comber, tossed high in the air, her propeller screaming as her stern came clear of the water, her engine starting to falter and her bow tilting down, down into the deep, dark trough of the waves. Then she slammed down heavily into the trough, water spraying and gushing everywhere, almost swamping her. She wallowed, the timbers of her wooden hull groaning as she strove to climb up out of the maw of the sea. I thought her bow would never actually rise again, and was sure our last hour had come.

John hung grimly on to the tiller and I on to the gunwale as, at last, *Sheena*'s bow eventually rose, incredibly slowly, on the next big wave, and her stern became submerged again. Her propeller bit into the water, gripped and started to function normally. Blessedly, her engine, which I had thought must be swamped, fired normally and at last we escaped into the relatively calm water of the river mouth.

"Whew, that was close," I gasped, spluttering as the sea water streamed down my face, into my eyes and into my mouth.

"Let's get her tied up safely then look to ourselves," said John, without further comment.

It was always a case of, "First see to the boat, and then to yourselves" in this job, so John steered the boat gently into her mooring and I attached *Sheena* firmly to the huge iron chain half buried into the shore, using the usual efficient rolling hitch. We put an extra line out from her stern for more security and walked stiffly up off the beach and into the shelter of "the hut" where John lit the oil lamp, then the fire in the little old-fashioned grate. I thankfully pulled off my oilskins and heavy rubber boots before collapsing weakly on to the piles of folded dry nets stacked on the floor opposite the fireplace, and rubbed face and hair with a nice, dry, comforting, fluffy towel out of the ancient sideboard drawer.

The Benedictine, which was always kept in the cupboard for just such occasions, was brought out, a dram of the golden liquid poured out into two cups, and each of us sat, sipping slowly and thoughtfully as its warmth spread gradually throughout our tissues. Our sodden persons gradually dried out in the gentle heat of the fire, and my shattered nerves began to recover a little.

Such events were commonplace on the west coast fishing grounds, from the Butt of Lewis to our Mull of Kintyre and all the islands in between and sometimes, alas, the fishing boats did not come back to port at all.

This was the reason why I never let on to my parents when an "incident" had occurred at Dunaverty. Fortunately they never did realise how dangerous it could be to go out in our relatively small boats in most states of the weather. In any case they considered John and Archie to be very nearly omnipotent in all matters pertaining to the sea. It would never have occurred to them that I might be in any danger when out on the water in the company of these two men.

The only faintly comic event I did tell them about concerned the local Ladies' Lifeboat Guild --- a most respected organisation in the whole of Kintyre. Such was the *esprit de corps* among the group that they enjoyed a good social life while at the same time doing a great job raising funds for the nationwide lifeboat charity, as well as for our own Campbeltown lifeboat.

Summer had come and the Secretary had arranged for the ladies to drive into the town of an evening. As the sea was blissfully calm --- and we were the Lifeboat Guild after all --- we were to venture forth upon Campbeltown Loch in a local fishing boat, hired along with her skipper for the occasion, for a trip to the island of Davaar at the entrance to the loch. All fifteen of us duly arrived at the New Quay and clambered down into an open boat about the same size as the *Sheena,* where the skipper placed everyone comfortably around the various thwarts before starting up the engine and setting off out into the broad, calm loch. It was a glorious evening and we sailed serenely towards the entrance channel between Davaar Island and Trench Point. The ladies chatted happily, even those who were not entirely at ease in any boat of any size, and looked forward to a visit to the local fish and chip shop when we arrived back on shore.

Then, without warning, the engine stopped and the boat came to a gentle, rocking halt opposite the MOD depot on Kilkerran Road. The skipper looked disconcerted, but told us not to worry as he would have us going again in no time, and he whipped the tarpaulin off the engine casing and dived in under the lidded top, whence lots of tapping, banging and scraping noises issued forth. But, after ten minutes or so, his embarrassed, oily face emerged from the engine housing and he admitted that he couldn't get the engine to start again and we'd have to get a tow from another boat in to the New Quay or, horror of horrors, in the worst case scenario, we'd have to call out the lifeboat.

One lady, probably because of fright, snapped at him, "Fine thing this, the Lifeboat Guild having to call out the Lifeboat! We'll never live this down, you know."

The poor man tried to explain that we were in no immediate danger, as the sea was so calm. But the tide was undoubtedly going out and although the boat was floating in a placid sea, we were definitely being carried, ever so unobtrusively, out towards the entrance to the loch and the open Firth of Clyde. The skipper and I met in eye contact and he raised his eyebrows inquiringly and nodded slightly towards the oars, thoughtfully placed under each gunwale many years ago when the boat was young. I nodded back and started to get the oars pulled out from their slings.

This action alarmed the passengers considerably and we had to reassure them that this didn't mean the boat was about to sink, and that we'd probably manage to row back to the shore even before any rescue boat reached us.

Shouts and hand-signals to the shore were made in explanation of our plight, and various persons walking along Kilkerran Road assured us that they would get a fishing boat out to rescue us. These were the bad old days before mobile phones.

Exclamations of disbelief greeted this idea, and the snappy lady insisted on taking one oar while I took the other one. We started to row while the boatman steered the stricken vessel round in a wide arc, back up the loch towards the town quays.

My fellow rower showed absolutely no understanding of how to row a boat, never mind a heavy, wide-bodied fishing boat whose engine had failed. It was undoubtedly a heavy row, and she tired after about ten minutes, having continually failed to keep the oar properly in contact with the water then, finally and spectacularly, "catching a crab" and falling backwards off the thwart into the well of the boat. The others rushed to pick her up, but the skipper immediately directed them back to their places as they were upsetting the balance of the boat, and the next volunteer timorously took up the abandoned oar.

Much the same thing happened and we went through a stream of willing, but totally ineffectual rowers, until no more remained. In the meantime I had to keep adjusting my stroke as, when the other rower failed to pull the boat through the water my stroke was too strong and the unfortunate boat was pulled round in a circle. Our progress back up the loch can only be described as "crab-wise". Quite a crowd had gathered along the edge of Kilkerran Road and the townsfolk watched our erratic progress, much to the acute embarrassment of our skipper.

A suggestion was made that I was bound to be tired and should be relieved of my stint at the oar, but he immediately blocked that idea.

"She's the only one o' you that can row," he challenged," so jist let'er get on wi' it. She'll row this boat till Kingdom Come, an' no bat an eyelid."

At this point he decided that the only way to make any definite progress was for him to delegate the helm to the strongest looking lady, tell her to keep the boat pointing straight ahead, and to take up the other oar himself.

This cause a varied reaction among the rest, who didn't trust their friend to steer the boat in a straight line, and who wanted the skipper to keep steering himself. An unseemly flurry of argument ensued until a frightened, quavery voice was uplifted in the hymn, "Oh, God our help in Ages Past", and the others all joined in sanctimoniously, as we floated along perfectly safely on a dead calm sea.

The skipper and I were squirming with embarrassment as the voices floated over to the spectators on shore, who thought it was some sort of joke and started to laugh uproariously. The ladies, halted in mid-verse, looked affronted and scandalised at this desecration but, thank goodness, stopped their hymn singing and subsided into silence while the skipper and I pulled together very effectively and brought the boat well up towards the head of the loch.

In a few more minutes I was glad to see a nice, big fishing boat surging out from her berth on the New Quay towards us. She circled us and, with absolutely no fuss at all, her crewman threw us a line and she towed us in to the quay where a sizeable crowd of interested spectators watched us disembark from our unfortunate boat.

I stayed behind to help the skipper put his boat to rights, and to commiserate with him over the incident, before running up the quay to catch up on the group before they went for their fish and chips. It turned out that this was the last thing on their minds, and all they wanted was to get away as fast as possible from Campbeltown Loch, fishing boats in general, and the sea in particular.

The Ladies' Lifeboat Guild never again ventured forth upon the loch in a small boat on their annual summer outing while I was a member.

I recounted this unexpected adventure to my parents on my return to Southend, and they certainly saw the funny side of it, while feeling sorry for the owner of the fishing boat.

"Well, at least the ladies have proved that they are good church attenders and know their hymns", I said.

Actually I was a bit disappointed we didn't make it to our planned destination of Davaar Island, as I had hoped for a repetition of the incredible sight I had already seen that week during the school lunch hour.

My colleague Christina and I, weary of sitting in the staffroom during the lovely summer weather, decided to drive down Kilkerran to the long, sandy spit which ran from the edge of Campbeltown Loch out to Davaar Island. This spit, known locally as the Doirlinn, ran out in a slight curve, thus causing a shallow bay to form when the tide was coming in, though it dried out at low tide and you could easily walk out to the island over the exposed sand of the bay.

Lunchtime at the Doirlinn

The sun shone brightly and we were glad we had made the effort to get out for some fresh air, as we drove down the single-track part of the road south of the town. We drew into the verge and climbed out of the car, over the fence and down on to the beach, where we wandered for a little while, eating our lunchtime sandwiches and revelling in the warmth of the June sunshine.

The tide was about halfway in towards the Doirlinn, and had already formed a shallow loch.

Christina jogged my arm. "Look over there," she said. "The surface of the bay is speckled all over its entire surface."

I looked. She was right --- gone was the smooth, unruffled surface of a few minutes ago, and now there was a continual disturbance all over the little bay formed by the Doirlinn.

Before either of us could speculate further we were riveted by the sudden, noisy arrival of a huge cloud of seabirds which started diving at a furious pace into the water, and coming up with beaks full of fish. The racket of their cackling and squawking was incredible as they wheeled like an attacking squadron of fighter planes all over the bay.

"They're gannets," shouted Christina. "Just look at their pointed beaks and the way they dive --- wings closed, and swooping down till you think they'll break their necks hitting the water at that speed. They're like dive-bombers."

"Yes, they're almost crashing into the sea," I said. "They're right into that big shoal of fish trapped in this little bay. That's what is causing the disturbance on the surface. It's the fish, frantically swimming about, and swept into the shallows by the gannets, where they can't escape, poor things."

Christina, jumping up and down with excitement said, "Look how the birds are diving, grabbing a fish, and swallowing it as they rise, barely above the surface of the water. Then another frantic dive and another fish. What an incredible sight! I've never seen anything like it!"

"Neither have I," I agreed. "Talk about a massacre of the innocents!"

"And talk about opportunists!" said Christina. "These gannets must have had their scouts out."

It had happened only because the shoal, coming in from the open firth, had obviously taken the wrong turning and instead of entering Campbeltown Loch at a safe depth, they had instead turned too soon and swum into the shallow bay where they were trapped and attacked by the hungry gannets.

This frenzied activity lasted for about fifteen minutes, then the flock of gannets began, noticeably, to thin out. Fewer and fewer dives were made, the birds gradually withdrew, the raucous squawking subsided into nothing and, within the space of a few minutes, the last bird had flown off into the distance. The surface of the little loch calmed down, returned to its smooth, unruffled state and, in no time at all peace and silence descended upon the area of the Doirlinn.

"You'd think nothing at all had happened here," said Christina, gazing in awe at the area now emptied of birds and, it seemed, of fish.

"What a gang of hooligans!" I said.

We suddenly returned to normality and became aware that the passage of time had caught up with us and we had, very reluctantly, to return to the school.

We were full of this spectacle when we got back to the staffroom, and intrigued so many of our colleagues that there was a steady progression of teachers down the loch side at lunchtime for the rest of the summer term. Alas, nobody else saw the phenomenon. Nor did we ourselves ever see this incredible sight again.

Indeed, there was a strong suspicion that Christina and I had made the whole thing up!

Tale no. 20: The Ball, the Baroness and Miss Julia Brown

The folk of Kintyre have always had a soft spot for the eccentric and the whimsical. This is exemplified in the hilarious tales of *Para Handy* by the Inveraray author, Neil Munro, many of which are set in Kintyre.

Although this is a fictional series the author hits the nail squarely on the head in describing the daily doings of Para himself, proud captain of the puffer *Vital Spark,* MacPhail the lugubrious engineer, Dougie the much put-upon mate and Sunny Jim the deckhand --- a most unlikely set of west coast heroes, whose well recorded antics accurately mirrored that of many good folk of today in the peninsula, though few of them would actually admit to being eccentric, or even recognise it in themselves. Unfortunately, with the arrival of many incomers to the district, many of the amiable eccentricities have, sadly and inevitably, died away.

But, years ago, end of the year celebrations were well marked in Campbeltown by the number of balls held in the town's main meeting place, the Victoria Hall. These were frequently preceded by whist drives with "basket teas" which went on for most of the evening, with the dance element beginning quite late, around eleven o'clock.

For some of the important events, such as the Farmers' Ball, the Red Cross Ball, the Drama Ball, the Police Ball and the Bankers' Ball, it was necessary to get your tickets well in advance, such was the desire to see and be seen on these important social occasions.

I remember Mary Taylor, of Keil Hotel, telling me that when she and her sister Sybil went to winter balls in the town before the Second World War they followed an unusual custom, as did every lady on entering the dance hall. She would drift elegantly over to a corner of the floor where a large carpet had been tastefully spread, and then was left standing on the carpet with other ladies until her partner came to claim her for a dance. Whether she was ever allowed to sit down I never did find out.

Mary boasted that she had been namely for her shapely back --- "So much nicer than Sybil's" ---so she always wore a low-backed dress and stood with her back to the throng while awaiting the arrival of a partner!

This lent a whole new dimension to the phrase, "being on the carpet".

Also, for the ladies there was the eternal headache about "what to wear" as the town had very few dress shops and everyone knew what was in their limited stock and, worse still, how much each dress cost! But there was a way to get round this, as the informed people knew. You had first to get a "line" from one of the big city stores, such as Daly's in Glasgow, or Jenner's in Edinburgh.

Well before the time of the ball the lady would contact the store, telling them her requirements, and giving exact information as to size, fabric, colour, style and so on, which would then be relayed to the Gowns Department. Several days later a large parcel would arrive for the customer, containing three beautiful ball gowns for her approval. She would choose the one she wanted and the other two would be sent back to the store.

The customers were mostly always satisfied with the choice offered to them, which suited the store as well as the lady, for there was sure to be a repeat order the next time a dress was required, if the customer was pleased. The lady's requests were always noted down and kept for future reference. It was obviously good practice for the shop to study its customer's needs and make sure it fulfilled them.

At one ball to which I was fortunate enough to have been invited Iona, my boss's wife, had gone through this procedure and turned up at the ball dressed in an exquisite oyster satin creation, surmounted by a black velvet cloak which hung elegantly from her shoulders. She looked positively regal. Other ladies were equally beautifully dressed that evening and, looking round the company, I thought that I could easily be standing in the ballroom of a castle or important civic building during a very grand occasion.

By this time, thank goodness, the carpet scenario had died out.

Just before eleven o'clock there was a bit of a clear out when the whist-and-basket tea came to an end, though some stayed on and joined an entirely different set of people who started arriving for the serious part of the evening --- the ball. Eleven o'clock came and went and gradually the hall filled with the cream of Kintyre society, while the band appeared and started tuning their instruments, and the inevitable bar was set up at the back of the hall.

There was a noticeable flutter of anticipation, with excited greetings being exchanged among the company and everyone looking around to see who had arrived.

It looked as if "everyone who was anyone" was here. Little groups settled themselves down in their chosen corners, all chatting amiably, and the band, at last, struck up the first waltz --- just to get everyone nicely warmed up for the livelier dances to follow.

Soon the hall was full of dancers and those who didn't dance, but stood in the bar area watching the couples whirling round the floor, and engaging in civil chat with all those standing nearby.

As soon as one dance was finished the next one was called and the more energetic sprang up immediately, eager to show how well they could perform, while the less energetic sat out the more flamboyant dances and congregated in happy huddles, chatting to friends and companions while watching the passing scene.

This pleasant state of affairs lasted right through midnight and into the small hours. It was all very civilised and well organised but, inevitably, the crowd started to thin out a bit towards two or three in the morning. By this time the organisers had finished counting the tickets and tallying up the money at the door, and took themselves off in order to enjoy a few last-minute dances themselves.

This was the point at which anyone who trundled up to the now unguarded doors could wander into the hall and join the company.

I was sitting out an old fashioned waltz, admiring Iona and other silk and satin clad friends swaying elegantly past when I became aware that the dancers were avoiding a certain part of the floor. It seemed that there was something unusual happening out there. Then I saw it ---.

Weaving in and out through the well dressed crowd was a local worthy attired in a battered old waterproof only partially covering what were, quite obviously, his pyjamas, and stumping about in a pair of wellingtons whose toes had long since parted company with the rest of the feet. The whole effect was topped off by a moth-eaten "bunnet" which sat at a rakish angle on his head. The dancers gave him a wide berth, taking serious avoiding action but, as usual in Campbeltown, no one made a fuss, and he managed a complete, solo round of the floor before the organisers quietly abandoned their partners and discreetly ushered the maverick out into the waiting arms of the police sergeant hovering outside the front doors.

east side of the estate, rebellious crofters refused to pay the increase on their rents.

Fortunately, a leader stepped forward --- a certain Norman Stewart, a crofter in Valtos. He was one who refused to pay the increased rent. His attitude had been hardened over the three years since 1877 as he had been imprisoned for a week for taking heather and rushes from the moorland to mend the thatch on his roof!

This is almost unbelievable to us nowadays, but shows the inhumane treatment handed out to many crofters in these days by many uncaring owners of estates.

In 1881 an eviction notice was imposed on Stewart and others who dared to rebel.

Things were threatening to become ugly, but surprisingly, in far away Glasgow, a groundswell of support was growing, and Parnell of the Irish Land League, along with the Glasgow sympathisers, pledged their help in whatever form might be necessary --- even if this meant resorting to force.

The crofters found, to their satisfaction, that the news of their struggle was not confined to the Hebrides, and that justice was demanded from many folk in Glasgow --- and not only from those who had relatives in Skye.

The groundswell rapidly grew to a tidal wave of protest but, before actual violence broke out the Kilmuir estate landlord was forced to back down and hold a meeting with the tenants, at which a reduction of rents was offered and accepted.

The Kilmuir rebellion was symptomatic of the anger of many humble folk across the broad acres of Highland Scotland, including the Isle of Skye, because of their treatment at the hands of factors, landlords and owners of estates since the catastrophic failure of the 2nd Jacobite Rising of 1745, and its infamous aftermath, the Clearances.

Down the road a bit from Kilmuir, at Braes, a township south of Portree, the capital of the island, very serious trouble broke out.

Some of the young Braes fishermen-crofters had sailed down through Hebridean waters, into the Irish Sea as far as Kinsale in Ireland where they heard of the struggle for Irish land reform, and came back to their native Skye all fired up over the possibility of getting reform for themselves and their families.

They were distraught to find that, during their absence, a violent storm in November had destroyed 250 of the island's fishing boats.

As fishing was an integral part of the livelihood of most crofters, there was an immediate shortfall in their incomes, thereby making the payment of rents a complete nightmare.

This exacerbated the earlier loss of common grazings on the hills around Braes when Lord MacDonald took them for sheep farming during the Clearances.

Poverty, and near starvation in many cases, was rife, and the young men persuaded the crofters to refuse to pay rent until the common grazings were returned to them. Although the rents were due to be paid that December no one appeared at the factor's office in Portree to pay them.

Inevitably, Sheriff Officer Angus Martin and his officials were despatched to Braes carrying eviction notices, but were met by a crowd of furious crofters who snatched the notices from them and burned them in front of their scandalised eyes. Prudently Martin and his officials retreated to the safety of Portree, complaining loudly.

Obviously the matter was not allowed to rest there and warrants were issued for the arrest of all those involved in the fracas. The Sheriff of Inverness, one William Ivory, along with forty Glasgow policemen, arrived on Skye in response to the Sheriff Officer's request for immediate help.

Ivory and the police marched immediately to Braes and managed to arrest the main organisers of the unrest, but brought down upon themselves the wrath of 300 Braes crofters who pelted them with stones and other missiles as they tried to take their prisoners back to Portree.

The situation escalated into a full scale riot with the police drawing their truncheons and attacking both men and women, seven of the latter being seriously injured as a result. A final violent baton charge allowed the police to escape the infuriated crofters and return to Portree along with their prisoners.

The infamous event was named the Battle of the Braes and now the event is marked by a cairn and a memorial reading:-

Near to this cairn on 19th April 1882 ended the battle fought by the people of Braes on behalf of the crofters of Gaeldom.

The non-jury trial of the Braes men took place on 11th May 1882. They were, of course, found guilty and sent to prison, but their plight was widely broadcast and even the people of the mainland cities and towns were outraged by their harsh treatment, to the point where MPs in the House of Commons demanded an immediate inquiry.

This encouraged the crofters in the Glendale area of Skye also to begin agitating for the return of their common grazings, and they started to put their cattle out on the previously forbidden pastures. Court orders for the removal of the animals were completely ignored, and the situation became fraught again with crofters assaulting anyone who tried to remove their cattle. Warrants were issued for their arrest and in January 1883 a small band of policemen was sent out to arrest the "agitators". This time the crofters won the ensuing fight and the police fled ignominiously for their lives.

At this point the government, in its wisdom, decided to crack an egg with a sledgehammer, and actually sent a Royal Navy gunboat to Skye. Aboard was an official charged with parleying with the "trouble-makers".

The deal was that the government promised to consider seriously crofters' grievances and, in return, five volunteers, now known as the Glendale Martyrs, would offer to take part in a token trial. Surprisingly, the crofters agreed to this.

Back on the mainland the newly formed Highland Land League was attracting members from socialist groups all over the country and, in 1885 declared its intention of selecting men to stand for Parliament. They eventually gained four seats --- a first triumph for the ordinary, working man.

Crofters everywhere were now emboldened to start rent strikes all over the Highland and Islands, while Lord Napier, in 1883 started gathering evidence for what became known as the Napier Commission, with subsequent limited land reforms. But nothing was as important as the passing of the Crofters' Holdings, Scotland Act in 1886 when, at last, every crofter was guaranteed security of tenure.

This brought a new heart and spirit, as well as new confidence, to the previously downtrodden, feudally ruled people of Gaelic Scotland, though even today much still remains to be done concerning the ownership of vast areas of land by a wealthy few.

The ancient landowners of the island of Skye were, of course, the three big clans --- the MacDonalds, the MacLeods and the MacKinnons, established in place from time immemorial and nowadays struggling to keep their lands and buildings intact, with varying degrees of success.

While travelling through the island I occasionally had the enjoyable experience of encountering some of the modern-day clan chiefs and heard, with great pleasure, John MacLeod, 29th chief of the Clan MacLeod --- and a professionally trained singer --- singing chamber music to his clansmen and women, as well as to other visitors, in his ancient castle of Dunvegan on north Skye.

I also encountered Lord Godfrey MacDonald, High Chief of the MacDonalds, in the formerly grand castle of Armadale in Sleat in south Skye, where the burned out ruins of the original building have been very successfully transformed into a highly successful MacDonald Clan Centre which is regularly visited by thousands of MacDonalds from all over the world.

After his father's death in 1970 Sir Godfrey MacDonald inherited 45,000 acres and 4 hotels but was forced to sell much of his land in order to pay death duties and the outstanding debts which he inherited on becoming Chief. This left him with 20,000 acres, now in trust as clan lands.

Suffice it to say that nowadays the long ingrained grudges held by the ordinary clansfolk against the undoubted tyranny of some of their clan chiefs have mostly been forgiven --- but never forgotten!

Wonderfully, Skye, in the 21st century, has a booming economy, mainly from tourism, and has such a lot to offer from climbing in the spectacular Cuillin Mountains, exploration of its magnificent scenery, castle and heritage buildings, to the highly successful Sabhal Mòr Ostaig, the Gaelic College which has been incorporated into the University of the Highlands and Islands.

The latter has become one of the outstanding successes of the island of Skye, but it took an outsider to realise the possibilities of regeneration in the southern peninsula of Sleat.

The outsider was the merchant banker, Sir Iain Noble who, in 1972, bought 20,000 acres fortuitously placed on the market at that time by Sir Godfrey MacDonald.This couldn't have happened at a better time for both parties, as Sir Godfrey got the money to pay the death duties and Sir Iain, the astute businessman, got the greatly desired 20,000 acres of Sleat along with other assets which he hardly noticed at the time.

Among these were several hotels and the imposing, but derelict buildings of Sabhal Mòr Ostaig, the Big Barn of Ostaig.

He was also aware that his uneconomic Sleat crofting estate was subject to the financial stagnation which blighted many island communities at that time, but had been impressed with the success story that was the Faroe Islands where economic recovery was based upon language regeneration.

He decided to follow that model in Sleat.

Sir Iain became almost fanatical about Gaelic language and culture, and taught himself the language with his usual enthusiastic application, expecting all employees on his newly acquired estate and in his hotel at Eilean Iarmain to speak Gaelic at all times, unless communication broke down and English had to be used instead.

But what was he to do with the derelict Sabhal Mòr Ostaig, lying in crumbling splendour in its spectacular situation on the Sound of Sleat?

Happily, this fell neatly into his great dream of a Gaelic revival on Skye, at least on his part of the island, so he founded, as he put it himself, "the first Gaelic college in Scotland since the days of Saint Columba".

The curriculum included subjects such as Gaelic music and singing, horticulture, Highland and Country dancing, visual arts, literature, history, business studies, etc, all to be taught in the medium of the Gaelic language --- as well as short holiday courses for those who wished to learn the language.

By this means he hoped to stop the flood of young Hebridean islanders to the mainland in order to further their education. Unfortunately they had rarely come back to find work in their native islands, thus increasing the depopulation of these areas.

As an incomer to Skye he had to put up with the merchants of doom who continually predicted failure for the venture, even some locals who benefitted financially from the establishment of the college, but this was an experienced businessman who was not accustomed to failure.

Sir Iain pressed on regardless.

With the input of such luminaries as Sorley MacLean, Iain Crichton-Smith, Gordon Barr, Dr Finlay MacLeod, D.R. MacDonald and others the college grew in scale and academic reputation, increasing its range of activities, its notable library and its actual campus to the point of worthy inclusion into the University of the Highlands and Islands.

It is evident that Sleat has flourished economically over the years, and there is a noticeably high proportion of Gaelic speakers in this district. Many young Hebridean islanders are educated here to full university standard, in the language of their ancestors, making it unnecessary for them to leave the islands to finish their education, and can now find jobs in the Gaeltachd without the draining loss of their skills to mainland Britain, as previously.

It would seem that Sir Iain's dream of economic revival through the resurrection of the Gaelic language, has been realised in Sabhal Mòr's great success.

Tale no. 30: Extracts from a Primary Adviser's Diary

11th April : Isle of Harris

Was warmly welcomed today at Sir E. Scott Junior Secondary School in Tarbert by the Head Teacher, who invited me to come over to the Schoolhouse after school to meet his wife.

An amazing pair. They have carpeted their entire house with shaggy woollen rugs which they have woven themselves. Apparently this took them two years of continuous effort!

H.T. asked me to sign his Visitor's Book, and showed me the page on which my Uncle Bob signed his name during his last visit to the school as an Inspector of Schools several years ago.

12th April

Still on Harris but over on the west coast all day. Again experienced the spectacular, white shell sand beaches. Took Roddy down on to totally deserted, fabulous Luskentyre beach stretching away ahead for glorious, gleaming white miles.

He went mad with joy and raced away into the distance with me tearing after him, shouting to him to stop. Eventually he did when both of us were completely out of breath. We sat on silver-white dunes gazing at this incredible place and I began to feel a bit nervous --- not a soul to be seen!

The teacher at Seilebost School told me the beach was safe but its emptiness began to intimidate me.

Where were all the people? Were there quicksands? Were the army about to fire rockets over this part of the Hebrides? etc. Very relieved to see, coming towards me, a man walking his Labrador. Naturally both dogs went to greet each other with the usual wagging tails.

The man came over and introduced himself as the manager of Luskentyre Estate. Said yes, the beach was completely safe, just very quiet, especially at this time of year.

Said he had recently been on his daily walk along the beach and came across a lady walking along on her own. He was struck by her close resemblance to the Queen and said, "Excuse me, but you look so like the Queen."

"That's because I am the Queen," she said smiling, "and there is *Britannia* anchored out there."

Manager said he felt a bit peculiar bowing to the Queen on an empty Hebridean beach!

13th April

Left Tarbert this am. and drove west for nine miles along the tortuous B887 road to Amhuinnsuidhe ("sitting on the river"--- and it is!) Castle, which suddenly appears like something out of *Brigadoon* --- dramatic and spectacular.

Mrs Mac at the Post Office asked me to hand-deliver a telegram to the castle as I was walking past there anyway. On arrival I found all the doors open but nobody answered at my knock. No one about, so I walked into the hall and shouted. Still no reply. Put telegram in an obvious place and left --- but I could have gone right through the place and pinched all the valuables!

Told Mrs Mac who phoned castle later to explain. All okay.

Asked Mrs Mac what was the greatest improvement in the place since her childhood. She said the road! Up till then most things had to come in by boat.

24th April: Fort William

Had an annoyingly slow 3-hour journey down Loch Ness-side this morning as I got caught up in a procession of lorries and caravans driven by persons apparently in a state of near coma, so was late in arriving at the Fort William schools which were awaiting me.

Most H.T.s quite understanding about my tardy arrival, except the man at Caol who is a law unto himself, and wouldn't let me into any of his classrooms!

May and Eileen [Staff Tutors] found this very amusing as they have had similar experiences here in the past. Can nothing be done about this, I asked, but they said he was really a good H.T., just very old-fashioned, so nobody likes to complain about him.

At Inverlochy they proudly showed me the mountain of newsprint donated to them regularly by the nearby Wiggins Teape Paper Mill who are most generous with presents of paper to all local schools. Only problem is in finding a place to store the huge, heavy rolls of paper which could easily kill any unwary person if they fell on them.

Nan Cooper has just phoned, full of indignation. She and other local ladies have been chosen to dress the entire W.T. plant with fresh flowers for a visit by the Queen, but Nan's contribution is to be a very small arrangement for the Ladies' Powder Room which will be put at Her Majesty's disposal for the duration of the visit.

She's been told to keep the arrangement low as it's to be just a simple bouquet for the dressing-table. Nan thinks H.M. probably won't even notice. Only the wives of local bigwigs are getting to do the more prestigious arrangements. Nan said she should have been given a bigger arrangement as she has got her certificate from the Flower Arranging Society. She is quite put out!

26th April: Isle of Skye

Back to Skye today. Got to Sconser in time for the little ferry over to Raasay. I missed it by a couple of minutes last time round.

Mrs Fraser has 14 pupils now in school --- amazing for a little island off the coast of Skye. She tells me that Calum's road is now finished. What a man --- single-handedly building the two miles of roadway between Brochel and Arnish with spade, wheelbarrow and a book on *How to Build a Road*, from the local library.

"A great job, very well done," according to the road engineer from Inverness. Well, you can't keep a MacLeod down, once he's put his mind to a job!

Glad to see that Raasay House, in such a state when I last saw it, has been bought out by the islanders, but what a cost --- £3.5 million --- phew! To think that awful businessman, John Green, bought it for a song --- £8,000 --- visited it only once, let it go to rack and ruin, then sold it to the HIDB for £135,000 in 1979. Talk about profiteering!

Visited my quaint old friends, the MacPherson sisters at Kilvaxter. Last time I saw them they kept going on about "the twins". I was quite puzzled till I discovered they were talking about their twin calves, born on the croft. Twins are now well-grown, but Flora and Peigi still love and dote on them. How on earth will they ever bring themselves to send them to market when the time comes?

They were pleased, as usual, to talk about my folk up the road at Bornaskitaig. They say that the place was really finished when there were no longer enough young men to carry a coffin up the road to

335

the cemetery at Kilmuir. Thank goodness for motor-hearses nowadays!

27th April

Had the misfortune to meet a Welsh, self-righteous, self-styled "evangelist" at Kilmuir Museum of Island Life. He prosed on with comments on the immorality, as he had the cheek to put it, of modern-day Highlanders. I desisted, with difficulty, from telling him that there was a great deal more immorality south of the Border, and he should gird up his loins and get back down there right away!

30th April

Nan has just phoned, in triumph, to tell me that not only did H.M. notice her little flower arrangement, but actually admired it and thanked Nan personally. Nan is in the Seventh Heaven!

1st May: Inverness

Summoned to the Longman estate for a meeting with HMI [Her Majesty's Inspectors of Schools] and other Primary Advisers of the Northern Division.

Meeting, as usual, completely taken over by Inspectors while the rest of us just sat and didn't manage to get a word in edgeways --- utterly boring. The Caithness PA dozed off and began to snore. His Staff Tutor jerked his elbow to wake him up. This was the only interesting happening in the entire meeting.

Amused to discover, in the Ladies' Toilet, that every sheet of toilet paper is stamped with HM Government stamp. Incredible!

2nd May: Speyside

Eileen left a note on my desk --- would I please go over to one of the Spey valley schools as a pupil there is so unmanageable and physically violent that he has been given doses of tranquiliser strong enough, HT says, to knock out a young lion! She is worried that this will damage child's health, though something must be done as all the other children (and the teacher) are afraid of him.

On arrival at the school I discover that the Schools' Psychologist has just been, and diagnosed the child as possibly autistic. I'll speak to the Assistant Director about offering him a place in a specialist unit in Inverness.

3rd May: Sunart

Went out to Strontian this morning, but was left feeling unwelcome as the entire school was in the local village hall rehearsing for end of term concert next month. I was definitely *de trop*. Offered to help but they were obviously too busy even to talk to me, so I slunk away feeling sad and unwanted. The HT told me, quite sharply, to phone before coming next time.

Mrs MacBain stopped me in the car park this afternoon, full of annoyance at the local doctor. She said he cares more for his posh car than for his patients. She wanted him to come out to the croft to see Robbie, who has been off school for a week.

He told her the track up to the croft is far too rough for his car's suspension so she should put Robbie in the baby's pram and push him down to the road-end! She thinks it's terrible that the doctor will only see Robbie out on the roadside and anyway, how is she to manage this as Robbie is a big 12 year-old!

I sympathise, and immediately have inner vision of a large Robbie, overflowing the baby's pram, being "hurled" down rough path to the road by his diminutive mother!

This district has more than its fair share of eccentrics. The O'Brians, up the hill from MacBain croft, still live in their own little world and don't keep the same time as the rest of us. Never move clocks forward at British Summer Time, and still milk their cows by hand. What a chore!

5th May: Isle of Lewis

Met Roderick Cameron in Stornoway this morning, on his way to meet Fabric Committee of his local church. All are distraught as their new, expensive, electronic organ, installed only last week, has to be returned to the builders. Roderick says that plastic coating round wiring has been chewed right through by mice so nothing works and the whole business will have to be started again. He hopes insurance will cover it. Poor Roderick.

14th May: Kintyre

Iona MacNeill phoned from Campbeltown to say Hector's boat *Faoileag*, has disappeared from its moorings in the loch. They are very concerned about what has happened to it.

16th May: Cowal

Another disappearance! Roddy went off with Uncle Donald for a walk, was let off lead in Hafton estate grounds, and vanished. Donald arrived back at the house in a panic. We all rushed out to comb district, fearing the worst, of course.

I was trailing back homewards in despair, and glanced in at the open doorway of Tina's Post Office. There sat smug Roddy, happy as could be, eating sweets offered to him by kind-hearted Tina and being patted by all her customers. What a relief! But he is a little brat. Had to revive poor Donald with a large dram!

20th May: Isle of Mull

Went off to Mull for a weekend sail on the ketch, *Ariadne,* with Duncan Morrison and friends. Very strenuous as we ran into a heavy sea and blustery northerly wind. Glad to tie up on Saturday night at Tobermory where Iain Ross invited us to a ceilidh and dance out at Salen.

Had to go by local bus driven by Smokey Stewart --- wild character--- as Iain's car was in the garage. Duncan opted to stay with the boat.

Ceilidh was lively and hall crammed with folk. Bar did a roaring trade. I have never danced a set of Quadrilles before and never will again! Found myself flying through the air after being swung off my feet by energetic partners. Alarming!

After midnight found Smokey in a heap behind front door. Said he was just having a kip as he was tired but insisted he was perfectly able to drive the bus back to T. He wouldn't give up the keys so we set off about 2am with him at the wheel. What a journey --- wheels over the verges several times and Morag slid off her seat on to the floor each time we swung round a bend. Arrived back at T. with a bush stuck to the radiator. Unforgettable journey!

Had to shout very loudly at Tobermory quay to wake up skipper Duncan on the ketch which was swinging at her anchor out in the bay. Must have wakened up the whole of T. Now we are very unpopular in the village.

Roddy and best friend, Donald

26th May: Mid-Argyll

Met Sir Iain MacFarlane --- staying at the local hotel while Lady Silvia entertains her relations back at the castle. Said he couldn't stand these chattering women any longer so moved out as anyway, he was going to a farm displenishing sale. He called the hotel a dump as he was sure his sheets were damp. However, he wrapped himself in his plaid and managed to get to sleep --- just like Highlanders of old.

He was also upset when, after buying a couple of young Highland bulls, his cattleman carelessly let them get out. They had a fight in the middle of the village, crashing into someone's garden wall and knocking down several yards of it, also scaring the wits out of the locals. Sir Iain was then sternly interviewed by the local constabulary --- so unfair!

Later, the rather large Sir Iain stepped on to the running board of a friend's vintage car, but his weight was too much for it, and it collapsed.

Altogether, Sir Iain is not a happy man!

14th June: Lochaber

Danny Fraser, colleague from Wester Ross, invited me to a ceilidh in one of his local primary schools. I turned up full of pleasant expectation. But it was dreadful.

New HT obviously imagined himself to be another Alfie Boe and hogged most of the programme, keeping the children, whom we had really come to see, off the stage. The man was a complete crow and must have been tone deaf as he seemed unaware of parental mutterings and kept on churning out songs from the musicals. What a racket --- all out of tune, as well as time.

The Fear an Tighe tried, unsuccessfuly, to get him off the stage. Kids and audience became increasingly restless. Eventually an irate parent shouted "Dùin do bheul!" ["Shut up"] and the place started emptying.

What a fiasco, and a bad beginning for a new HT.

Danny was furious and gave him a flea in his ear. "We didn't realise he was such a limelight case when we appointed him," he growled.

Received a phone call from Iona to say that Hector's boat had apparently dragged its anchor during a severe summer gale, and was found drifting near Ailsa Craig by a Royal Navy minesweeper, which towed her, fortunately undamaged, into Girvan harbour. Hector, very happily, has gone over to collect her, but, not so happily, has to pay the considerable salvage fee to the Royal Navy!

19th July: Isle of Barra

At low tide stood on the sand at Traigh Mhòr near Eoligarry, and watched Loganair's little Twin Otter plane dramatically touch down on the beach. It always looks as if the aircraft is landing in the sea.

Amused to watch the pilot jump out, go forward to the nose cone, open it --- much to intense interest of spectators --- and remove his lunch from its nice, cool storage place!

Looked around, but no trace of the wonderful, annual display of primroses all over the grassland around the bay.

Eoligarry School roll was about 40 when I last visited. Nice to see a true Barra MacNeill in charge today.

Loganair landing on Eoligarry Beach, Barra

25ᵗʰ July: Isle of Coll

Cattle sale today. Met Ronald out here testing sheep for the Ministry (Agriculture).

He was rather hot and bothered in spite of chilly wind. Seems he had sent word on ahead to a farm that he would arrive in the morning to blood-test the flock, and would they please gather the sheep into the fank ready to be tested, but on arrival found only a fuming farmer's wife and two daughters. No farmer.

Wife said that after the sale her absent husband was sure to be found now propping up the hotel bar, and she was going to kill him on his return!

So Ronald and the girls had to start gathering the sheep off the hill on their own, and get them into the fank, but daughter no.2 hadn't closed the back gate so all the sheep went in the front, straight through the fank and out the back, on to the hill again. Sheep went round and round several times before they discovered this! Wife was incandescent and blamed non-appearance of farmer.

Daughter no.2 realised it was all her fault and went away in a huff, so Ronald and daughter no.1 were left to shut the back gate, get the sheep into the fank again, and start the testing. Girl was very helpful and held each sheep while it was being tested, though she was quite small.

Wife was increasingly furious so Ronald left immediately after testing completed, not wishing to witness possibly violent reception of farmer on his return!

30th July: Wester Ross

Took the road out of Torridon and drove west towards Diabeg this evening. Dusk beginning to fall as I reached Upper Diabeg --- breathtaking views out to northern Applecross, island of Rona and Trotternish in Skye in the brilliant sunset. *Abair sealladh!* [What a view!]

7th August: Kintyre

Went out to Sheep Island with John and Archie in *Sheena* and *Zena,* taking some visitors, including Dr Taylor, to see the nesting seabirds. Dr T. is a bit eccentric --- her choice of suitable clothing being a flowery nylon dress and heavy climbing boots.

She brought along her dog which kept trying to leap out of the boat. John very alarmed as Dr T. nearly fell out after it --- dreadful currents and rip tides out there. Then a flock of disturbed gannets swooped down and attacked her! The other passengers managed to beat them off. All very alarming.

We couldn't land as birds now thoroughly alarmed, so didn't see the puffins which were object of the trip. Had to turn back early. Talk about a Jonah! Dr T. thoroughly unpopular!

9th August

Back to Inverness for new schools' session and, hopefully, many more encounters with the folk who live in the west.

Translation of the Gaelic verse on the Dedication page:

Thig crìoch air an t-saoghail   The world will come to an end
Ach mairidh gaol is ceòl   but love and music will endure.

Translation of two verses from Runrig's beautiful song, *Cearcall a'Chuain:*

We are all on the ocean
Steering a course through our lives
Sailing a dark ship
Lost in the grip of the seas
The wind is behind us
The ship keeps moving forward
And neither the time nor the ocean
Can provide us with purpose or reason

But it is my desire, my intention
When the sun finally sets
They will find me sailing west
Across to Uist on the circle
The ocean circle
It will forever keep turning me
To the white machairs of the west
Where day first began

Lightning Source UK Ltd.
Milton Keynes UK
UKHW050834140922
408847UK00006B/29